Children's Toys
and Furniture

Children's Toys and Furniture

**Monte Burch
and the Editors of U-Bild**

CREATIVE HOMEOWNER PRESS® 24 PARK WAY, UPPER SADDLE RIVER, NEW JERSEY 07458

Manufactured in United States of America

Current printing (last digit)
10 9 8 7 6 5 4 3

Produced by Roundtable Press, Inc.

Editorial: Judson Mead
Design: Caliber Design Planning, Inc.
Illustrations: Norman Nuding
Jacket photo: David Arky
Rocking horse on cover: Courtesy U-Bild Newspaper Syndicate

LC: 81-71606
ISBN: 0-932944-57-4 (paper)
        0-932944-56-6 (hardcover)

CREATIVE HOMEOWNER PRESS ®
BOOK SERIES
A DIVISION OF FEDERAL
MARKETING CORPORATION
24 PARK WAY, UPPER SADDLE RIVER, NJ 07458

How to Use this Book

There is nothing more satisfying for you or for your children than building their toys and furniture. You get the full pleasure of the shopwork and the accomplishment of the finished product of your craft. At the same time, your children get safe, sturdy wooden toys and furniture pieces that will last and have the special touch of handmade objects. Also, beyond whatever pleasure you find in working with your hands, you will also enjoy the economy of making pieces yourself.

The projects in this book are all fairly simple to build, and their degrees of difficulty and the time required are indicated with each. Only basic familiarity with woodworking techniques and tools are needed to finish the easier projects, and slightly more advanced techniques are enough for the rest. Many of these projects can be made with hand tools only. Since power tools make various operations go faster, you will always find them listed among the materials needed to build a toy or piece of furniture, but you can certainly substitute hand tools wherever it is practical. If you are just starting out as a woodworker, read Chapter 1 on Materials and Tools to get an overview of what is called for in this book.

The materials list that accompanies each project specifies the material required. If no specific mention is made of wood type, any solid stock that you have on hand will serve.

To build any of these projects, first read the step-by-step instructions all the way through, looking at the drawings and pictures as you go along. By constructing the project in your imagination in this manner, you will discover the skills you might want to practice first, as well as any special tools you may need. After familiarizing yourself with the procedures, gather the materials listed in the materials list accompanying each project. The materials are listed by the dimensions required for each piece, which means there may be a large number of parts, but they may all be obtained from a single, large sheet of plywood. Reading the directions first will tell you this. When you have the materials in hand, read the instructions through one more time, reminding yourself of the whole assembly sequence, then proceed with the first step. When you complete the sequence, you will have transformed an assortment of boards and fasteners into something you and your child will value more than anything you can find in a store.

Contents

Projects

1. Materials and Tools

The proper choice of materials—wood in particular—and tools is vital for completing the projects in this book.

Choosing Woods
The basic material for all the projects in this book is wood: either softwood, hardwood, or one of the manufactured woods, like the various kinds of plywood, Masonite, or hardboard. When the kind of wood is important to the project, the directions will say so; in many of the toy projects, scrap pieces from other projects are all you'll need. Before purchasing materials for any of these projects, familiarize yourself with the basics of the available woods and how to order the correct sizes and grades.

Dimensions
The named, or nominal, wood sizes—1 × 4, 1 × 6, 1 × 8—are not the actual sizes. Dressing the boards at the mill reduces the size somewhat. As the boards increase in nominal width, they lose more and more stock. Nominal length remains the actual length. The accompanying table shows actual and nominal sizes, and it is essential that you be conscious of them when planning your project.

NOMINAL SIZE	ACTUAL SIZE
This is what you order.	This is what you get.
INCHES	INCHES
1 × 1	3/4 × 3/4
1 × 2	3/4 × 1 1/2
1 × 3	3/4 × 2 1/2
1 × 4	3/4 × 3 1/2
1 × 6	3/4 × 5 1/2
1 × 8	3/4 × 7 1/4
1 × 10	3/4 × 9 1/4
1 × 12	3/4 × 11 1/4
2 × 2	1 3/4 × 1 3/4
2 × 3	1 1/2 × 2 1/2
2 × 4	1 1/2 × 3 1/2
2 × 6	1 1/2 × 5 1/2
2 × 8	1 1/2 × 7 1/4
2 × 10	1 1/2 × 9 1/4
2 × 12	1 1/2 × 11 1/4

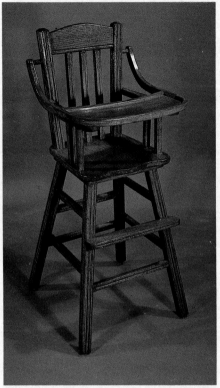
This red oak highchair, stained and finished with a satin varnish, is constructed almost entirely with angled mortise-and-tenon joints.

Softwoods
Pine and fir are softwoods, which means they come from conifers, or cone-bearing trees. The term *softwood* does not mean that the wood is necessarily softer than the kind called hardwood: indeed, balsa, a lightweight wood that can be cut with a knife, is a hardwood. Softwood is a good deal less expensive than hardwood because it grows faster. Most of the toys in this book are made of softwood, while most of the furniture calls for hardwood or plywood. Pine, especially, will be readily available in the size and grade you need at any lumberyard, but such softwoods as cedar (for a large toy chest) or redwood (for a sandbox) may be harder to find.

Grading
Finished softwood comes in various grades. The best type is Clear, so called because it does not have knots or blemishes. It also is not commonly stocked and is therefore expensive. One grade down from Clear is Select, which is cheaper and comes in three subdivisions: Nos. 1, 2, and 3. No. 1 is the best of the three, with only a few blemishes on one side of the board and perhaps more on the other. Nos. 2 and 3 will have more blemishes—and will cost less. Usually, lumberyards will carry Nos. 2 and 3 Select but not No. 1.

The lowest grade, but still a perfectly good wood, is Common; this will have more than a few blemishes and knots. It is often used in a project that will be painted or covered in some way. When you need Clear stock, an excellent money-saving trick is to buy Common and cut out only the unblemished portions you need. You will have a lot of waste but will probably still save money over buying all Clear or all Select. You would have to estimate the percentage of the Common that would be usable and then buy enough wood to compensate for the waste. You must also check that the sizes of the pieces you would cut for the sides, back, doors, and so on, could be cut from the individual pieces of Common wood left after cutting out the blemishes.

Choosing the Best Wood
When selecting wood, always look at each board with the following quality criteria in mind. Ask yourself these questions.

1. Is the board flat? Does it lie flat on the board beneath it?

2. Is it straight? Raise the board and sight down it to the other end; any curve will show up right away.

3. Is the board warped? Look at the end nearest you and sight to see if it is parallel with the end farthest away. To double-check, lay it on the floor. The end farthest away should be flat. You can adjust for a little warpage, but nothing drastically warped will be usable.

4. How many knots are there and in what condition are they? Some grades will have knots, but if these are tight the wood is acceptable.

5. When you cut up the board for your project, can you eliminate the knots? By carefully positioning the pieces to be cut out, you may be able to avoid most of the knots.

6. Are you finishing the wood with a clear finish or with paint? If with paint, the knots may be unimportant.

7. Are there pith pockets? Pith is a soft brown exudation that looks like a brown line running lengthwise on the board. Do not buy wood with these pockets. Pith usually causes a board to warp.

8. Does the board have sap pockets? If so, avoid such stock unless you can cut the sap pockets out. Sap can also cause a board to warp.

Hardwoods

Hardwoods come from deciduous, or leaf-bearing trees. In general, hardwoods—mahogany, oak, birch, and maple are some examples—come in random lengths from 8 to 16 feet and in widths from 4 to 12 inches milled to the same dimensions as softwood. But what you will be able to find varies from region to region. The hardwood you buy will be Clear; dealers do not bother to stock other grades. Hardwoods are generally better looking than softwoods—hardwoods have nicer grain and color and are easier to tool than softwood. Most of the furniture projects in this book call for hardwood.

The wood you buy, if a softwood, will come dressed on all four sides. If you buy hardwood, it will come in the rough unless you specify that it be dressed on two or more sides. But this is mill dressing. Before you work with it, ensure that the surfaces are smooth. In almost all cases, this requires that you sand imperfections from the top and bottom and then smooth the edges with a plane and sandpaper.

Grain

The grain pattern of the wood you buy will be dictated by whether the wood has been quarter-sawed or plain-sawed. Quarter-sawed wood produces a tighter, parallel grain pattern. Plain-sawed wood has a characteristic loop. Quarter-sawed is better wood but, again, you can expect to pay for it. If the grain makes a difference in your project, make sure that all the pieces you purchase have been sawed in the same way.

Plywood

Plywood is often used in these projects. It commonly comes in 4 × 8-foot sheets $1/4$-, $1/2$-, and $3/4$-inch thick. It consists of two veneers of wood (which can be one of many different types) sandwiched over a core—usually bonded wood chips or lumber. The edges of plywood with a wood-chip core are more difficult to finish than are the edges of plywood with a lumber core—called, logically enough, "lumber-core plywood."

One major distinction between plywood and regular boards or lumber is that for plywood the nominal size is the actual size—a $3/4$-inch-thick panel is really $3/4$ inch thick.

Plywood Grades (Softwood)

The quality of the face veneers is indicated by letters: A designating the best and D the worst. A-face plywood is free from blemishes; it is absolutely clear and free of knots or visible mars and, after a light sanding, is ready for finishing. Grade B will have a few defects, but the knotholes will have been cut out and the area patched. Grade C Plugged has repaired knotholes. Grade C has unfilled knotholes and checks (splits). Grade D plywood often has large knotholes. There is also a Grade N (natural) that designates furniture-quality wood veneer free of all defects. This must be specially ordered and is in limited supply in most areas.

Plywood Grades (Hardwood)

The exposed plies for this type of plywood are designated as Premium, Good, Sound, and Backing. A Premium sheet may have two sides of Premium veneer or one side of Premium and one of Backing grade. The latter plywood is suitable for a piece that will have one side hidden from view. The next category is a Custom sheet. This allows a combination of Premium and Backing grades, or a Premium and a Good side for two exposed faces. The final category is an Economy sheet. This permits faces to be combined as Good and Backing, Good and Sound, or two faces Sound.

The Premium and Good designations indicate that the exposed surface is nearly perfect and suitable for a clear finish. The only difference between the two grades is that Premium grade allows only small, inconspicuous patches, while the Good grade allows larger, but carefully matched patches. The Good grade allows mismatching of grain but not of color. Sound grade is intended for a painted finish.

Choosing Plywood

The following recommendations are based on long experience. For furniture parts that will be stained or covered with a clear finish so that the wood will show (i.e., the color and grain will be exposed), the top grade, Premium or A, is recommended. If both sides will show, A-A, A-B, or Premium should be used. The use of Custom grade, A-C, or A-D depends on how attractive you feel the back or hidden face should be. If you intend to apply paint to the plywood, then grades B-B and B-D should be used. If you wish, you may even obtain a plywood that has been primed at the factory.

Handling Plywood Edges

Plywood can be worked easily with good power tools or hand tools, as needed. You prepare and finish it as you would solid stock. The only areas that present potential problems are the edges. Lumber-core plywood has nearly solid board edges that may be handled in the same way as any solid wood. However, if the edges on furniture are exposed layers of plies, the appearance may be unattractive and you will want to hide them.

The most popular way to finish plywood edges is with a veneer tape. This material comes in a roll and is applied to the exposed edges with contact cement. Instructions vary a little from brand to brand, but all are applied essentially in the same way.

If you are simply going to paint the plywood, there is no need to use any special edge-finishing technique or material. Instead, choose one of the many wood putties, either in powder or semisolid form, and apply it as directed to fill and smooth the edges. The putty will seal the edges of the plywood and keep the fibers from absorbing excess amounts of paint. The filled and painted edges will look like the rest of the plywood.

Basic Tools

The projects in this book were developed in a fairly well-equipped woodworking shop, but most of them can be built without an extensive collection of tools. The following are the basic hand and power tools you will need for simple woodworking, and you can add some of the stationary power tools as you become more advanced. Tools should be neatly organized to keep them easily accessible, sharp, and clean. With all power tools, safety is a paramount concern. *Never* operate a power tool without fully understanding all the cautions in the manufacturer's directions, and always observe all the cautions as if your hands and eyes depend on it—because they do.

Standard Claw Hammer

The best quality claw hammers are

Always buy a hammer to last a lifetime. Left, straight; right, claw.

drop-forged and have hickory handles. Look at the claw before you buy. It should have fine inside edges that will slide under the head of a nail easily, and the curve of the claw should be sufficient to provide good leverage. Claw hammers come in a variety of weights, starting at 7 ounces. The best all-around sizes are 13 or 16 ounces.

Rubber Mallet

The rubber mallet is one of the handiest tools to have because it enables you to pound on toy and furniture parts without denting or marring them. It is ideal for tapping newly glued joints firmly together.

Screwdrivers

You'll find mostly large screws used in the projects in this book, so you should have a good collection of large-bladed screwdrivers. The secret in using a screwdriver is to match the width of the blade to the slot on the screw. A blade that is smaller than the slot won't provide the leverage you need to turn the screw in or out easily. A blade that is only half the size of the slot may bend under the pressure you apply or may damage the slot in the screw. Your best buy is a matched set of good-quality steel screwdrivers, with handles large enough to allow a comfortable grip. There are a good many cheap screwdrivers available, but it is best to avoid these "bargains."

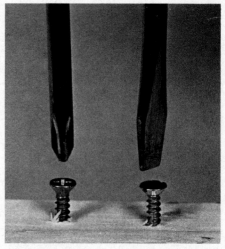

Never use a screwdriver that doesn't perfectly fit the screw. Left, Phillips; right, straight.

Good ones will last longer and give much better service.

You won't need screwdrivers with Phillips heads for these projects, but to work with metal units, you will need several sizes.

Nailsets

In those instances when you use finishing nails in toy or furniture construction, you want to hide all traces of them. This is done by countersinking the nailhead and then filling the hole with wood putty. To countersink a nail, use a nailset to tap the nail $1/16$-$1/8$ inch or so below the wood surface.

Carpenter's Handsaw

The familiar carpenter's handsaw consists of a steel blade with a handle, usually wood, at one end. The lower edge of the blade has cutting teeth, which are *set* (bent alternately side to side) to make the *kerf* (the groove cut by the teeth) wider than the thickness of the blade. This is necessary to prevent the blade from rubbing against the sides of the kerf and then binding. Carpenter's handsaws are described by the number of teeth per inch (given as the point size). In general, the lower the point size, the easier and faster the saw will cut; the higher the point size, the finer and smoother the cut.

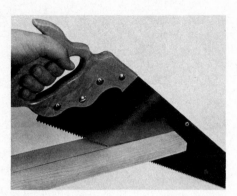

Handsaws are one of the most basic tools in the woodworker's shop.

There are two broad classifications of carpenter's handsaws: the rip saw and the crosscut. Rip saws are designed to cut with the grain of the wood; crosscuts saw across the grain. The latter will probably be your first purchase. For general use, an 8-point crosscut saw is recommended. If the saw will be used primarily for fine work—such as cutting trim or hardwoods—a 10- or 12-point may be preferred. Most rip saws have 5½ or 6 points per inch.

Coping Saw

A *coping saw* consists of a thin, fine-toothed (10–20 points per inch) blade

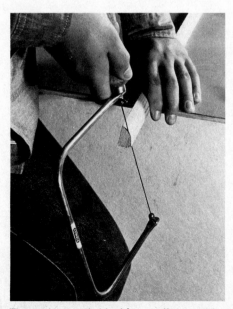

The coping saw is ideal for small cuts and delicate curves; it has many blades.

held in a U-shaped metal frame. The blade is removable, and it can be inserted in the frame so that it cuts on either the push or pull stroke and in any direction. Some more expensive blades are round with spiral cutting edges; these will saw in any direction, making possible tight-radius curves. To start an internal cut with a coping saw, the blade is removed from the frame and passed through a predrilled hole in the work; then the blade is reattached to the frame for the cut.

When using a coping saw, the work should be held firmly in a vise as close as possible to the cutting line to avoid the possibility of splitting the wood and excessive blade twisting and breakage.

Clamps

Almost no tool is more important to complete the projects in this book successfully than clamps. Make it a basic rule from the beginning to clamp every glue job, no matter how big or how small. If you do, you will make neat, successful glue joints every time. There are four basic types of clamps at your hardware store, and you'll need all of them in a variety of sizes if you do much shop work.

Hand Screws

These are the traditional wooden-jawed clamps that woodworkers have been using for centuries. They consist of two blocks of shaped hardwood with two steel, wood-handled clamping screws running through them. To tighten the clamp, you turn the screws. Because the clamping screws are mounted in pivots, the jaws can be set at any desired angle. They range from miniature ones to big ones with jaws that open to 14 inches. A good basic starter group might include a 3- or 4-inch and an 8- or 10-inch model.

Bar and Pipe Clamps

These are called furniture clamps in

Bar clamps are used for clamping large pieces of work to set a strong glue bond.

some tool catalogues. They consist of two movable metal jaws, one of which has a built-in clamping screw, fitted over either a long steel bar or a long pipe. They are used to span big work such as a desk top, the seat of a chair, or the side of a toy chest. You can buy them in lengths from 12 to 48 inches. The longer lengths are the most practical, because even the 48-inch clamp can be fitted to work of 12 inches—though sometimes fitting larger clamps to smaller work is clumsy. For big gluing jobs, you may need as many as three or four at a time; two is a minimum for most shops.

Strap and Web Clamps

Some woodworkers think these are the handiest tools in the shop. They are inexpensive and often can be made to do the work of the more costly hand screws and bar clamps. Strap and web clamps are just like tourniquets.

The clamps you buy consist of a fabric strap fitted with a metal clamp body. Put the strap around the work to be clamped; then tighten it by pulling the strap through, not unlike the way you tighten an airplane seat belt. Most clamp bodies are made so you can do the final tightening by turning a nut on the side of the body with a small wrench. Most straps are 12 to 15 feet long, so they can go around big work.

C-clamps

The C-clamp is shaped like the letter C, with the open mouth of the letter used for clamping. The clamping surfaces are small metal pads, adjusted by turning a screw handle, which moves the lower pad. C-clamps are available with jaw openings from 1 to 8 inches or more. It is best to buy the sizes you need for each job as required instead of trying to purchase a whole collection immediately. Always insert pieces of scrap wood between the work and the metal pads of C-clamps before tightening. Otherwise the pads will make ugly dents in the surface of the furniture or toy.

Other Clamping Devices

Anything that can hold two pieces together while they are being glued can be called a clamp. You can use spring-type clothespins for small work, and sometimes a rubber band is as good as anything else. You can buy metal spring clamps, which work the same as the spring-type clothespins but have jaw openings in sizes ranging from 1 to 3 inches. It is good to have a few of these around.

Doweling Jig

Many toys and pieces of furniture have parts joined by dowels—wooden pegs that fit into holes drilled in each of the joined pieces. Dowel joints are strong, neat, and long-lasting, and they eliminate the need for screws. To do dowel joining, you need a doweling jig. Basically, the jig positions the drill in the proper place on the pieces to be joined, so that the holes are perfectly aligned after drilling. It is nearly impossible to make a precise dowel joint without the jig, and it is a worthwhile investment if you plan to do much furniture work. Each brand is slightly different, so follow the instructions that come with the one you buy.

Bench Vises

It takes two hands to do most woodworking jobs. Unless you have a third

A doweling jig is necessary for making a successful dowel joint.

arm, there is no way to hold the wood while you work on it. This means you should have a bench vise into which you can clamp the work. A bench vise is not only a convenience but also a safety device, since a lot of woodworking accidents occur when people attempt to work on loose pieces and a tap of the hammer causes one of the unclamped pieces to fly.

If you already have a good workbench, it is probably fitted with a bench vise. If you don't have a workbench, then buy a clamp-on vise, which clamps to the edge of any sturdy table. Just be sure to put little wooden pads between the clamping areas on the vise and the table top to prevent marring. Some vises have heads that swivel, allowing you to change the angle of the work by adjusting the angle of the clamp. These are the most useful for general work.

Woodworking vises are a special variety of bench vise mounted on the side of the workbench, with jaws flush with the top of the table. They are lined with wood to protect anything clamped in them and are the most practical for furniture work. Clamp-on models are available, but swivel models are not. If you are buying your first vise and intend to work a lot with wood, the woodworking vise is best. However, you can use a bench vise to hold most woodwork by padding the jaws with thin wooden boards to protect the work.

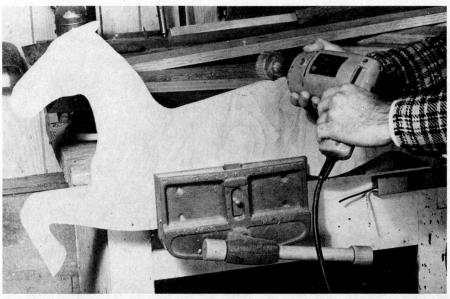

No workshop is complete without one or more vises for holding work in place. Vises used for woodworking should be padded with wood liners so they don't mar surfaces.

Rules

A rule, of course, is a device for measuring, and you need one constantly to measure the work. Three types are helpful in making good toys and furniture: the folding rule; the steel-tape rule; and the try square, commonly known as the T-square. The folding rule is most convenient for general measurements, especially of outside dimensions. The steel-tape rule is handy for making inside measurements, such as the inside of a drawer or cabinet. The T-square is held against the outside of a cabinet, drawer, or other square construction to show whether or not the corners are truly square.

Choosing and Using Power Tools

Power tools do any job quicker and often better than hand tools. The costs of good power tools have come down in recent years, so they are generally affordable and they pay for themselves in time saved and in work quality. As with any tool, however, you must practice with a power tool to find out how to get the most out of it.

There are two classes of power tools: the portable ones and those that mount on a workbench or stand alone. The bench tools and stand-alone units include the wood lathe, the band saw, the drill press, the joiner, the jig saw, the shaper, and the radial arm saw. Any of these is wonderful to have in a workshop, and you can find all kinds of uses for each of them. Each of them, however, requires a major investment in money and in workshop space—and you can make most of the projects in this book without them.

The portable power tools you can use for making toys and furniture include the electric drill, the saber saw, and the electric sander. A router is a good versatile addition to your tool collection.

Sanders

Three kinds of sanders are available at most hardware and home centers:

The electric oscillating sander makes quick work of smoothing large surfaces.

the oscillating sander, in which the abrasive paper moves back and forth rapidly and imitates the back-and-forth motion of hand sanding; the orbital sander, which moves the abrasive paper in a small-diameter circle; and the belt sander, which has a continuous belt of abrasive paper or cloth that runs constantly at high speed. Some units now available combine oscillating and orbital sanders. You control the motion of the abrasive paper by turning a switch.

Each of these sanders has its specific use. The oscillating sander is the best all-around sander for most people. Its sanding action is straight and relatively slow, so the novice doesn't make as many mistakes with it. The orbital sander is specifically a finishing tool, used for putting a final smooth finish on wood. It doesn't remove much material, even when used with coarse abrasive paper. The belt sander, on the other hand, cuts into wood fast, even with fine and medium abrasive papers. Handle the belt sander carefully or you will cut deeper than you intend.

Your best buy is a combination oscillating/orbital unit. If your budget allows it, add a belt sander later.

Electric Drill

An electric drill can do a lot of jobs in addition to drilling holes. It can be converted to a circular sander, a drum sander, or a disc sander. It can be used with a wire brush to remove

An electric drill is an indispensable time- and labor-saving power tool.

rust, paint, and finishes. It is, with the addition of attachments, the most versatile tool you can buy. Electric drills come in $1/4$-, $3/8$-, and $1/2$-inch sizes, with these numbers referring to the size of the chuck (the device that grips the drill bits and other attachments). The power rating of the drill generally varies with the size, ranging from $1/3$ to $1 1/2$ horsepower. For most home workshops, the $1/4$-inch model is fine. If you expect to do some heavy-duty work on occasion, buy the $3/8$-inch model.

When buying a drill, features to look for include a variable speed trigger, which permits you to control the speed of the drill by squeezing the trigger, and double insulation. This allows the use of a two-prong plug because the shell and the chuck are completely insulated from the wiring. The cheapest units have minimum horsepower and low-quality bearings, and they may burn out if used for heavy-duty work: they are fine for light-duty chores. As a rule, if you buy a recognized brand name, you can assume that the more expensive models are made to survive heavier work. Units in the middle to top price range are the best buy for the kind of work in these projects.

Attachments

Attachments add to the versatility of your drill. Good ones to consider at the start include: screwdriving units; a buffing and sanding set consisting of a rubber pad, a lamb's wool buffing pad, and sanding discs; and a collection of drill bits. Bits come in small storage cases containing a range of sizes. Your collection should include wood/metal twist bits in sizes from $1/32$ to $1/2$ inch. Add to these some wood spade bits from $1/2$ to $1\frac{1}{2}$ inches. If you drive many screws, a set of screw-mate bits can be helpful. Use these to drill pilot holes for screws. The bit not only drills a hole of the correct depth; but also widens the top of the hole so that the screw is automatically countersunk when you drive it.

Stands

A drill can be turned into a small workshop if you buy a stand for it. The stand holds the drill so that you don't have to. You can then use grinding wheels, disc sanders, and other fittings in the drill and have both hands free to hold the work. The drill also can be converted into a small but effective drill press with the purchase of a drill-press stand. With a disc sander in the chuck, you can hold small wooden parts to the spinning sander wheel and do some very good sanding work.

Saber Saw

The saber saw is a portable jig saw used to make curved and interior cuts in plywood and boards up to 2 inches thick. If you have to make curved cuts for a project, like those for the body of a rocking horse or the rockers for a cradle, the saber saw is a good tool for the job. It is not the

Saber saws cost little and do many cutting jobs easily, especially curved outlines.

One of the basic carpenter's tools, the circular saw is familiar in most shops.

best tool for making long, straight cuts; those are jobs for the circular power saw.

Router

The router is made for furniture work and although it is not required to complete the projects in this book, it can be handy in several of them. Among other things, it cuts grooves, rabbets, dovetails, and dadoes. You certainly can have a lot of fun with a router, and it is essential if you make your own furniture from scratch.

Routers cut complicated joints, round edges, and carve at several thousand rpm.

Circular Saws

The circular saw is a major time- and labor-saver in building some of the

larger projects in this book. It is also a dangerous tool, so it needs careful handling.

Circular-saw sizes are designated by the diameter of the blade. For do-it-yourself usage, these range from 6 to 8 or 9 inches. Amperage ratings run from 6 to 13. For frequent, heavy-duty cutting, a higher-amperage model is best. However, you can cut the same material with an economy saw if you work slowly and guard the motor against overheating.

The housing of a circular saw encloses the motor, electrical parts, and gears, and it also incorporates blade guards, a base plate or "shoe," cutting-depth and cutting-angle adjustments and, usually, a removable ripping guide. The blade guards consist of a stationary upper guard—covering the front, top, and back of the saw blade—and a lower guard that covers the blade bottom (below the shoe) when the saw is not in use. The lower guard moves backward and upward as the saw is pushed into the work and springs back automatically to cover the blade after the cut is completed. Never tamper with or remove this guard.

Stationary Power Tools

If you want to do a lot of fairly complex projects, you will need some "heavy hitters," the stationary power tools that can turn out work far more quickly and accurately than any hand-held tool.

Table Saws

The table saw is probably the most frequently used tool in a home workshop (except among those who prefer a radial arm saw). It can crosscut, rip, miter, bevel, and—with the proper accessories—cut dadoes, make moldings, and even sand. Various guides help it perform with a high degree of precision.

Many older table saws were made with tilting tables—that is, the saw table was adjusted to make angle cuts while the blade remained vertical. Today, almost all bench saws have tilting arbors; the table remains horizontal, and the blade is adjusted for cuts from 45 to 90 degrees.

Table-saw size is designated as the largest-sized blade the tool will accommodate. An 8-inch saw is a minimum choice for most home workshops. It has a depth of cut of about $1\frac{3}{4}$ inches at 90 degrees and $1\frac{3}{8}$ inches at 45 degrees. 9-, 10-, and 12-inch models are also available, with the latter having depths of cut of about 4 inches and $3\frac{1}{4}$ inches at 90 and 45 degrees respectively. This may be more capacity than you will ever need, so consider size before you buy a bench saw.

Radial Arm Saw

The radial arm saw performs basic sawing operations such as crosscutting, ripping, mitering, and beveling, along with more complicated jobs such as compound angle cutting. With accessories and attachments, it can be quickly adapted to dadoing, shaping, molding, sanding, drilling, boring, and routing—all with speed and great accuracy.

The radial arm saw differs from a table saw in that the blade cuts into the work from above. For many operations, this gives the user a better view of what is being done. Another big difference is that for most opera-

The radial arm saw has a pivoting blade that cuts from above. It is a superior power tool for cutting angles, many dadoes, and other work of variable depth.

tions, the work is stationary—the saw, mounted on an overhead arm, is moved through the work.

The saw head and blade can be swung 360 degrees on most models and can also be tilted for angle and compound cuts. A 10-inch saw typically has a maximum depth of cut of 3 inches at 90 degrees and $2\frac{1}{4}$ inches at 45 degrees. A 12-inch model can cut stock up to 4 inches or more. Cutting depth is adjusted by means of a crank.

Band Saw

The band saw consists of two large pulleys over which a continuous, flexible steel blade is looped. It can be used for crosscutting and ripping, but it is best suited for cutting curves and fine scrollwork. Most band saws have tilting tables to allow work to be cut at an angle.

Band-saw size is stated as the diameter of the pulleys. The width of work that can be cut is limited to the distance between the blade and the frame—usually $\frac{1}{4}$ to $\frac{3}{8}$ inch less than the pulley size. For example, a 10-inch band saw may handle work up to $9\frac{5}{8}$ inches wide; a 14-inch saw

unit may take work up to $13\frac{3}{4}$ inches wide. Most band saws can cut wood up to 6 or $6\frac{1}{4}$ inches thick.

Jig Saw

A jig saw, or scroll saw, is used for light-duty cutting of straight lines and intricate curves. Its blade is fastened at top and bottom and moves up and down. Its size is determined by its cutting clearance: the distance between the blade and the frame.

A bench top jig saw makes light work of curves on almost any small job.

Popular sizes range from 18 to 24 inches. A unique feature of the jig saw is its ability to make interior cuts. The blade is removed from the saw first, and a pilot hole is drilled into the work. The blade is then passed through the hole and retightened in the saw.

Drill Press

There are many tools for making holes in wood, but for precision drilling, angled holes, or repetitive drilling of holes to a specified depth, there is only one tool: the drill press. With the proper fittings and accessories, a drill press can also make square holes and mortises, plane, shape, rout, and sand.

A drill press has four basic parts: base, column, table, and drilling head. The table is adjustable and holds the work. The head contains the motor, chuck, feed arm, and controls. The head tilts up to 90 degrees for angle drilling and swivels a full 360 degrees around the column, offering almost unlimited flexibility. On some models, the table also tilts.

Shaper

The shaper is a high-speed tool that cuts various shapes in wood and is limited only by the number of cutters or bits you have. It can make moldings, decorative beads on panel edges, and flutings, adding a professional-looking touch to any do-it-yourself project.

Jointer

Although the jointer does a limited number of jobs, it does them extremely well, and fine cabinetry would be next to impossible without it. Most readily available commercial lumber, though dressed, is rough-cut and imperfect. The jointer is used to finish the lumber surface prior to cutting on a bench or radial arm saw. The jointer is so named because it planes wood so flat and smooth that when pieces are joined together in a glue joint they fit perfectly.

If you plan to do much precision drilling, get a drill press. They're invaluable.

The shaper is a stationary tool that performs many of the functions of a router. It can round edges quickly and cut plain stock into molding.

2. Measuring and Patterns

Measuring parts to fit is a basic operation in any woodworking project. If the parts don't fit snugly, the toy or piece of furniture will not be sturdy. You will need a few special measuring tools, and, in addition to the ones described below, keep a compass in your shop for marking circles (for wheels). Mark your measurements with a sharp edge or a pencil, and remember to make all cuts just to the outside (waste side) of your mark, or else the kerf (the portion of wood cut by the saw) will slightly reduce the dimensions of the piece you are cutting. Another aspect of measuring that you will encounter frequently in these projects is enlarging patterns from their smaller-than-real sizes, given here on grids. The following are three measuring tools every shop should have in addition to straight rules.

Framing Square
The framing square is an L-shaped piece of flat steel, with one leg of the L measuring 16 inches and the other measuring 24. You can lay it across a board with one leg tipped down so that it butts against one edge; then mark the board for crosscutting.

Try Square
The try square, or T-square, has a movable metal blade and a wooden handle. It is used for quickly checking the accuracy of 45° and 90° angles. It also works well for checking the ends of boards to see if they have been cut square. Just hold the try square against the board. If the fit is snug, it is square; if there is space, it is not square.

Adjustable Square
Another operation that may be required for your project is marking lines that are parallel to the edge of the stock. For this, use an adjustable square. The metal part of the tool rides along the edge of the stock while the blade part slides along the surface, with a pencil held against the end to make the mark. This tool can also be used for determining 45° and 90° angles.

Measuring Tips and Tricks
For every measuring operation—including marking angles and other measuring-related steps—repeat the sequence of measurements to ensure that you get the same result both times. If they do not agree, recheck, and remark if necessary.

Whenever possible, try to avoid measuring—use a precut length or width of material as a guide, or hold the piece of stock to be cut in place against parts that are completed, and then mark and cut it to fit. Many of the following projects call for cutting all components to size beforehand to save time. For other projects, however, the cut-to-fit method offers less chance of wasted material.

Enlarging Patterns
Many of the designs in this book are presented on grids that make possible the reproduction of the designs without a full-sized pattern. Each grid in this book consists of squares that, if enlarged to 1 inch, will increase the pattern to its proper size. You can enlarge the pattern on brown kraft paper or tracing paper—or, if you have a good hand, directly onto the wood itself.

To enlarge a pattern, number the lines, horizontals and verticals, on the grid given in the book. Then draw a full-sized grid (of 1-inch squares) on paper (or on the wood) and number the lines exactly as on the original. Pick a starting point in relation to the lines on the grid (where the outline of the pattern crosses one of the grid lines). Mark this point on your full-sized grid. For example, if you start at a point that is near the intersection of lines 6 and 24 on the grid in the book, put it in the same point on your enlarged grid. Follow the original pattern, marking all the points where the outline crosses a line on the grid. Once you have plotted the position of all these intersections, draw in the connecting lines between the dots; use a straightedge or a flexible adjusting curve to make one continuous line, as smooth as possible.

The framing square is used to check that a piece is square, and for measuring.

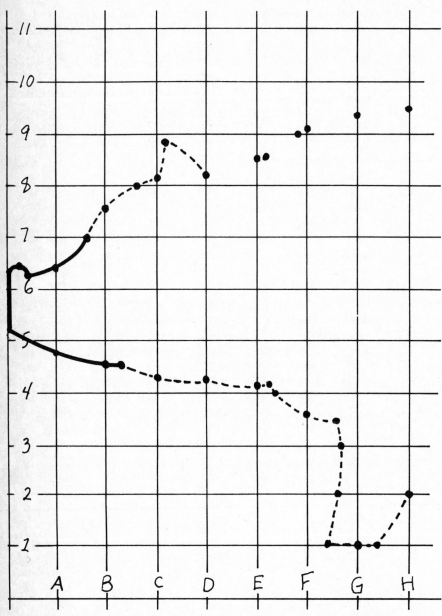

Don't hesitate to erase, correct, or make adjustments as you go along: the shape you draw is the shape your project will be. When you are finished with the drawing, you will have a full-sized pattern.

To transfer the pattern from paper to the stock you are cutting, lay a piece of carbon paper between the pattern and the stock, and draw over the design to impress it on the wood. For large patterns, where sheets of carbon paper are inconvenient, you can rub the back of the pattern, along the outline, with a carpenter's pencil, creating your own carbon backing on the pattern. Then put the pattern on the stock and follow the outline, pressing hard to leave a mark from the pencil on the back of the pattern. You can also cut out the pattern, making a template, and mark around the edges onto the stock. As with any shop technique, enlarging patterns gets easier with practice. If you aren't sure of your skills, make some practice enlargements before you tackle the real thing.

To make a pattern, draw a grid of squares to the size indicated, label the lines on the pattern and your own grid; make dots where the outline crosses grid lines and connect.

3. Fasteners

Almost all the parts of the toys and furniture projects in this book are held together with glue and either screws or nails. Screws hold a job together better than nails, and you will need far more of them for these projects. In almost every case, where nails are used, they are finishing nails—the kind that can be sunk slightly below the surface and covered with wood putty. Everything you can make from this book is likely to get a thorough pounding, so glue is necessary in almost every joint to keep these toys, tables, and chairs in one piece.

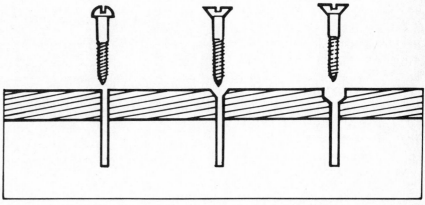

You can pre-bore for screws several ways: to sit on the surface (left), countersink to sit flush with the surface (middle), or counterbore below the surface (right).

Types of Screws

A screw can come with any of three different head styles: flathead, roundhead and ovalhead, described in the chart on page 21.

Screwheads may have straight slots or criss-cross (Phillips) slots. It is said that the Phillips type allows more turning force to be applied to the screws, but in practical terms it does not matter which type is used in these projects.

Working with Screws

In most of these projects the screw used is 1/4–1/2 inch less than the combined thicknesses of the pieces being joined, depending on whether it is countersunk or counterbored. In some cases, such as when screwing into the end grain of wood, this formula does not work. In these instances, it is suggested that you use a screw that is twice as long as the top piece of the two materials being secured. The screw diameter should be in proportion to the item being assembled: large screws will split thin wood, small screws won't hold large pieces.

If you are drilling into a hard wood—i.e., wood that is physically hard, not the species category—then you should drill pilot holes for the screws. The hole should be the diameter of the threaded part of the screw without the threads. With a

soft wood, pilot holes are not required. You can tell if a pilot hole is required by driving a test screw. If it goes in easily, no pilot hole is required. If the test screw is difficult to drive and springs back—moves counterclockwise slightly after you lift the screwdriver from it—then the wood is hard enough to need pilot holes.

In some of these projects you countersink flathead screws. Sink them flush to—not below—the surface. There is a countersinking bit available that makes the job simple. It is a cone-shaped bit designed to make a countersink as deep as you require, i.e., as deep as and the same diameter as the head of the screw. First drill the pilot hole (if required); then use the countersinking bit to drill the countersink. Remember to allow for the depth of the countersink when calculating how long a screw must be.

Counterboring involves drilling a hole deep enough to recess the head of the screw sufficiently so that it can be covered by wood putty or a plug. To do this, drill a hole equal to the length of the screw plus the depth of the counterbore. If you are just filling the hole with wood putty, a 1/4-inch counterbore is sufficient; if installing a plug, make the counterbore depth 1/2 inch. The hole diameter should be that of the screw without the threads.

Use another bit to drill a hole that is the same diameter and length of the shank of the screw used. Finally, use another bit, the same size as the screwhead diameter, to drill the counterbore.

If you expect to be making a fair number of counterbores of a particular size, then it is suggested that you buy a screwmate such as the one put out by Stanley Tools. This bit drills the pilot hole, shank hole, and counterbore in one operation. The screwmate comes in various common screw sizes. If, for example, you will be using No. 10 × 1 1/4-inch screws, then you would buy a screwmate of the same size to drill the counterbores for it.

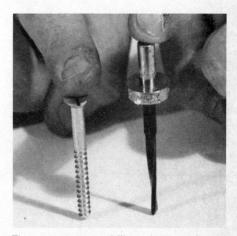

The screwmate pre-drills and counter bores for specific screw sizes.

Driving screws is tedious work, but it can be speeded up with some automatic mechanical assistance. One of the best devices available is an electric screwdriver drill. This drill accepts screwdriver bits and drives or removes screws. Another alternative is the Yankee screwdriver. When you push on the drill bit, it turns on and drives the screws. If you are working with very large screws, use a brace and bit. Incidentally, do not confuse the electric screwdriver drill with a screwdriver bit used in a regular drill; the latter does not work as well.

Covering Screws with Plugs

One way to cover screwheads is with wood plugs. There are various plastic and metal types available, but you can also buy ones made of wood, called "boat plugs," at marine-supply stores. These are commonly available in mahogany, teak, and oak in various diameters—3/8, 1/2, 5/8, and 7/16 inch. In cases where the plugs do not match the grain and color of the wood, they can provide an attractive accent.

If you need plugs made from a specific type of wood, you will have to cut them yourself as demonstrated here. This is done with a plug cutter and drill press or drill. Set the

A plug-cutter in a drill press can provide you with all the wood plugs you need to cover screw heads for the fine finish called for in several of these projects.

Wood plugs, which are popped loose with a screwdriver or small chisel, are usually cut from scrap of the kind of wood they will mate with.

Glue the wood plug lightly, then tap it in place. If any of the plug protrudes above the surface, shave it off with a chisel, then sand it smooth.

cutter so that the plug will be about 3/8-1/2 inch thicker (longer) than the counterbore. Then slice the board horizontally to separate plugs from board. Plugs are normally counterbored 1/2 inch deep.

1. Dip the plug halfway in white glue.

2. Stick the plug in the counterbore hole.

3. Gently tap the plug with a hammer until it is securely in place.

4. Using a very sharp wood chisel, chip off half—or a little more than half—of the protruding plug.

5. Use the chisel again to chip off some more of the plug, directing your blows from the high side (this guards

against the plug splitting) to within $1/16$ inch of the surface of the board. Sand to remove the rest of the plug.

When installing any plug made of the same wood as that used in a toy or piece of furniture, rather than using the plug as an accent, install the plug with the grain running in the same direction as the stock used for the project. The plugs will thus be as unobtrusive as possible; indeed, when installed properly they are nearly invisible.

Selecting Nails

A brief consideration of how nails are characterized may be useful. First, the length of a nail is indicated by the letter d, which used to be the symbol for the English penny and which goes back to the times when nails were sold for a penny a pound. Sizes run from 2d, which is 1 inch long, up to 60d, or 6 inches. As a nail becomes longer it becomes thicker; i.e., the diameter increases.

Common nails are the nails most often used by the average do-it-yourselfer. It has a flat head and the top of the shank is grooved to allow a good grip. Its most common application is in general construction work; common nails rarely turn up in building these projects.

A finishing nail is the nail that will be most useful in building toys and furniture. It is a thin nail with a small head that is designed to be hidden or set below the surface. Once a piece is assembled, these nailheads are hit with a nail set of appropriate size to sink them slightly below the surface. The resulting depressions are then filled with wood putty. After the finish has been applied, it is difficult to determine exactly where the nailheads were placed—and that is just what you want.

Brad is the name given to finishing nails $1\frac{1}{2}$ inch or smaller. This type of nail is used when strength is not the prime factor, as when attaching the back of a display case or similar nonload-bearing pieces, and to secure molding.

Screw Sizes

Screws are designated by both length and diameter. Length is designated in inches. Diameter is designated by a gauge number. Lengths available run from $1/4$ inch to 6 inches. Gauges available are 0 ($1/16$ inch) to 24 ($3/8$ inch). The label on the box of screws might read 1×6, meaning the box contains 1-inch screws of No. 6 gauge. Most common gauges are Nos. 2–16. The heavier the work required of the screw, the larger the gauge should be.

Types of Screwheads

Standard slotted woodscrews come in three headstyles: flathead (flat across the top); ovalhead (the top is rounded and the underside of the head is beveled); and roundhead (top rounded, underside of head flat). For most furniture work, you will use flathead screws, but the others have uses, too.

Flathead Use flathead screws when the head of the screw is to be flush with the surface. Use a countersink bit in your electric drill to drill out a place for the head, or use a screwmate bit, which both predrills a hole for the screw and a wider place at the top for the head. You can also countersink the head slightly below the surface.

Ovalhead Ovalhead screws are pleasing in appearance and are easier to remove than flatheads. As a rule, the underside of the head is countersunk, and the oval top remains above the surface. Use where the screw will be seen and appearance is important.

Roundhead Most important use for roundhead screws is in applications where you expect to remove the screw and the work is to be disassembled. They also can be countersunk covered.

There are a variety of wood putty products on the market to use for filling nailsets and other blemishes on a surface in preparation for finishing.

White glue, or carpenter's glue, is the glue used most often in these projects.

Glues and Adhesives

There are more than a dozen different types of glues and adhesives available, from library paste to the new instant adhesives that will glue your fingers together if you aren't careful. Only a couple of these are suitable for the projects in this book. Modern adhesives for making wooden toys and furniture include the polyvinyls, resorcinol resin, and contact cement.

Selecting the right glue is not hard. Applying it properly takes some practice. But neither the right glue nor the proper application means much unless you clamp the work and give the glue all the time it needs to dry. A well-made glue joint is strong, neat, and durable. A poorly made joint is sloppy looking and comes apart quickly under stress.

Always read the label on any new adhesive you buy. The manufacturer wants you to get good results with the product, and the instructions are designed to help you get those results.

Gluing Techniques

Some people feel that if a little glue holds firmly, then a lot of glue holds even better. That's not the case. In fact, the opposite is true. Too much glue makes a weak joint, chiefly because glue in itself is not a strong substance—not nearly as strong as the wood it bonds.

If you place two pieces of wood 1/8 inch apart, fill the space between them with glue, and let it set, you will have a weak joint that can be easily broken. On the other hand, if you apply a thin coating of glue to each of the surfaces and clamp them firmly as they dry, you will have a joint that in many cases is stronger than the wood itself. If you try to break the joint apart, the wood on either side of the joint will probably fracture before the joint breaks.

And therein lies the secret of making a good glued joint. Apply thin coats of glue, clamp securely, and allow ample drying time.

Adhesives

The chart below describes some of the properties of the adhesives you should use in putting together these toys and pieces of furniture.

Adhesives

The cardinal rules in making an adhesive do its job are: (1) the surfaces to be glued must be absolutely clean; (2) the adhesive should be applied as directed—and not too heavily; (3) the glued material must be clamped tightly until the glue has dried; (4) the glue must be allowed to dry completely. When waiting for glue to dry, remember that humid conditions can more than double the drying time listed on the container.

White Glue   Elmer's and polyvinyls like it: these glues are the white creamy liquids in plastic bottles. They are good for most toy and furniture work. A polyvinyl should not be used on anything that will be subjected to excess moisture. The most recent type of this glue is yellow in color, is made especially for woodwork, and is stronger than the white variety. Polyvinyls dry clear, losing their yellow or white appearance.

Resorcinol   A syrup and powder are mixed just before use to make a resorcinol glue. It has great strength and durability and should be used where moisture could be a problem, since it is absolutely waterproof. It will stain light-colored woods, so apply with care. Drying time is long, up to 16 hours.

Contact Cement   Two types are available, water-based and chemical-based. The chemical-based type must be used in a well-ventilated area; the water-based type needs no special precautions. Contact cement comes ready to use as a thick liquid and dries in a few minutes (much like rubber cement). To use, coat both surfaces, allow each to dry until tacky, and press together. The bond is instantaneous and permanent. You can't take the pieces apart to try again.

4. Common Joints

There are many different types of joints that can be used to build a project. You can, for example, use rabbet joints to connect the tops and sides of an item, but you could also use the simpler butt joint. It depends upon the look and sturdiness you want for the finished piece. A rabbet joint will give a seamless look, while a butt joint will not; the butt joint is not as strong. The kinds of joints used for each project in this book are specified in the directions.

There are a number of tools you can use to make these joints; these can be either hand or power tools. But it is strongly suggested that you use power tools unless you are willing to expend inordinate amounts of time and muscle.

Butt Joint
This is the easiest and simplest of the wood joints. It involves butting the end of one board or wood section against another. Butt joints can be made using one of a variety of saws: the important point is to cut the stock carefully to ensure that the two pieces will meet flush, with complete contact. Test the joint for fit after cutting, then use a plane or sandpaper—or recut the wood if required—so there will be continuous, total contact between the two adjoining pieces.

Miter Joint
The miter joint can be thought of as a butt joint, except the pieces are cut on a slant, or diagonally.

This joint is very popular in making frames and boxes. It is also used for trim because it results in a clean, finished appearance.

You can cut miters with a table saw or a radial arm saw, but they are most commonly cut with a miter box and backsaw—a handsaw designed for cutting miters. There are many kinds of miter boxes available. The rule is to get the best you can afford. In addition, a good backsaw—one that is long, sharp, and solidly

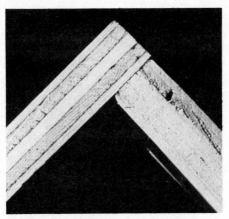
The butt joint is the simplest, but weakest of the common joints.

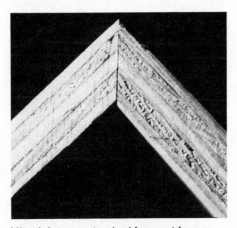
Miter joints are standard for most frames, with mating edges cut on a 45° angle.

constructed—is essential. Once again, buy the best you can afford. To cut a miter joint, first set the miter box at the angle at which you want to cut the wood. Instructions that come with the tool detail this step, and it is not difficult.

Set the piece that will mate to an adjoining surface firmly in the box and cut off an inch or two. The purpose here is just to get a clean, finished end. Take the piece of stock (you may have to cut it down into smaller pieces to facilitate working with it) and set it in position on the item on which you are working, at the point where you want the end of the piece you are cutting to fall. Mark the shape of the adjoining face onto the piece. Position the piece in the box

so that when you make your second and final cut the saw will follow and obliterate the drawn line as it meets the edge of the stock.

Dado Joints
A dado joint gives one of the strongest connections between parts; you need it, for instance, to hold the Rocking Horse together. Basically, a dado is made by cutting a square-edged slot or groove in one piece of wood so the end of another piece will fit into it snugly.

You can create a dado using a chisel and handsaw. However, this is the hardest method. It is far better to use a table saw, a radial arm saw, or a router.

If you have a table saw, there are several ways to proceed. First, consider dado blades, a selection can be found at your hardware store. There are two round blades, as well as knifelike rakers. Each has a certain thickness—usually 1/4 inch for the round blades and 1/8 inch and 1/16 inch for the rakers. To achieve the desired width of the dado, you use as many round and raker blades as required in order to add up to the width you require; then set the depth that you wish.

Another useful tool accessory when making dadoes is the dado head. This looks like a mini–saw blade. It comes with an attachment

A dado joint consists of one structural member sitting in the notch of another.

that allows you to install it on a standard table saw: the dado head is designed (twisted) to provide a cut that is wider than the blade edge. Full instructions for its use come with the device. It is important to practice on scrap until you have the correct cut.

A dado can also be made with a radial arm saw, but the easiest method is with a router. There are many sorts of router bits available to cut whatever width and depth you wish. Before you begin to cut the dado, use C-clamps to secure a straightedge in line with the cut you want to make. The straightedge will act as a guide for the baseplate of the router. Clamp the straightedge so that the cutter will make the dado in the exact spot you wish. You can use a ruler and square to measure and mark dimensions, or you can work it out first on scrap material.

No matter what tool you use to make the groove for the dado, make sure the cut is smooth and the edges sharp so that it can readily accept the mating piece of wood. A piece of tightly folded sandpaper usually works to clean the cut after it has been made. If the cut is very rough, go over it again with the router.

Dowel Joints

Another useful joint is the dowel joint, in which members are joined using glue and spiral-grooved dowels made for the purpose. It looks like a difficult joint to make, but is not hard if you use a doweling jig. This tool ensures that you drill holes at the correct locations in the pieces of wood that will be joined by the dowels.

Cut the parts to be joined (for the purposes of illustration we will assume that there are four parts—top, bottom, and two sides, as on a child's blackboard). Lay them out in their final relation to one another. Label the joints (for each of the pieces) A, B, C, and D, or number them. It is necessary to do this

Dowelled joints are butt joints reinforced with sturdy pegs, always drilled with a jig.

because you will be drilling many holes—in this instance, 16—and you want to avoid mixing up the pieces.

Instructions for use of the jig come with the device, but here is a brief summary of its use and operation. The jig clamps onto the ends of the piece of stock and has holes to guide the drill bit. There is also a guideline on the jig that is lined up with the one(s) you have marked on the ends of the stock. These lines are made to indicate the center of the hole(s) to be drilled.

Mark the boards 1/2 inch in from each side edge: these marks will indicate the positions of the hole centers. Clamp the jig in place, setting it so you can drill a 3/8-inch-wide hole that is half as deep as the glue dowel. Use a 3/8-inch bit for the drilling. As a preventive measure, so you don't drill deeper than you wish, wrap a piece of tape around the bit at the depth to which you wish to drill. Repeat the clamping-drilling process until all holes have been drilled. Half-fill each hole with white glue.

Stick glue dowels (each is 3/8 inch in diameter) into these holes, gently rotating them in place until they bottom in the holes. Lay out the cut-out pieces with dowel-sides up: apply glue to the top of each dowel. Let the glue dribble down to coat each dowel well. Place the mating pieces in posi-

tion but do not attempt to drive them snugly together.

After loosely assembling the unit, set it on a flat surface. Position one bar clamp over one end of the assembly, and the second clamp at the other end. Gradually tighten the clamps, bringing the pieces of the assembly snugly together, alternating the pressure by tightening first one clamp and then the other—just a little each time. If you are doweling stock for more width, drive the pieces together (with a rubber mallet, if you have one) and clamp them.

Rabbet Joints

The rabbet joint is made by cutting a rectangular recess out of the edge of one piece of stock to the width of the mating piece. When the pieces are joined, the joint does not show.

The rabbet can be cut in several ways: with stationary power tools, with repeated passes of a circular saw, or with a router with an appropriate bit. Bits are commonly available, but the sizes you can make are limited, up to 1/2 inch wide. This cut can also be made in one pass with a dado head.

To make the rabbet on a table saw, first draw the outline of the piece to be cut out onto the end of the stock. Set the blade at the depth required (half the thickness of the stock is standard) and run the stock through.

Turn the wood on its side to make the width cut. You can simply set the saw to the intended width, but it is also a good idea to mark the dimension along the top of the board so you can be sure the cut is correct. Run the board through.

That is all there is to the rabbet— make two cuts and a neat rectangular piece of waste will drop out. To ensure that the edges of the cut are square, stick the mating piece of stock in place to see how it fits. If it does not fit well, then adjust the blade or stock position as necessary, and run the joint through again. Sand the cut.

5. Sanding and Finishing

Children's toys and furniture demand truly fine finishes both for appearance and safety—you want your child to get fond memories, not splinters, from the projects you build. In many of the projects in this book, sanding should take as long as all the other steps combined. There are proper techniques for sanding, and they are not hard to learn. The most important thing to keep in mind is that not all sanding is a removal process. You will, of course, have to sand away rough edges and sometimes sand a piece to make it the right shape. But much of the sanding required in these projects is simply smoothing to a perfect finish. Remember that patience is probably the most important ingredient in a successful sanding job. Remember also that a good sanding job is more important than any other single aspect of these projects.

Selecting Sandpaper
Technically, there is no longer an item called sandpaper. Today, these gritty sheets are called *abrasive papers,* because they are made of abrasive materials other than sand. Five kinds of abrasives are used: flint, garnet, silicon carbide, aluminum oxide, and emery. The cheapest papers use flint. They neither cut as fast nor last as long as the better papers. If you expect to do much sanding, it will pay you to buy better papers coated with one of the other abrasives.

Abrasive papers come in half a dozen thicknesses. The thinner papers are good for working in tight places because these weights fold easily. However, they are not as good for use on sanding blocks or power sanders because the paper will tear. The heavier papers feel very stiff and may crack when folded, but they stand up longer in the power and hand sanders. You should have some of each weight.

There are two kinds of papers, *open grain* and *closed grain.* The open-grain type has only a light coating of abrasive material so that the material being sanded doesn't cling to the abrasive granules and clog the paper. The closed-grain type has a dense coating of abrasive material and does its work more quickly. For general smoothing and finishing, the closed-grain type is better. Buy some light-weight papers for sanding in and around corners, but buy mostly heavier papers for their longer mileage.

The accompanying chart shows the relationship between the different grading systems for indicating the coarseness of grit for abrasive papers and tells the most common use for each type.

In addition to standard abrasive papers, you can buy waterproof sandpaper. This is usually sold only in the finer grits and is made to be used with water or oil for the final rubdown in hand finishing.

Using a Tack Cloth
When you finish sanding, wipe the sawdust from the surface of the work with a tack cloth. (You can buy tack cloths already made at your home center, or you can make one by moistening a cloth with a mixture of one part turpentine and three parts varnish.) The advantage of a tack cloth over a regular dust rag is that the sawdust clings to the tack cloth; it doesn't fly into the air, only to settle on the work again in a few minutes.

Sanding Blocks
A sanding block, in its simplest form, is a rectangular block of wood around which you wrap a piece of abrasive paper. A typical sanding block is about 2 inches wide and 4–6 inches long. For smaller work, you can make smaller blocks. Holding the sides of the block, you apply one face of it to the surface to be sanded, and work the block back and forth with straight-line motions. The job is much smoother if a small felt pad is placed on the block before the paper is wrapped around it. This cushions the paper and prevents the problem of uneven sanding.

It takes only a few minutes to make a sanding block, but you will find several types of hand sanders at your home center that are both convenient and inexpensive. All have some type of clamp to hold the abrasive paper in place, built-in felt padding, and (usually) a comfortable

Always clean a surface you have sanded; a tack cloth picks up the finest sawdust.

A sanding block, whether homemade or purchased, should be standard .

gripping surface that makes them easy to control.

Whether you buy one or make one, you certainly should own a sanding block and use it in the great majority of your sanding work. As a matter of principle, always use a block when sanding flat surfaces.

Power Sanders

The proper way to use an oscillating sander is to let the sander do the work. Your job is to guide it in a straight line with the grain of the wood, to move it slowly over the surface, and to apply light pressure. In other words, don't try to use it like a hand sander and move it back and forth by hand. Start at one end of the area to be sanded and slowly move it toward the other end. Then go back to the beginning and run the course again. Do this until the whole surface is sanded down.

Sanding Techniques

Sanding is easy if you are aware of the basic techniques. Follow these instructions.

1. Always sand with, not across, the grain of the wood.

2. Use a straight back-and-forth movement of the sanding block. Don't use a circular or irregular motion.

3. Apply even pressure to the top of the sanding block. Don't lean more heavily on the front or back of it. The pressure should be light, not forced.

4. When sanding a flat surface, be especially careful as you approach the edge. There is a tendency to lean on the block at this time, which results in heavier pressure near the edge of the work. Keep the sanding surface level and the pressure even to avoid tapering the work surface downward.

5. Tap the sawdust out of the sandpaper at regular intervals. The sawdust clogs the paper and prevents the paper from cutting properly. You can use a small brush (an old toothbrush will do).

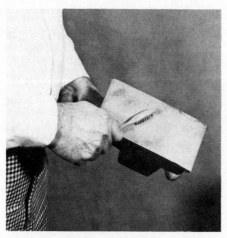

A toothbrush is a good tool for cleaning sandpaper. Sandpaper loses its cutting power when it clogs with sawdust, so it must be cleaned periodically.

Finishes

In most cases in this book, the choice of finish for a project is left up to you. In a few instances, the projects demand to be finished a certain way; if so, the finish is specified in the directions. The single most important thing to remember when choosing a finish for your toys and furniture is that many of these projects will get chewed on when they are in use. For this reason, always check the labels on the finishes you are considering to be sure you choose one that is nontoxic. Toxic finishes must be labeled as such.

The finish you choose will be dictated by the kind of wood the project is made of: if it is handsome, you will want a clear finish that shows off the grain; if the wood is less attractive, paint will do. Some projects and some parts of projects, like the handle on a toddler's rocker, are best left unfinished. As with sanding, the time you spend finishing a project will be well invested. Many coats, each thoroughly sanded down, will enhance the toys and furniture you build.

Sandpapers

Manufacturers grade their abrasive papers by one of three methods, and there are no national standards to serve as a guide. Some give their papers a name (fine, medium, etc.); some rate them by grit number (30, 180, 400, etc.), referring to the abrasive particle size; and others use a numbering system (3/0, 5/0, 8/0), the oldest of all grading methods. The chart below shows all three methods in relation to each other, so that no matter which rating is used, you can buy the paper you need.

Number	Grit	Name	When to use
10/0	600, 500, 400	Superfine	Last sanding of a new furniture or toy finish; final sanding of fine woods; hand-rubbed finish
9/0	360		
8/0	320, 280	Extra fine	Same as above
7/0	240		
6/0	200, 220	Very fine	Sanding between coats of paint or varnish
5/0	180, 150	Fine	Sanding hardwood and softwood before and after you stain, seal, or apply a priming coat
4/0	120, 100		
3/0			
2/0			
1	80, 60	Medium	Removing deep scratches, shaping of parts, or rough sanding
0	50		
1/0			
1/2			
1 1/2	40, 36	Coarse	Wood removal, shaping, rough sanding
2	30		
2 1/2			

Projects

Old Time Auto

Materials List
Base (1), ¾ × 3½ × 10″
Cab uprights (6), ¾ × ¾ × 5″, square
  molding
Cab doors (4), ¾ × 1½ × 2½″
Cab ends (2), ¾ × 2 × 2½″
Engine base (1), 1½ × 2½ × 3⅜″
Engine top (1), ½ × 2½ × 3⅜″
Roof (1), ¾ × 3½ × 6″
Wheels (5), ¾ × 2¼″ diameter
Furniture buttons (6), ½″
¼″ dowel
³⁄₁₆″ dowel
¾″ wooden bead
Glue

Tools
Band saw, coping saw, or saber saw
Drill
Sander or sandpaper
Drill press (optional)
C-clamps

Level of Difficulty
Easy

Length of Time Required
Afternoon

Safety Precautions
Safety goggles

**To obtain a full-sized traceable pattern
for this project, use the order form at the
back of this book and order pattern
number 632.**

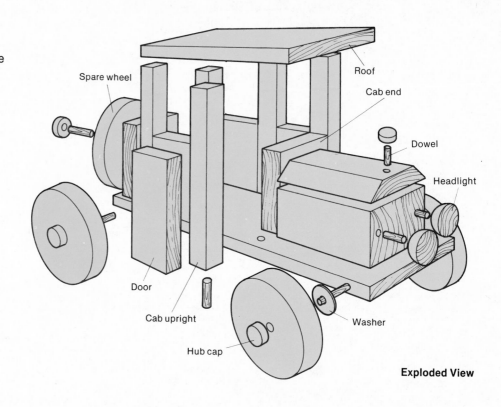

Exploded View

This chunky, old-fashioned automobile can stand up to a generation of kids. It is one of the easiest projects in this book to complete but it requires a lot of sanding to make it smooth enough for two-year-old owners. Take extra care making the wheels: for the best roll, they should all be exactly the same size and perfectly round. Make the auto from clear pine or fir scraps. Leave it natural, or finish it with any nontoxic finish. Remember, this toy will probably get chewed on, too.

STEP 1
Cutting and Drilling the Parts
Cut the base to the given dimensions, sand it thoroughly, and round the edges and corners slightly. Drill ¼-inch holes 1 inch deep into the long edges on the center line ¾ inch in from the ends. Cut the cab roof, uprights, doors, ends, and the engine base and top, to the given dimensions. Cut the edges of the engine top to the angle shown in the Front View. Sand all the pieces except the engine bottom and top and round their corners and edges. Scribe five 2¼-inch circles (marking the center point so you can drill it out later) and carefully cut out the circles with a coping saw, saber saw, or band saw, cutting just outside the marked circles. Then sand down to the lines. You can also cut out the wheels with a 2¼-inch hole saw in a drill press. However you cut them out, be sure to sand and round their edges.

STEP 2
Constructing the Cab
Glue the uprights and doors together, as shown in the Top View, with the bottoms and sides flush; clamp until the glue is set. Drill a ¼-inch hole ½ inch deep in the center of one of the cab ends; then glue and clamp the ends between the cab sides, flush with the bottom, with the drilled end at the rear, as shown. Glue and clamp the roof to the uprights, flush with the back and sides, overhanging the front uprights ¾ inch.

STEP 3
Assembling the Engine
Glue and clamp the engine top to the engine bottom, as shown in the Front

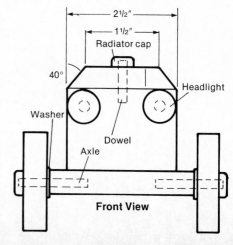

Front View

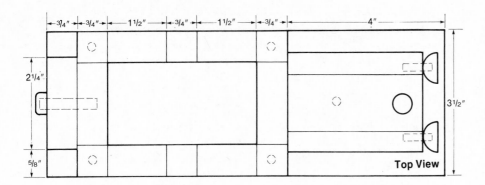

Top View

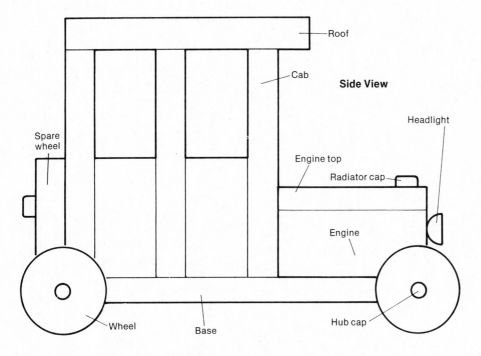

Roof

Cab

Side View

Spare wheel

Headlight

Engine top

Radiator cap

Engine

Wheel

Base

Hub cap

the points shown in the Top View. Glue in 1½-inch pieces of ¼-inch dowel and sand down the ends.

STEP 5
Finishing the Auto and Attaching the Wheels

Drill ¼-inch holes halfway through five furniture plugs (from the flat side); mark your drill bit with masking tape so you can tell when you have reached the proper depth. If you don't have furniture plugs, use ⅜-inch slices of ½-inch dowel. Drill a ¼-inch hole through the center of one of the wheels. Glue a 1½-inch length of ¼-inch dowel into the hole in the back of the cab; glue on the drilled wheel, and a furniture-plug hubcap on the end of the dowel. Glue 2-inch lengths of ¼-inch dowel into the axle holes on the edge of the base; drill ³∕₁₆-inch holes through the center of the remaining wheels. Finish the auto and wheels as you wish; then install the wheels. They will turn more easily if you put plastic washers between them and the base; you can make these by punching out ½-inch discs of plastic from a coffee-can top (with a lipstick cap or something similar), then punching out ³∕₁₆-inch of the center with a paper punch. Put the optional washers in place, mount the wheels, and glue on the furniture-plug hubcaps.

View. When the glue is set, sand the engine, rounding the corners. Drill a ³∕₁₆-inch hole, 1 inch deep, ½ inch in from the center of the engine top and ½ inch in from the front end. Glue in a 1⅛-inch length of ³∕₁₆-inch dowel. Drill a ³∕₁₆-inch hole halfway through the center of a furniture button and glue it on the end of the dowel, gluing it also to the top of the engine. Drill a ³∕₁₆-inch hole through the center of a wooden bead (through the smaller hole) and then cut the bead in half across the hole (hold it in a vise to perform this delicate operation). Drill ½-inch deep, ³∕₁₆-inch holes into the front of the engine at the points shown in the Front View. Glue in ¾-

inch lengths of ³∕₁₆-inch dowel and glue the headlights onto the dowels, as shown in the Top View. Sand the ends flush with the beads.

STEP 4
Attaching the Cab and the Engine

Glue and clamp the cab to the base, with the rear of the cab ¾ inch in from the rear of the base; then glue and clamp the engine to both the center of the front of the cab (¾ inch in from either side) and the base. When the glue has set, drill ¼-inch holes 1½-inches deep through the base into the cab and the engine at

Clown Stacking Toy

Materials List

³/₄" softwood, large enough for the 6 disks required
³/₄" dowel, 5" long
Felt, 4¹/₂" in diameter
Glue
Paint and stain

Tools

Band saw
Sandpaper
Small dowel
Wood lathe (optional)

Level of Difficulty

Easy

Length of Time Required

Afternoon

Safety Precautions

Safety goggles

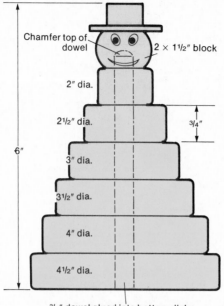

Chamfer top of dowel
2 × 1¹/₂" block
2" dia.
2¹/₂" dia.
³/₄"
3" dia.
3¹/₂" dia.
4" dia.
6"
4¹/₂" dia.

³/₄" dowel glued into bottom disk

Stacking Toy Disk Dimensions

STEP 1
Making the Disks

Cut the disks from ³/₄-inch softwood with a bandsaw to the diameters given in the drawing above; sand smooth. Bore a ³/₄-inch hole through each disk; then sand the hole on all but the largest disk with sandpaper wrapped around a small dowel. This ensures that the disks will slip easily over a ³/₄-inch dowel. Paint the disks, each with a different color, and, if you like, add small circles of one color down the front to create the buttons on a clown's suit.

STEP 2
Installing the Dowel

Cut a ³/₄-inch dowel 5 inches long, sand it smooth, and round off one end with sandpaper. (If you are making a stacking toy with no head, make the dowel 4¹/₂ inches long.) Finish the dowel with a stain—paint may make it fit too tightly in the stacking disks. When the finish is dry, glue the unsanded end into the bottom disk. After installing the dowel, glue a round of felt to the bottom of the disk to protect surfaces on which the toy sits.

STEP 3
Shaping the Head

Turn a 2 × 2 × 1¹/₂-inch piece of softwood on a lathe to whatever shape you like—the drawing shows a round head with a plug hat on top. Sand the head smooth and bore a ³/₄-inch blind hole in the center of the bottom to fit over the end of the dowel. Paint and decorate the head as you like.

The simplest toy is often the best one. This toddler's stacking toy is a good case in point, and it is easy to make. The toy consists of six progressively smaller wooden disks; the largest is the base with a dowel standing up in the center; the others slide over the dowel. The toy is crowned with a clown's head, which is created by turning a block of wood on a lathe. If you don't have a lathe, simply make the toy without a head, shortening the dowel that holds the disks so that it comes flush with the top disk. The result may not be a "clown" stacking toy, but toddlers seem to think it works just as well.

Blue Bear Toothbrush Holder

Materials List
Body (1), $3/4 \times 6 \times 7''$, hardwood
Arms (1), $3/4 \times 6 \times 3''$, hardwood
Base (1), $1/2 \times 7 \times 6''$, hardwood or
   plywood
No. 8 finishing nails
Paint

Tools
Band saw, saber saw or coping saw
Sander or sandpaper
Hammer

Level of Difficulty
Easy

Length of Time Required
Afternoon

Safety Precautions
Safety goggles

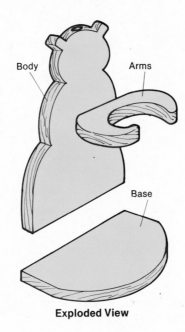

Body   Arms

Base

Exploded View

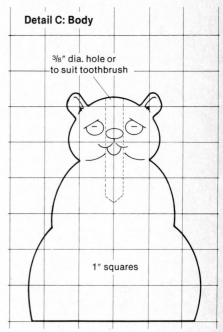

Detail C: Body

$3/8''$ dia. hole or
to suit toothbrush

1" squares

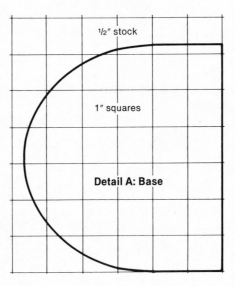

$1/2''$ stock

1" squares

Detail A: Base

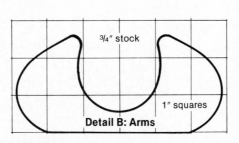

$3/4''$ stock

1" squares

Detail B: Arms

Getting kids to brush their teeth can be a lot easier if they have a whimsical toothbrush holder to visit. Just remind your youngsters that this particular bear likes plenty of attention.

The bear is simple to make, and the project takes just an hour or so, plus the time for the paint to dry. The body and arms are made of $3/4$-inch hardwood stock, and the base is $1/2$-inch hardwood or plywood stock. The holder can serve one brusher or a whole family.

STEP 1
Cutting the Body, Arms, and Base
Enlarge the squared drawings, transfer the pattern to $3/4$-inch stock for the body and arms, and $1/2$-inch stock for the base. Cut out the pieces on a band saw and sand thoroughly.

STEP 2
Assembling the Bear
Attach the arms to the body with glue and No. 8 finishing nails where indicated on the squared drawing, driving the nails in from the back of the body. Attach the body to the base with glue and the same size nails.

STEP 3
Drilling the Toothbrush Holder
Bore a $3/8$-inch hole down through the top of the head, as indicated on the squared drawing; you may have to make it a little larger, depending on the size of the toothbrush it is to hold. Additional holes can be drilled at angles into the shoulders to hold more toothbrushes.

STEP 4
Finishing the Bear
Paint the bear a bright color. When dry, apply the facial features, following the pattern on the squared drawing or one of your own design.

Crayon Holder

Materials List
$1\frac{1}{2} \times 4 \times 6\frac{1}{2}''$ scrap (1 required for
   each crayon holder)
Paint (2 contrasting colors)

Tools
Band saw
Sander or sandpaper

Level of Difficulty
Easy

Length of Time Required
Afternoon

Safety Precautions
Safety goggles

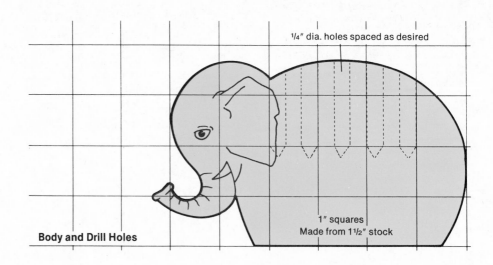

¼" dia. holes spaced as desired

1" squares
Made from 1½" stock

Body and Drill Holes

STEP 1
Cutting the Holder
Enlarge and transfer the pattern to a piece of 2 × 4, 2 × 6, or other stock scrap of appropriate size. Cut out the shape with a band saw.

STEP 2
Drilling and Finishing the Holder
Bore ¼-inch holes (or larger ones,

depending on the size of your child's crayons) in the top to the same depth—about 2 inches from the bottom—for the crayons. Sand the block thoroughly and paint with a bright color. Use two coats for the best finish. After the base coats are dry, use a contrasting color and a fine brush to add the facial features. You can also use India ink or a thick felt-tip marker.

An elephant table-top crayon holder will delight any youngster. These holders make great little stocking stuffers for Christmas and fun birthday presents. Best of all, they can be made in minutes; waiting for the paint to dry is the only part of the project that takes time. If you decide to make one, you might as well make several at the same time to keep as a supply of ready gifts. All you need are blocks of scrap wood large enough to fit the pattern.

Animal Puzzles

STEP 1
Cutting Out the Puzzle

Enlarge the squared drawing and transfer the pattern to any solid wood stock. Or draw your own pattern directly on the stock. Use a band saw first to cut out the whole shape, then to cut apart the pieces.

STEP 2
Finishing the Puzzle

Be sure to sand all the pieces and round any sharp corners with sandpaper or a sander. Check to see that there are no splinters or sharp edges that could injure a small child. Paint the pieces and, when they are dry,

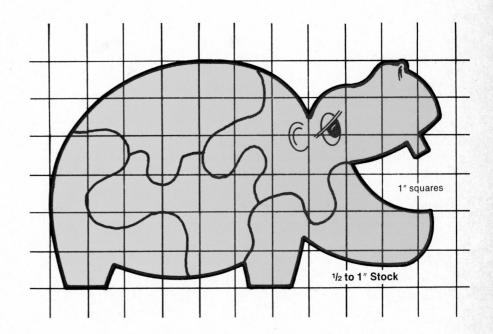

1″ squares

½ to 1″ Stock

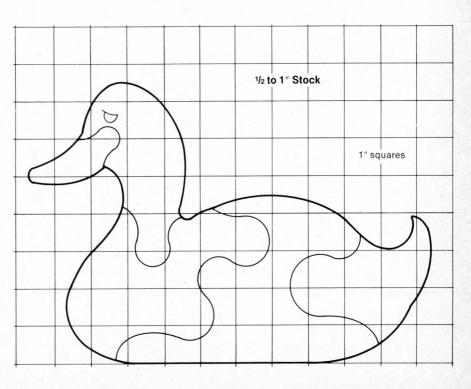

½ to 1″ Stock

1″ squares

Animal puzzles provide an enjoyable and whimsical way to spend an hour or two in the shop and a great way to use up some scrap material. After you've had the fun of making them, they will give plenty of good times to the youngsters who play with them. The four drawings given here can get you started, but you should let your imagination go and create patterns of your own. The difficulty of the puzzles should depend on the age of the child who will be playing with them (notice that the puzzle in the photo has only three pieces, while the drawing of the same shape has five—you can make the cuts any way you like from the same basic shape).

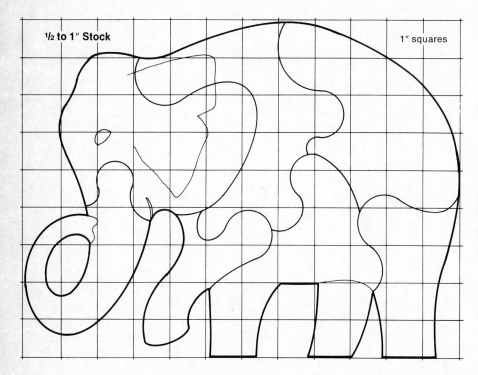

add decorative features. For very young puzzle-workers, you may want to add dots on the top side to make it easier to match up the parts. Some of the dots on the hippo shown here are painted across the parts to give an additional hint of how the pieces go together.

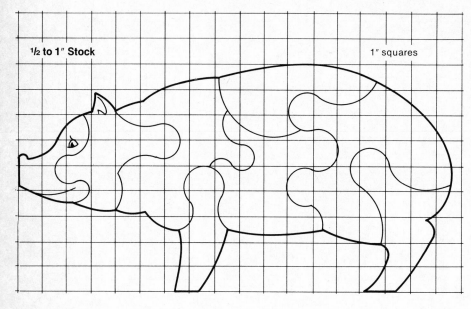

Initial Bookrack or Wall Plaque

Materials List
¾″ solid stock or plywood, large enough for 2 letters if building bookrack
½ × 8 × 16″ stock, for bookrack base
1″ wood screws (4), for bookrack
Glue
Plaque hangers (2), for wall plaque
Paint or stain

Tools
Band saw, saber saw, coping saw, or jig saw
Drill
Sandpaper
Small dowel or emery board
Screwdriver

Level of Difficulty
Easy

Length of Time Required
Afternoon

Safety Precautions
Safety goggles

Any youngster likes personalized items, so a bookrack or wall plaque made of his or her initial will be very popular. These items are easy to make, requiring only an hour or so in the shop, and can be made of scrap materials you probably have lying around already. You can enlarge letters from the alphabet given here or design your own to suit your fancy.

Stock for the bookrack ends should be at least ¾-inch thick. You can use either solid stock or plywood—each has advantages and disadvantages. Solid stock has a tendency to split and break on the thinner parts of some letters; plywood is stronger. On the other hand, the edges of plywood letters are harder to finish unless you plan to paint them. If you are making a wall plaque, the strength of the letter is not a concern. The strength requirement for the bookrack unfortunately precludes certain letters—namely F, I, P, T, V, and Y—because the bases of these letters are too narrow to support much weight.

STEP 1
Cutting the Letters
Enlarge the squared drawing of the letters you need to the size desired for a wall plaque or to 6 inches along the bottom edge for a bookrack. Transfer this pattern to a piece of stock for as many letters as you need (two for a bookrack). Use a band saw, saber saw, or coping saw to cut out the outline of the letter. For letters with inside cutouts, such as 0 or B, drill a starting hole with a ¼-inch bit inside the area to be cut out, then insert a saber-saw, coping-saw, or jig-saw blade and make the necessary cut. Always cut as exactly on the pattern as you can in order to eliminate as much sanding as possible; it is difficult to sand in small crevices on the letters. For hard-to-sand areas, use sandpaper wrapped around a small dowel or thin piece of wood; you can also use a standard fingernail emery board. Sand the letters thoroughly until they feel smooth to the touch.

Initial Book End Alphabet
1½″ squares

STEP 2
Assembling and Finishing the Bookrack

To make the bookrack, attach the letters a sanded, 8-inch wide piece of ½-inch stock with glue and countersunk 1¼-inch wood screws (see drawing). The materials listed here are for a bookrack 16 inches long, but you can vary the length to suit your needs. When the glue is dry, stain and finish or paint the rack. To use the letters as wall plaques, finish them as desired with stain or paint, then attach small plaque hangers to the back. These are available at hobby or craft shops.

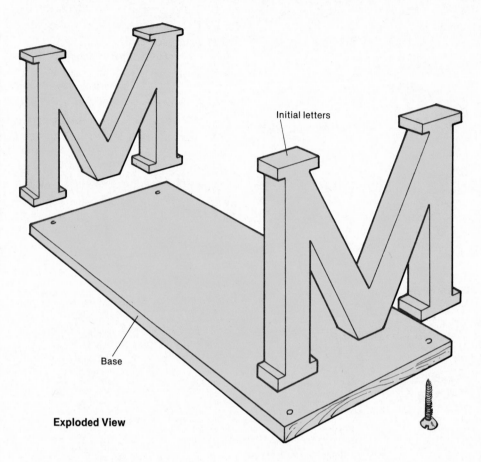

Initial letters

Base

Exploded View

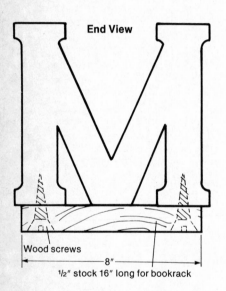

End View

Wood screws

8"

½" stock 16" long for bookrack

Personalized Coat-and-Cap Rack

Materials List
3/4" plywood, large enough for child's name in 5" letters and rack below
1/2 × 3³/4" dowels, as many as needed
Nails or screws (2), for mounting on wall
Paint or stain

Tools
Band saw
Saber saw
Drill
Sandpaper
Hammer or screwdriver

Level of Difficulty
Easy

Length of Time Required
Afternoon

Safety Precautions
Safety goggles

One good way to encourage your youngster to hang up clothes and keep a tidy room is to put up a coat-and-cap rack with his or her name running across the top in large letters: seeing the name, the child may be reminded that the pegs below have a purpose. Parents of particularly forgetful children might consider making a coat-and-cap rack with the word COATS along the top.

Making the coat-and-cap rack is fairly simple, although it does require a bit of time and patience to cut out all the letters. The rack can be made of plywood or solid wood, but I recommend plywood because it makes for a sturdier rack.

STEP 1
Making a Pattern
Enlarge the letters you need to 5 inches high from the alphabet on page 35 or in a style of your own design. Arrange the letters as you wish—try different positions. Some children's names have letters that can touch, like the R and the K in the photo below; others don't. As you arrange the letters, remember that you will have to cut them out, so don't create any crevices you won't want to tackle with a saw.

STEP 2
Creating the Nameplate
Transfer the letter patterns in the arrangement you like to a piece of 3/4-inch stock and mark off an area 3 inches deep below the bottom line of the letters; then mark off length of the name (see drawing). Use a band saw to make all the open cuts. For cutouts inside letters, drill 1/4-inch starter holes and insert a saber-saw blade in the hole to make the cut. On

cutouts that have sharp corners, such as the bottom triangle in the letter K, drill pilot holes at each corner, then saw from hole to hole.

STEP 3
The Hangers and the Rack
Bore 1/2-inch holes through the rack for the dowels that will serve as the coat and cap hangers; these should be about 3¹/2 inches apart along the center of the portion below the name. The longer your child's name, the more pegs you can have. Cut 1/2-inch dowels to 3³/4 inches and sand smooth the ends that will protrude from the rack. Glue the dowels in place in the rack. After the glue dries, sand surfaces and paint or finish.

STEP 4
Hanging the Rack
Hang the rack on the wall by nailing or screwing it to a stud, first checking the reach of the youngster who will be using it.

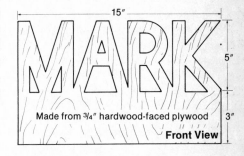

15"
5"
3"
Made from 3/4" hardwood-faced plywood
Front View

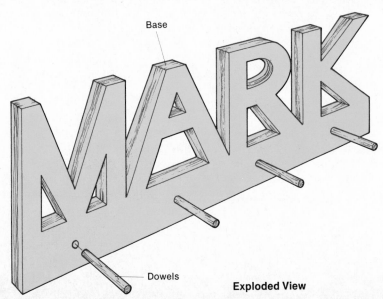

Base

Dowels

Exploded View

Bad-Guy Bean-Bag Game

Materials List
Target face (1), 24 × 30″, tempered
¼″ hardboard
Braces (2), 16 × 16″, ¾″ plywood
Bottom support (1), 16 × 24″,
¾″ plywood
1¼″, 1½″ flathead screws
Paint
Canvas or stout cloth
Dried beans
Strong thread

Tools
Saber saw, coping saw, or band saw
Screwdriver
Sandpaper or sander

Level of Difficulty
Easy

Length of Time Required
Afternoon

Safety Precautions
Safety goggles

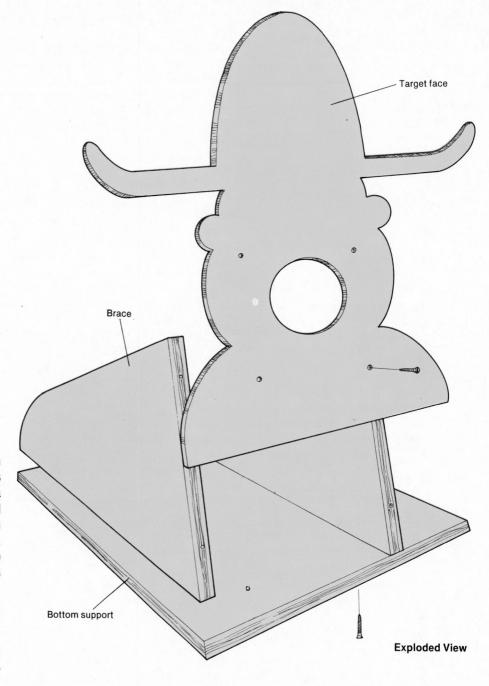

Target face

Brace

Bottom support

Exploded View

Throwing bean-bags at a target is an age-old game that never loses its appeal—grownups can't resist a toss any more than a four-year-old can. This bean-bag game is fun because a good throw makes Mr. Bad swallow the beans. Plan to make several bean-bags; your youngsters will want lots of ammunition.

STEP 1
Cutting Out the Head
Enlarge the squared drawing and transfer the pattern to a sheet of tempered ¼-inch hardboard. Cut it out with a saber saw or coping saw. Drill a starting hole inside the mouth and cut out the opening.

STEP 2
Cutting the Supports and Bottom
Make a pattern for the braces as indicated in the Side View. The curved edge does not have to look exactly as shown, but it should be rounded off

to eliminate sharp corners where the braces meet the bottom support. Be sure to mark off the correct angle or the face won't tilt back. Cut two braces from ¾-inch plywood. Cut the bottom support to size from the plywood, cut one edge to the same angle as the braces as indicated in the drawing, and round the corners on the other edge.

STEP 3
Assembling the Target
Sand all the pieces; check the fit among the face, braces, and bottom; and make any necessary adjustments. Attach the face to the bottom with four ½-inch flathead screws, countersunk to avoid rough edges. Next attach the face to the braces in the same way, and finally affix the

Side View

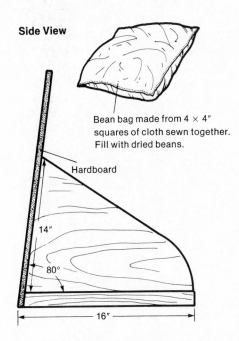

Bean bag made from 4 × 4″ squares of cloth sewn together. Fill with dried beans.

Hardboard

14″

80°

16″

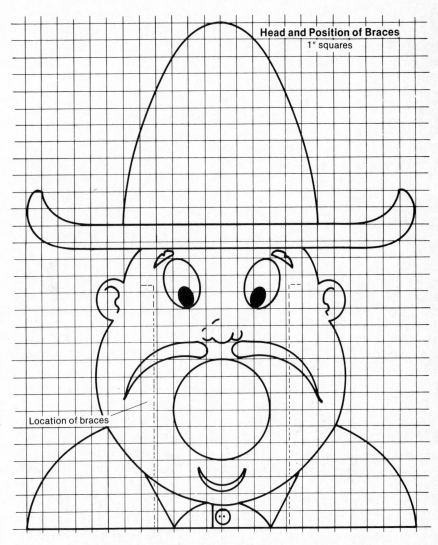

Head and Position of Braces
1″ squares

Location of braces

braces to the bottom support, driving countersunk 1¼-inch screws up through the bottom. Follow the pattern on the squared drawing to paint the face or use your own imagination. As you can see by comparing the photo with the pattern, bean-bag games vary every time you make one.

STEP 4
Making the Bean-Bags
Stitch together 4-inch squares of sturdy cloth, leaving an opening on one side. Fill the bag with dried beans—don't overfill it; the bag should be limp—and stitch closed.

Children's Blackboard

Materials List

Frame, top and bottom (2), ¾ × 2 × 20½", any stock

Frame, ends (2), ¾ × 2 × 14", any stock

Blackboard back (1), ¾ × 14½ × 17", hardboard

Chalk rail (1), ¾ × 2 × 20", any stock

Chalk-rail lip (1), ½ × 1 × 20", any stock

1⅜" spiral dowels

¾", 1" wood screws

Glue

Wood putty

Flat black latex paint for blackboard

Paint or other finish for frame

Picture hangers

Tools

Table saw, band saw, radial arm saw or router

Doweling jig

Drill

Screwdriver

Sander or sandpaper

Clamps

Level of Difficulty

Easy

Length of Time Required

Afternoon

Safety Precautions

Safety goggles, filter mask

A blackboard not only gives young children lots of fun while they draw and practice writing, but it can also be a good reminder board for older children. In place of the traditional slate, this blackboard uses a piece of hardboard painted with several coats of flat black paint, so the project is easy to make from readily available materials.

If you want to construct a more elegant blackboard, read the directions for the Double Easel on page 137, and follow the steps for building the blackboard portion of that proj-

ect. You can make it in place of the simpler model described here, and you can hang it the same way as this one.

STEP 1
Making the Frame

Cut the frame pieces from any ¾-inch stock. If you are using a softwood stock such as pine, you can hold the frame together with glue and chevron-joint fasteners, but I recommend doweling the pieces together for added strength. With hardwood stock, doweling is a necessity. To dowel the joints, lay the pieces of the frame in place exactly as they are shown in the drawing. At each corner, mark a line at the center of the end pieces across the top and bottom pieces; then use a doweling jig to drill 1-inch-deep holes at each end of the end pieces and in the top and bottom pieces where marked on inside edges. These holes will accept the joint dowels. Before assembling the frame, cut a ¼ × ¼-inch rabbet along the length of the inside back edge of the end pieces and along the inside back edge of the top and bottom pieces to within 1½ inches of either end. You can use a table saw, radial arm saw, or router for this job. Finally, round the outside corners of the top and bottom pieces and sand the pieces of the frame smooth.

STEP 2
Assembling the Frame

Squeeze glue into the dowel hole at one end of the bottom piece, insert a 1⅜-inch spiral dowel, glue the corresponding hole on the end piece, glue the edge of the end piece that will butt against the bottom piece, and fit together. Complete the joints at the other three corners in the same manner, then clamp the finished frame in a bar clamp or picture-frame clamp and wipe away all excess glue with a warm, damp cloth. Allow to dry overnight. When dry, finish the frame with paint, stain, or varnish.

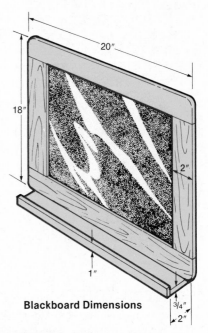

Blackboard Dimensions

STEP 3
Installing the Blackboard Back

Cut the blackboard to size from ¼-inch hardboard and paint with several coats of flat black latex paint. When the last coat has dried, glue it into the rabbets at the back of the frame and fix tightly with small C-clamps. Allow to dry overnight.

STEP 4
Building and Installing the Chalk Rail

Cut the pieces for the chalk rail and sand them smooth. Attach the chalk-rail lip to the chalk rail, as shown in the drawing, with countersunk ¾-inch flathead wood screws. Fill the holes with wood putty and, when the putty is set, sand smooth. Attach the chalk-rail assembly to the bottom of the blackboard in the same manner.

STEP 5
Hanging the Blackboard

Because the blackboard will move when written on if it hangs from a single picture hook, install picture hangers on either side of the frame and wall hangers on corresponding places on the wall. If you won't want to move the blackboard, you can nail or screw it through the frame into studs in the wall.

Cork Bulletin Board

Materials List

Frame, top and bottom (2), $3/4 \times 2^1/2 \times 36''$, any hardwood stock, molding, or picture-frame stock

Frame, ends (2), $3/4 \times 2^1/2 \times 24''$, any hardwood stock, molding, or picture-frame stock

Back (1), $1/4 \times 19^1/2 \times 31^1/2''$, hardboard

Cork tiles (enough to make $19 \times 31''$) or sheet cork

Glue

Contact adhesive

Brads or $1/2''$ flathead brass screws

Paint or other finish

Tools

Table saw or radial arm saw

Picture-frame clamp

Screwdriver or hammer

Sander or sandpaper

Level of Difficulty

Easy

Length of Time Required

Afternoon

Safety Precautions

Safety goggles, filter mask

Bulletin Board Dimensions

36″

3/4″

24″

2½″

Shop-made molding or picture frame molding

Cork

1/4″ hardboard

1/4 × 1/4″ rabbet

Every youngster needs a place to organize and pin up photographs, newspaper clippings, baseball cards, ribbons, and so on. This project fits the bill, and once you make one for the kids' room, you will probably make another for the kitchen or your workshop. The bulletin board is simply a frame made of scrap stock, molding, or picture-frame stock, holding a 1/4-inch hardboard back with cork tiles or sheet cork glued in place.

If the walls of your children's room are crowded, one good place to hang this bulletin board is on the inside of a closet door. True, it won't show off a collection as nicely as it would if it were hanging on the wall, but if the board is intended for reminders and other things that needn't be so public, hanging it inside the closet uses an otherwise wasted space effectively. To mount the bulletin board, simply screw it onto a hardwood door or, in the case of a hollow-core door, use wall anchors short enough that they won't pierce the outside of the door.

An even simpler, equally effective closet-door bulletin board can be created by gluing cork tiles or sheet cork directly onto the door. In this way you can make a bulletin board as large as you wish in a matter of minutes. For gluing the cork to the door, follow the directions given in the last step of this project.

STEP 1
Cutting the Frame

The materials listed here make a 24 × 36-inch bulletin board, but the project can be made to any size. The procedures of construction are the same regardless of size. Use any hardwood stock you have on hand, or buy picture-frame stock and cut it to the size you desire. Cut the pieces for the frame and use a table saw or radial arm saw to cut a 1/4 × 1/4-inch rabbet along the length of the inside back edges. Miter the corners at a 45° angle. Sand the pieces smooth.

STEP 2
Assembling the Board

Glue the corners of the frame together, make sure the frame is squared, and secure it in a picture-frame clamp. Allow to dry overnight. Cut the 1/4-inch hardboard to the dimensions given or, if you are making a larger or smaller bulletin board, to 1/2 inch longer and wider than the inside dimensions of the frame (so that it will fit in the rabbets). Glue the back into the frame and secure with small brass screws or brads for extra strength. Finally, finish the frame as you desire.

STEP 3
Applying the Cork

Use cork tiles, or sheet cork, if you can find it, for the face of the bulletin board. You will probably have to cut the tiles along two of the sides to fit inside the frame; the sheet cork can simply be cut to fit the whole area. To apply the cork, use contact adhesive or ordinary white glue. If you use white glue, press the tiles or sheet cork in place and hold them with weights, overnight, until dry.

Palomino Stick Pony

Materials List
Head (1), ¾ × 10 × 10″, any light stock
Handle (1), ½ × 5″ dowel
Stick (1), ½ × 36″ dowel
Glue
Paint

Tools
Band saw, saber saw, or coping saw
Drill with ½-inch bit or drill press

Level of Difficulty
Easy

Length of Time Required
Afternoon

Safety Precautions
Safety goggles

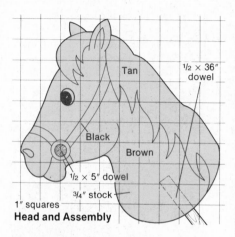

Tan

½ × 36″ dowel

Black

Brown

½ × 5″ dowel

¾″ stock

1″ squares
Head and Assembly

The easiest way to cut out the pony's head is with a bench top jig saw.

STEP 1
Cutting Out the Head
Enlarge the squared drawing and transfer the pattern to whatever stock you choose. Cut out around the pattern with a band saw, saber saw, or coping saw. Sand the edges. Sand the head thoroughly, taking care that all the edges are smooth.

STEP 2
Fitting the Handle and Stick
Fix the head in a drill press or a vise and bore a ½-inch hole 2 inches deep in the bottom edge, where indicated on the drawing. Then bore a ½-inch hole through the head at the bridle, as indicated on the drawing. Sand away any rough spots caused by the drill. Cut the two dowels to length and glue them in place. Allow the glue to set overnight; then paint as indicated on the drawing or to your own taste.

Stick ponies, or some variation on them, must be one of the oldest toys known, and they happen to be just about the simplest of all to make. As any youngster can tell you, even a broom turned around with the brush for the pony's head will do fine. For fancier riding, the pony shown here is a good example of what an hour's work can produce. You can vary the basic pattern or the painting scheme to suit your imagination or the specifications of the rider.

The pony's head can be cut from almost any ¾-inch scrap, such as plywood left over from a larger project or a piece of white pine; for the best balance, the lighter the material the better.

Wooden Biplane

Materials List

Fuselage (1), 2 × 3 × 12″ or 2 × 4 × 12″

Wings (2), ¼ × 1½ × 12″ molding

Tail pieces (2), ¼ × 1½ × 6″ molding

Front wheel supports (2), ⅛ × ¾ × 9″ molding

Propeller (1), 3 ice–cream sticks

Propeller shaft hub (1), ⅜″ wooden bead

Dowels (various lengths) ¼″, ⅛″, 3/16″

Front wheels (2), 1¼″ wooden spool

Rear wheels (2), ⅞″ wooden spool

Heads (2), 1″ wooden drawer pulls

Glue

Tape

Tools

Table saw, band saw, radial arm saw, or saber saw

Coping saw

Drill

Sander or sandpaper

Level of Difficulty

Easy

Length of Time Required

Afternoon

Safety Precautions

Safety goggles

To obtain a full-sized traceable pattern for this project, use the order form at the back of this book and order pattern number 632.

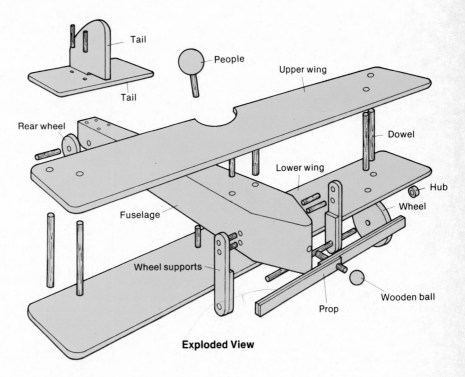

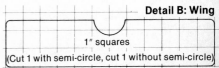

Exploded View

Wooden toys that roll are a great favorite with woodworking parents and their young children. The following three plans produce durable, safe toys, constructed without nails or screws, that cost almost nothing to make. Because they are intended for youngsters, it is important to make surfaces as smooth as possible. Spend a lot of time sanding the pieces to make the toys soft on the cheek. This project requires careful drilling for the installation of long dowels and a complicated cut to make the fuselage; otherwise it is

very simple. Make the plane from clear pine or fir and leave it natural or finish with any nontoxic finish—remember that this toy will probably get chewed on.

STEP 1
Cutting the Fuselage and Wings

Enlarge the squared drawing of the fuselage Top View in Detail A, transfer it to a piece of 2 × 3- or 2 × 4-inch pine or fir, and cut out the shape. Then enlarge the fuselage Side View in Detail A, transfer it to the side of the partially cut out fuselage, and make the required cuts. Sand all the surfaces and softly round the edges. Enlarge the squared drawing of the wing in Detail B and transfer one pattern with the semicircle and one without it to ¼ × 2½-inch molding.

Cut out the pieces and sand them smooth.

STEP 2
Drilling the Wings

Tape the wings together so that the upper wing (the one with the semicircle cut out) extends over the leading edge of the lower wing by exactly ¾ of an inch, as shown in the Top View. Mark the position of the six holes on the upper wing, shown in the Top View, and drill ¼-inch holes through the two wings at those points. Also drill ¼-inch holes on the rear edge of the lower wing where indicated in the Top View.

Detail B: Wing

1″ squares

(Cut 1 with semi-circle, cut 1 without semi-circle)

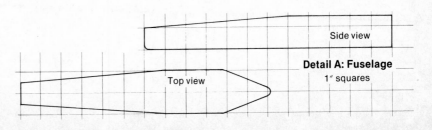

Side view

Detail A: Fuselage

1″ squares

Top view

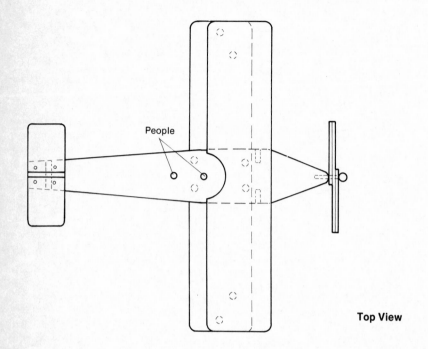

People

Top View

points. Turn the fuselage over and align the corresponding holes on the lower wing with the holes through the fuselage and mark through the two holes at the back edge of the wing. Drill ¼-inch holes ¾ inch deep at those points.

STEP 5
Cutting and Mounting the Tail
Enlarge the squared drawings in Detail D, transfer the patterns to ¼-inch molding, and cut out the parts. Sand the pieces and glue the vertical piece onto the horizontal piece. Glue the assembled tail onto the back of the fuselage (as shown in the Top and Side views) and reinforce it with ¾-inch pieces of ⅛-inch dowel drilled and glued in place, as shown in the Top and Side views.

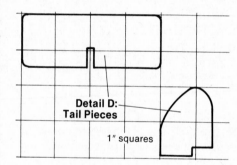

**Detail D:
Tail Pieces**

1″ squares

STEP 3
Cutting and Assembling the Front Wheel Supports
Cut two 2½-inch pieces and two 1¾-inch pieces of ⅛ × ¾-inch molding. Glue the two shorter pieces to the longer pieces as shown in Detail C and when the glue is dry, round the ends with a coping saw—use a penny to mark the outline. Drill two ³⁄₁₆-inch holes through the long end at the points shown in Detail C, and a ¼-inch hole through the double thickness as shown.

STEP 4
Drilling the Fuselage
Position the front wheel supports on the fuselage (first one side then the

other), as indicated in the Side View, with the edge of the shorter piece on the inside butted against the bottom of the fuselage, mark through the two upper holes onto the fuselage, and then drill ½-inch deep, ³⁄₁₆-inch holes straight into the fuselage at those points. Drill a ¼-inch hole through the tail of the fuselage where indicated on the Side View. Drill ¼-inch holes 1 inch deep for the biplane's crew at the points indicated in the Top View. Drill a ⅛-inch hole ½ inch deep in the center of the nose of the fuselage. Position the top wing on top of the fuselage as shown in the Top View, mark through the two holes in the wing and drill ¼-inch holes through the fuselage at those

STEP 6
Mounting the Wheel Supports
Cut a 3½-inch length of ¼-inch dowel for the front axle and slip it through the lower holes in the wheel supports. Glue the wheel supports to

Detail C: Front Wheel Supports

Edge view, two parts glued

Rounded ends

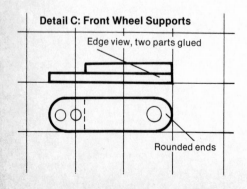

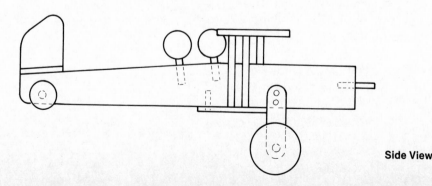

Side View

either side of the fuselage (line up the dowel holes) with the double thickness on the inside, butted against the bottom of the fuselage. Glue 1/2-inch lengths of 3/16-inch dowel through the wheel supports into the fuselage and sand the ends flush with the wheel supports.

STEP 7
Attaching the Wings
With the wheel supports hanging over the edge of your work surface, drive two 3-inch lengths of dowel through the front fuselage holes—if they stick, sand the dowels until you can just get them through. The fit should be tight enough so that you won't need glue to hold them in place; glue may start to set before you can get the dowels all the way through. Drive the dowels through so that they protrude 1/4 inch from the bottom. Glue the remaining 3-inch lengths of 1/4-inch dowel to the holes in the lower wing so that the dowels are flush with the bottom of the wing; then glue the wing onto the dowel ends protruding from the fuselage. Make sure that the wing is facing in the right direction, or else the dowels won't fit the holes in the upper wing. Glue two 1-inch lengths of 1/4-inch dowel through the lower wing into the fuselage at the rear of the wing. Finally, glue the top wing onto the dowels so that they are flush with the top of the wing. Sand the top of the upper wing and the bottom of the lower wing so that all the dowel ends are flush with the wing surfaces.

STEP 8
Making and Installing the Wheels
The wheels are easy to make if you have a 1 3/8- and a 7/8-inch wooden spool. All you have to do is slice off the beveled ends from the shaft of the spools—the ends are the wheels. The front wheels fit loosely enough on the front axles to turn, and the rear wheels fit snugly on the ends of their axle which turns in its axle hole.

If you have wooden spools that are the wrong size, you can turn them into wheels by boring out the center hole with a 5/16-inch bit and gluing in a piece of 5/16-inch dowel. When the glue has set, redrill the centers for whatever dimension you need, then slice off the beveled ends.

The wheels can also be made of slices of dowel: 3/16-inch thick slices of 1-inch dowel for the rear wheels; 1/4-inch thick slices of 1 1/4-inch dowel for the front wheels. Drill the centers of these dowels to the appropriate dimensions. When the wheels are made, slip the rear axle through its hole at the back of the fuselage and glue the rear wheels onto the ends of the dowel. Slip the front axle into place and glue on chair buttons or 3/8-inch slices of 3/8-inch dowel drilled halfway through to accept the axle.

STEP 9
Making and Installing the Propeller
Cut and glue pieces of ice-cream sticks together in the position shown in the Exploded View. Drill a 3/16-inch hole through the center of this assembly. Glue a 1 1/4-inch length of 1/8-inch dowel into the hole at the front of the fuselage and place the propeller on the shaft when the glue is dry. Drill. a stopped 1/8-inch hole into the center of a 3/4-inch wooden bead and glue this onto the end of the propeller shaft, taking care that the propeller can turn freely.

STEP 10
Adding the Pilot and Passenger
Drill out the center holes of two 1-inch round wooden drawer pulls to 1/4-inch diameter, 1/2 inch deep. Glue 1 1/2-inch lengths of 1/4-inch dowel into the drawer pulls. Try the fit of these "bodies" in the holes in the top of the fuselage and sand the dowels as necessary to make the fit loose enough to allow the dowels to be pulled out, but not so loose that they fall out easily. Keep testing the fit as you sand. Finish the plane or leave it natural, as you wish.

Baseball Bounce-Back

Materials List

Sides (2), ¾ × 30 × 40", exterior-grade plywood

Bottom (1), ¾ × 30 × 36", exterior-grade plywood

Top frame, top and bottom (2), 1 × 3 × 54¼", any stock

Top frame, sides (2), 1 × 3 × 30", any stock

½" hardware cloth (1), 36 × 51"

Target canvas (1), 18 × 20"

Nylon cord (1), 84"

Small screw eyes

Shock cords (4), 12"

1½" roundhead wood screws

Staples

Corrugated fasteners

Waterproof glue

Paint

Tools

Table saw or band saw

Screwdriver

Sandpaper

Staple gun

Large-gauge needle and heavy thread

Level of Difficulty

Easy

Length of Time Required

Afternoon

Safety Precautions

Safety goggles

In baseball, as in any other sport, practice is essential for a good athlete, and this backyard baseball bounce-back is an ideal target for any aspiring mound star. Some of the great pitchers of the past got their start throwing at nothing but an upturned bushel basket propped against the barn door; this project goes that tried-and-true target one better by bouncing the ball back at the pitcher. A hard throw in the strike zone will roll back to your young hurler, and he (or she) can get in more practice instead of chasing the ball.

This project is easy to put together. Constructed of exterior-grade plywood, it will last a long time. When you get it all finished, be sure to make the first test pitches

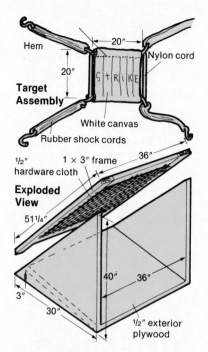

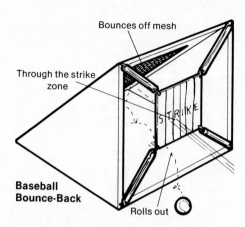

yourself. Once you turn it over to the kids, you probably won't get a chance to use it again!

STEP 1
Cutting and Fitting the Sides and Bottom

Cut the sides and bottom to the given dimensions from ¾-inch exterior-grade plywood. Sand all the edges. Use waterproof glue and 1½-inch roundhead wood screws to fasten the bottom in place, flush with the bottom front edges of the sides and 3 inches up from the back corners of the sides, as shown in the Exploded View.

STEP 2
Building and Installing the Top Frame

Cut the top-frame pieces to the given dimensions. Sand the pieces, and attach the top and bottom between the sides with waterproof glue and corrugated fasteners. The ball receives its impulse to bounce back when it strikes a ½-inch wire mesh, called hardware cloth, that is stretched across the top frame. Hardware cloth is available at hardware stores and can be cut to fit with shears. When the frame is set, cut the hardware cloth to fit and staple it

to the underside of the frame with a strong staple gun. Shoot the staples close together along all the sides to ensure strength. When the frame is complete, install it on the back of the sides with waterproof glue and 1½-inch roundhead wood screws.

STEP 3
Making the Target

The target is a piece of canvas, hemmed with a loop at the top and cut in strips that hang down, allowing the ball to pass through. Cut the canvas to the given dimensions and stitch the hem, leaving a 1-inch loop, so that you have an 18 × 18-inch target. Paint the word STRIKE across the front of the target, with the letters spaced as shown in the Target Assembly drawing, and cut the target into strips, as shown. Then run an 84-inch (7-foot) piece of nylon cord through the loop at the top of the target and tie the ends. This serves as a suspension system for the target.

STEP 4
Installing the Target

Drive small screw eyes into the top and bottom corners of the sides at the front of the box. Attach 12-inch shock cords with S-hooks at both ends to the screw eyes and to the loop of nylon cord on the target so that the cord is pulled into a square from which the target hangs. Take off the shock cords to paint the bounce-back and reinstall them when the bounce-back is dry. Test the finished project until your arm gets tired.

Baseball Rack

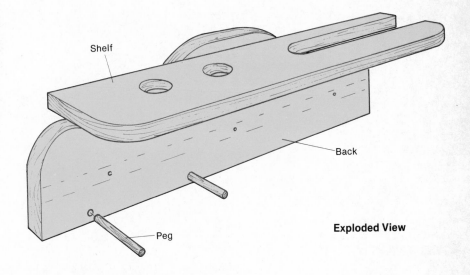

Materials List
Back (1), $3/4 \times 7 \times 15''$, any hardwood stock or hardwood-faced plywood
Shelf (1), $3/4 \times 5 \times 15''$, any hardwood stock or hardwood-faced plywood
Pegs (2), $3/8 \times 3''$ dowels
No. $8 \times 1\frac{1}{2}''$, No. $8 \times 1\frac{3}{4}''$ flathead wood screws
Paint or stain

Tools
Band saw, saber saw, or coping saw
Drill press with fly cutter
Sandpaper
Screwdriver

Level of Difficulty
Easy

Length of Time Required
Afternoon

Safety Precautions
Safety goggles

Shelf

Back

Peg

Exploded View

Baseballs, bats, and gloves have a tendency to stray in different directions when they aren't put away. One good way to keep them in one place, and to give yourself an easy project for an afternoon, is to make a wall unit that holds two baseballs, bats, and gloves. This rack can be made from any $3/4$-inch stock, including hardwood-faced plywood; the one shown here is solid oak, finished to

show off the handsome wood. It is attached to a stud in the wall with roundhead screws.

STEP 1
Cutting the Pieces
Enlarge the squared drawings for the back and the shelf and transfer the pattern to $3/4$-inch stock. Cut out the pieces with a band saw, saber saw, or coping saw. Mark the shelf for the $1\frac{3}{4}$-inch holes for the baseballs and cut the holes through with a fly cutter in a drill press. Drill the $3/8$-inch holes for the pegs in the back, as indicated in the drawing. Round all the edges of both pieces except for the back of the shelf and the inside of the notch for the bats. Sand both pieces smooth.

STEP 2
Assembling the Rack
Cut two 3-inch lengths of $3/8$-inch dowel and glue them in place with the ends flush with the back of the rack. Wipe away any excess glue around the dowels. Fasten the shelf to the back with its top edge 3 inches above the bottom of the rack, driving three No. $8 \times 1\frac{1}{2}$-inch flathead wood screws in from the back of the rack. Finish the rack as you like. When dry, hang it on the wall with two No. $8 \times 1\frac{3}{4}$-inch roundhead wood screws driven into a stud.

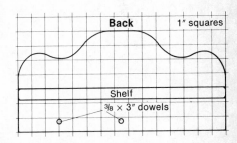

Back
1" squares
Shelf
$3/8 \times 3''$ dowels

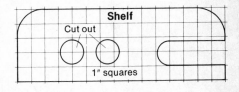

Shelf
Cut out
1" squares

Collection Display Case

Materials List

Frame, top and bottom (2), ¾ × 2 × 18″, any stock

Frame, sides (2), ¾ × 2 × 18″, any stock

Glass (1), 17 × 15″

Back (1), ¼ × 17 × 15″, hardboard

Back lining, 15 × 17″, felt, velvet, mat board, or other appropriate material

Stand pieces (2), ½ × 1½ × 6″, any stock

Back support (1), ½ × 1 × 6″, scrap

½″ butt hinge (optional)

Glue

Wire and picture hangers

½″ roundhead wood screws

Paint or other finish

Tools

Table saw or radial arm saw

C-clamps

Picture frame clamp

Level of Difficulty

Easy

Length of Time Required

Afternoon

Safety Precautions

Safety goggles

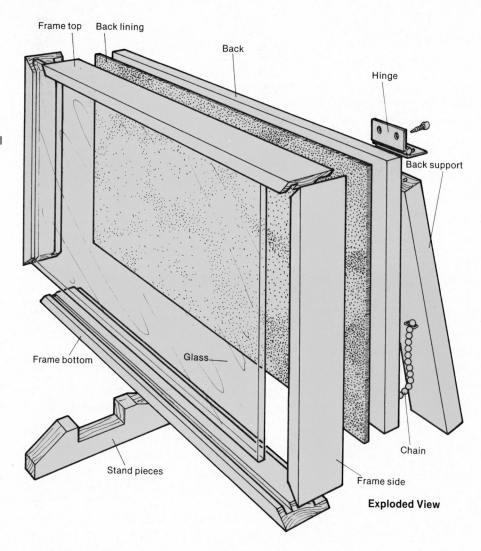

Exploded View

There are albums for stamps and coins and shoe boxes for baseball cards, but some things that youngsters collect—like bottle caps or butterflies—need homemade cases to show them off at their best. This project suits a variety of proud possessions, it is easy to make, and the dimensions can easily be varied to fit your young collector's special needs.

The display case is basically like a deep picture frame, with a glass front held in place by a ⅛ × ¼-inch dado. The case can hang on the wall like a picture, or it can be made to stand on a table with either of the two stands given in the directions.

STEP 1
Cutting the Frame Pieces

Cut the pieces for the frame to the size given or to whatever dimensions you like, as long as you make all measurements in proportion to the dimensions given. Cut a ⅛ × ¼-inch dado the length of each piece, ¼ inch in from one edge as shown in the Edge View. Cut a ¼ × ¼-inch rabbet the length of each piece on the other edge of the same side. Then miter the corners at a 45° angle. Sand the pieces and paint or finish as you wish.

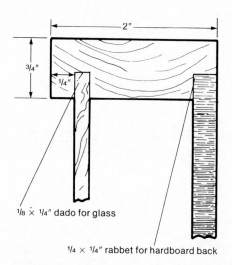

2″

¾″

¼″

⅛ × ¼″ dado for glass

¼ × ¼″ rabbet for hardboard back

Frame: Edge View

STEP 2
Gluing the Frame
Run glue along the mitered edge and assemble the frame with the glass in place (if you are making a case with dimensions different from those given, you will need a piece of glass ½ inch larger in each dimension than the inside dimensions of the frame). Clamp the frame with a picture frame clamp and wipe away any excess glue with a damp cloth. Allow to dry overnight.

STEP 3
Mounting the Collection
Cut the back to the dimensions given or to fit the frame if you are building a different size case. The nature of what you are mounting in the case

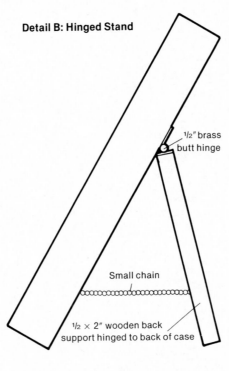

Detail B: Hinged Stand

½" brass butt hinge

Small chain

½ × 2" wooden back support hinged to back of case

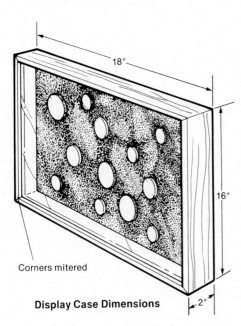

18"

16"

2"

Corners mitered

Display Case Dimensions

determines how you should line the back. If you are mounting butterflies, you will need something like mat board (available at artist's-supply stores) to push the mounting pins into. If you are mounting something like bottle caps, which can be glued to the back, then you can simply cover it with a piece of felt or velvet. Whatever material you use should be cut to the same size as the back and glued on; press it with a flat weight so that it will set flat. When dry, mount the items to be displayed. (For bottle caps, glue plugs of dowel slightly higher than the rim inside the cap; then glue the plugs to the cloth.)

When the items are securely attached, attach the back in the rabbet at the back of the frame with ½-inch brass roundhead wood screws. Use the glue sparingly so that it won't squeeze out inside the case—you won't be able to get at it to wipe it away.

STEP 4
Hanging or Standing the Case
You can hang the display case on the wall with wire and picture hangers. If you want it to stand up straight, cut the two stand pieces to the proper dimensions given in Detail A, finish them the same as you did the case, and glue them onto the bottom an inch or two from either end, as shown in Detail A. If you want to have the case stand at an angle attach a back support with a ½-inch butt hinge as shown in Detail B.

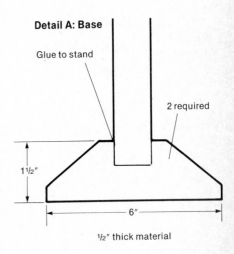

Detail A: Base

Glue to stand

2 required

1½"

6"

½" thick material

Paddle Boat

Materials List
Main deck (1), ¾ × 5½ × 12″
Upper decks (2), ¼ × 3½ × 6½″
Cabins (2), ¾ × 1½ × 4⅜″
Wheel supports (2), 1 × 1 × 1½″
Axles (2), 3 × ¾ × ¼″ dowel
Wheels (4), four identical wooden
   spools
Paddle blades (2), ¼ × 2½ × 3⅛″
Deck supports (12), 3 × ¼″ dowel
Tall smokestacks (2), 2¾ × ¾″ dowel
Short smokestacks (4), ¾ × ¾″ dowel
⅛″ dowel, 3/16″ dowel
Yellow wood glue
Tape
Waterproof paint or varnish
Rubber band
Cord

Tools
Band saw or saber saw
Table saw
Drill
Sander or sandpaper

Level of Difficulty
Easy

Length of Time Required
Afternoon

Safety Precautions
Safety goggles

**To obtain a full-sized traceable pattern
for this project, use the order form at the
back of this book and order pattern
number 632.**

Both a rolling toy and a floating toy
with a rubber-band engine, this easy-
to-build paddle boat will please kids
on land and in the tub. It needs a lot
of sanding to make it smooth enough
for little hands, and a seal to keep out
water. Because the paddle boat is
often in the water, the parts are pin-
doweled to keep them in place. Use
yellow wood glue rather than white
glue for assembly. If you just want to
construct a water toy, leave off the
wheels.

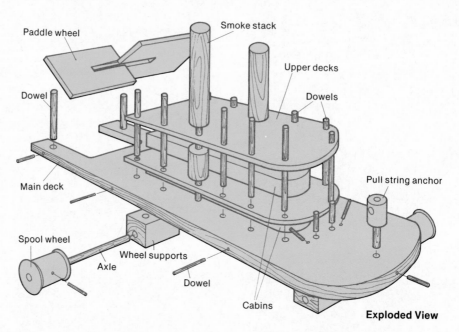

Paddle wheel Smoke stack Upper decks Dowels Dowel Main deck Spool wheel Axle Wheel supports Dowel Cabins Pull string anchor **Exploded View**

STEP 1
Cutting the Parts
Enlarge the squared drawings for the
main deck (Detail A), the cabins
(Detail B), and the upper decks
(Detail C). Transfer the pattern for the
main deck to a piece of 1 × 6-inch
clear pine stock, the patterns for the
two cabins to a piece of 1 × 2-inch
stock, and the pattern for the two
upper decks to ¼ × 3½-inch molding. Cut out the parts. Cut the wheel
supports to the given dimensions.
Sand the main deck and round its
edges softly; do not sand the other
pieces yet. Cut the following lengths
of different-diametered dowels (use
an egg carton to keep them sorted
out): ¼-inch dowel—12 pieces 3
inches long, 2 pieces 1½ inches
long, and 5 pieces 1¼ inches long;
3/16-inch dowel—2 pieces 3¾ inches
long; ¾-inch dowel—2 pieces 2¾

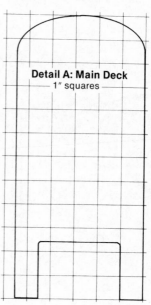

Detail A: Main Deck
1″ squares

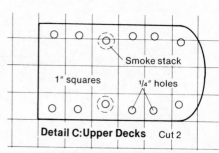

Smoke stack
1″ squares
¼″ holes
Detail C: Upper Decks Cut 2

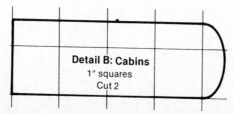

Detail B: Cabins
1″ squares
Cut 2

inches long and 5 pieces ¾ inch
long; ⅛-inch dowel—11 pieces ¾
inch long, 4 pieces 1 inch long, and 4
pieces 1½ inches long.

STEP 2
Attaching the Wheel Supports
If you want to build this boat strictly for water travel, you can skip this step and omit the wheels.

Bore a ¼-inch hole lengthwise through both wheel supports, centered, ⁵/₁₆ inch in from one edge, as shown in Detail D. Tape the wheel supports to the main deck, as indicated in the Top View, and bore ¼-inch holes through the deck and ½ inch into the wheel supports at the points shown. Remove the wheel supports from the deck and glue 1¼-inch pieces of ¼-inch dowel into each of the holes in the supports. Drill ⅛-inch holes ¾ inch deep from one side of each support into the ¼-inch dowels. Glue ¾-inch lengths of ⅛-inch dowel into these holes, fixing the ¼-inch dowels in place. Glue the wheel supports to the main deck (with the protruding dowels through the holes in the deck) and sand down the tops of the dowels if they are not flush with the deck. Finally, bore ⅛-inch holes on a diagonal into the dowels that secure the wheel sup-

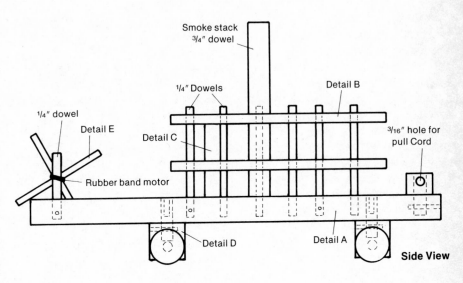

ports to the deck (see Detail D), glue 1-inch pieces of ⅛-inch dowel into these holes, and sand the ends flush with the deck.

STEP 3
Installing the Forward Pull-String Anchor
Bore a ¼-inch hole ½ inch deep on the top side of the main deck at the point indicated in the Top View. Bore a ¼-inch hole through the center of a ¾-inch length of ¾-inch dowel. Glue a 1¼-inch piece of ¼-inch dowel in this hole, with one end flush with one end of the larger dowel. When the glue has dried, drill a ³/₁₆-inch hole midway through the side of the ¾-

inch dowel—this hole is for the pull-string. Then glue the protruding ¼-inch dowel into the hole on the main deck as shown in the Side View, positioning the hole through the pull-string anchor at a right angle to the length of the boat. Finally, drill a ⅛-inch hole into the front edge of the main deck about ¾ inch deep, so that it goes through the dowel holding the pull-string anchor, as shown in the Side View. Glue a ¾-inch piece of ⅛-inch dowel in this hole and sand the end flush with the main deck.

STEP 4
Sanding the Cabins and Drilling the Main Deck, Upper Decks, and Smokestacks
Tape the two cabin pieces together and sand them as one so that they will be identical. Do the same for the upper-deck pieces; then mark them for ¼-inch drill holes, as indicated in Detail C. Drill the holes through both upper decks, separate the pieces, and tape one to the main deck in the position indicated in the Top View; use it as a template to drill ¼-inch holes ½ inch deep into the main deck. Drill ¼-inch holes through the centers of four ¾-inch lengths of ¾-inch dowel and ½ inch deep into the center of the two 2¾-inch pieces.

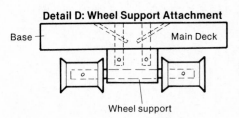

Detail D: Wheel Support Attachment

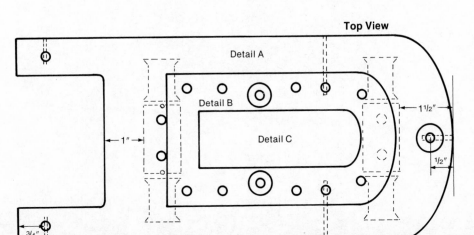

Top View

STEP 5
Assembling the Superstructure

Glue one of the cabin pieces to the main deck in the position shown in the Top View. Put 3-inch lengths of dowel through two of the predrilled ³/₄-inch dowels and glue to either side of the main deck, as shown in the Side View. Now fit one of the upper decks over the two dowels and glue it to the top of the cabin. Work the other ten 3-inch dowels through the holes in the upper deck and glue them into the main deck. Glue the remaining two short pieces of smokestack in place and glue the second cabin piece to the upper deck directly above the first one. Then fit the remaining upper deck over the dowels and glue it in place. Glue the long pieces of smokestack in place. Finally, drill ¹/₈-inch holes 1¹/₂ inches deep into both sides of the main deck at the points indicated in the Side View and glue in 1¹/₂-inch pieces of ¹/₈-inch dowel.

STEP 6
Assembling and Installing the Paddle Wheel

Cut the two paddle blades to the given dimensions, tape the pieces together, and sand the edges smooth. With the pieces taped together, cut the notch shown in Detail E. Separate the pieces and slip

one notch into the other to make the paddle wheel. Drill two ¹/₄-inch holes ¹/₂ inch deep in the stern of the main deck at the points indicated in the Top View. Glue in 1¹/₂-inch lengths of ¹/₄-inch dowel and fix them in place with ³/₄-inch lengths of ¹/₈-inch dowel drilled in from the sides of the main deck, as shown in the Side View, sanding the ends of the ¹/₈-inch dowel flush with the sides of the boat.

STEP 7
Making and Installing the Wheels

To make the boat stable on land, use a whole wooden thread spool for each wheel. To adapt spools for use as wheels, enlarge the hole in the spool by drilling through it with a ⁵/₁₆-inch bit. Cut lengths of ⁵/₁₆-inch dowel the length of the spools and glue them into the enlarged holes. When the glue has set, drill through the filled holes to a depth of 1 inch

with a ³/₁₆-inch bit so the spools will fit on the ³/₁₆-inch dowel axles. Glue one wheel onto the end of a ³/₁₆-inch dowel axle, fix it to the axle with a ¹/₂-inch length of ¹/₈-inch dowel drilled and glued through the side of the wheel into the axle, then slip the axle through one of the wheel supports. Attach the other wheel in the same manner. Repeat the procedure to mount the wheels on the other wheel support.

STEP 8
Finishing the Boat

Finish the boat with a few coats of paint or varnish. Then tie a cord through the hole in the pull-string anchor, place a rubber band between the paddle blades, fixing the ends over the posts. Put the boat in water, wind up the paddle wheel four or five times, and watch it go. This toy will amuse kids for hours.

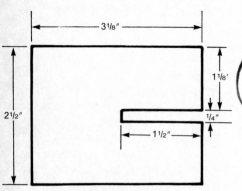

Detail E: Paddle   (Cut 2)

Big-Rig Toy Box

Materials List

Sides (2), ¾ × 11 × 29", any stock or plywood

Back and front ends (2), ¾ × 11 × 8½", any stock or plywood

Bottom (1), ¾ × 8½ × 22½'', any stock or plywood

Cab front (1), ½ × 5 × 8½", any stock

Cab top (1), ½ × 3½ × 8½", any stock

Window rails (2), ½ × ½ × 3", scrap

Bumper (1), ⅛ × ½ × 10", scrap

Headlights (2), ¼–⅜ × ½" dowel

Axles (3), ¾ × 1 × 10", any solid stock

Wheels (6), ¾ × 4", any hardwood stock

No. 8 × 1¼" roundhead wood screws (6)

Washers (12)

Paint, two colors

No. 4, No. 6 finishing nails

Glue

Tools

Band saw, saber saw

Fly cutter or wood lathe (optional)

Sander, sandpaper

Screwdriver

Hammer

Level of Difficulty

Easy

Length of Time Required

Afternoon

Safety Precautions

Safety goggles

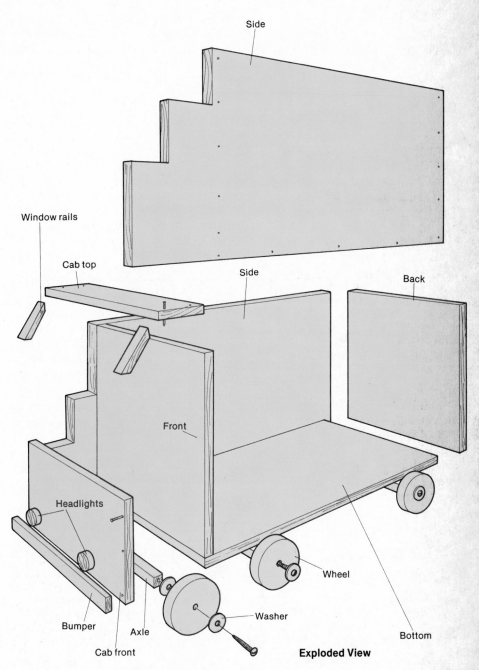

Exploded View

Labels: Side, Side, Back, Window rails, Cab top, Front, Headlights, Bumper, Cab front, Axle, Wheel, Washer, Bottom

This project is both a toy and a toy box, designed to look like the big trucks that seem to fascinate all youngsters. It can be loaded with the dolls or cargo a child wants to take for a ride, or it can store the toys that may be used in one room but kept in another. The box is easy to roll from room to room, and it adds fun to the job of "putting away." The construction of the big rig is quite simple—like the large toy chest on page 83, this is an excellent project for hand-tool work, except for cutting out the wheels, for which a band saw, fly cutter, or a lathe does the best job. The basic box is made either of scrap pieces of 1 × 12's left over from a shelving project or of ¾-inch plywood. The details, like the cab front and roof, require ½-inch pieces of scrap.

STEP 1
Cutting and Assembling the Box

Mark the shape of the two side pieces on ¾-inch plywood or scrap 1 × 12, according to the dimensions given in Detail A; cut these pieces out with a band saw, saber saw, or coping saw. Then, using the same material, cut the front and back ends of the trailer and the bottom piece to the given dimensions. Sand the pieces thoroughly. Attach the back and front end pieces between the sides, as shown in the Side View, with glue and No. 6 finishing nails set

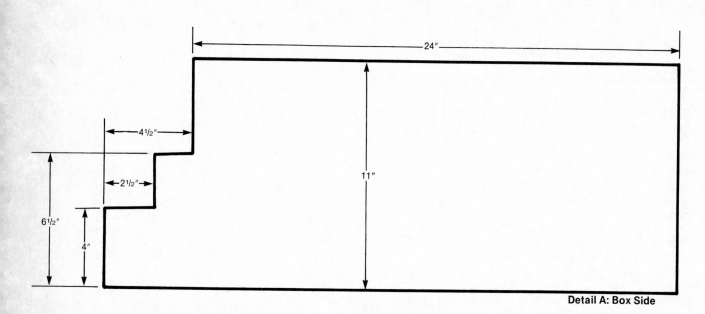

Detail A: Box Side

below the surface. Attach the bottom inside the box so that it is flush with the bottom edge, as shown in the Side View. Use No. 6 finishing nails set below the surface. Fill all nail holes with wood putty, allow the putty to set, and sand smooth.

STEP 2
Adding the Cab
Cut the cab front to the given dimen-

sions, sand it, and attach it between the sides at the front, flush with the front edges, with No. 6 finishing nails set below the surface. Cut the cab top to the given dimensions, sand it, and install it on top of the cab, butted against the trailer end, in the same manner. Then hold a piece of $1/2 \times 1/2$-inch scrap against the side of the cab where the window rails should be positioned (see the Side View) and

mark the angles at the bottom and top. Cut two pieces, as marked, sand them lightly, and install with glue; then allow to dry. Cut the front bumper from a piece of $1/8$-inch hardboard or other scrap to the given dimensions and glue it in place, as shown in the Front View. Cut $1/4$- or $3/8$-inch slices from a $1/2$-inch dowel for the headlights and glue them in place, as shown in the Front View.

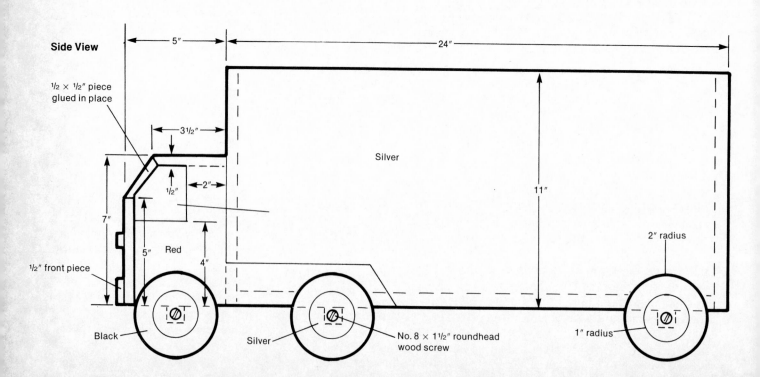

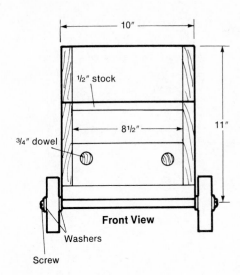

10″

½″ stock

8½″

11″

¾″ dowel

Front View

Washers

Screw

the wheels to the given size with a fly cutter, with a band saw, or on a lathe. Sand them smooth, paying special attention to the rims to make sure the wheels will roll smoothly. When the wheels are done and the glue on the truck is dry, sand the truck all over one last time; then paint it according to the pattern shown in Side View. Give the truck a few coats of each color—use tape to mark off the colors. Paint the wheels. When the wheels are dry,

drill a hole the next size up (¼ inch) through the center of each so they will turn on the screws that hold them to the axles. Attach the wheels to the axles with No. 8 × 1¼-inch roundhead wood screws and a washer on either side of each wheel. Don't screw the screws all the way in; leave enough room for the wheels to turn. Screw a screw eye into the front of the truck, inside the cab near the bottom, and attach a pull rope.

STEP 3
Finishing the Truck and Attaching the Axles and Wheels

Cut the axles to the given dimensions from ¾-inch stock, sand the axles, and attach them to the bottom of the box and cab, as shown in the Side View, with glue and No. 4 finishing nails. Allow the glue to dry. Cut

Circus-Wagon Toy Box

Materials List

A (2), ¾ × 2 × 16½" pine
B (2), ¾ × 2 × 34¼" pine
C (1), ½ × 18 × 34¼" plywood
D (4), ¾ × 2 × 14" pine
E (4), ¾ × 2 × 18½" pine
F (1), ¾ × 1¼ × 32¾" pine
G (1), ½ × 1¼ × 34¼" pine
H (1), ¼ × 18 × 24" Masonite
I (1), ¼ × 14 × 14½" Masonite
J (1), ¼ × 18 × 24" Masonite
K (2), ¼ × 24 × 34¾" Masonite
L (2), ¾ × 21" dowel
M (4), ¾ × 6" diameter (wheels)
N (4), ⅛ × 1" dowel
O (1), ¾ × 1½ × 24" pine
P (2), ¾ × 2 × 2½" pine
Q (1), ¾ × 2½" dowel
R (1), ¾ × 6" dowel
S (1), ½ × 16½ × 34" plywood
T (2), ¾ × 1¼ × 14½" pine
Knobs (2), 1¼"
Utility hinges (4), 1½"
Finishing nails 1¼", ¾"
No. 8 × 2" flathead wood screws
1 bar latch
Glue
Acrylic latex high-gloss enamel (See color code)

Tools

Hammer
Saber saw, table saw
Screwdriver
Sander or sandpaper

Level of Difficulty

Moderate

Length of Time Required

Overnight

Safety Precautions

Safety goggles, filter mask

To obtain a full-sized traceable pattern for this project, use the order form at the back of this book and order pattern number 630.

This is a larger, somewhat more complicated version of the Big-Rig Toy Box. At 18 inches high, 18 inches wide, and 34 inches long, it can hold more than six cubic feet of children's toys—almost a roomful if spread out

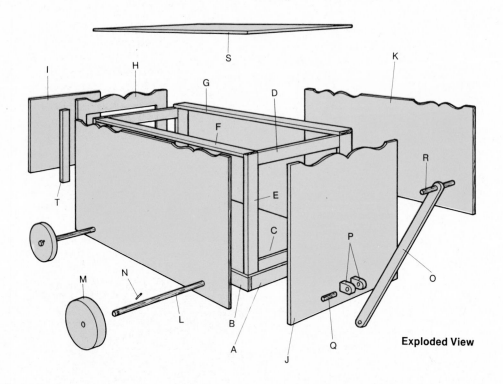

Exploded View

on the floor. Like the Big-Rig Toy Box, the Circus Wagon can be pulled from room to room. Although this project is simple to put together, there are enough pieces to make it look a lot more complicated than it really is. To make this project easier to assemble, I have given all the parts a letter code and the step-by-step instructions refer to each part by its code letter. For painting the wagon and its lion in a cage, use the color code for the side panels (K), the wheels (L, M, N) and the handle parts (O, P, Q, R). Paint the rest of the wagon blue (2 on the color code).

STEP 1
Cutting the Parts

Cut all parts to the given dimensions (except I, which will be cut from the

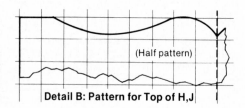

(Half pattern)

Detail B: Pattern for Top of H,J

middle of H later on). Enlarge the squared drawings in Details A (for K) and B (for H and J), transfer them to the tops of the parts, and cut out the patterns. Label all the parts lightly in pencil so you can keep them sorted out.

STEP 2
Assembling the Frame

Use glue and 1¼-inch finishing nails to attach A and B (with the shorter parts A between the longer parts B).

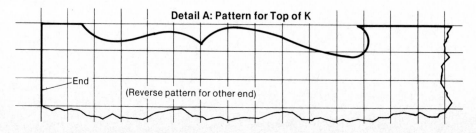

Detail A: Pattern for Top of K

End

(Reverse pattern for other end)

Use glue and the same-sized nails to attach framing piece C to this frame. Glue and nail parts D between parts E to make two frames and clamp until the glue is dry. When the frame is dry, use 1¼-inch finishing nails to toe-nail the two frames at either end of C. Then use glue and the same-sized nails to attach F between the two parts E, flush with the top, and on the opposite side, G across the tops of E. This completes the basic frame.

STEP 3
Cutting and Attaching the Ends and Sides

Mark the dimensions of the door (I), shown in Detail C, in the center of H and cut it out with a saber saw. Then use glue and ¾-inch finishing nails to attach H to one end of the frame,

flush with the bottom, and J to the other end in the same manner. Attach the two sides K to the frame with glue and ¾-inch finishing nails, flush with the bottom of the basic

frame. Finally, mark the sides K for the axle holes at the points indicated in the Side View and drill ¾-inch holes through the sides and frame at those four points.

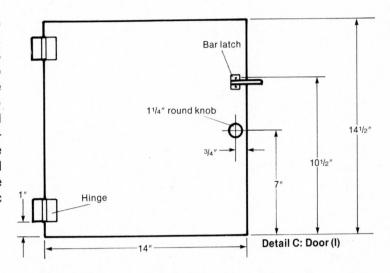

Detail C: Door (I)

Orange—1
Blue—2
Red—3
White—4

Black—Outline and detail on lion

Side View

STEP 4
Attaching the Axles and Wheels

Sand the ends of the two axles (L); then drill 3/16-inch holes through the center lines of each end, 1/4 inch in from the ends. Sand the wheels (M), and drill 3/4-inch holes in the centers, sanding out the holes with a piece of sandpaper wrapped around a dowel so that they slip easily onto the axles. Slip the axles through the axle holes in the side of the wagon, put the wheels on the ends of the axles and glue 1-inch pieces of 1/8-inch dowel (N) into the holes at the ends of the axles.

STEP 5
Attaching the Tongue Brace and Painting the Handle Parts

Attach the tongue-brace parts (P) to the center of the bottom of end J, 1 inch apart, with glue and four No. 8 × 2-inch flathead wood screws. Round the ends of the tongue (O) and bore 3/4-inch holes 7/8 inch in from each end, as shown in the Exploded View. Paint the parts according to the color code, and, when dry, glue the dowel handle (R) through one end of the tongue. Wait until the wagon is complete and painted before attaching the tongue to the braces with dowel Q with glue.

STEP 6
Attaching the Door and Top; Painting the Wagon

Glue and nail parts T flush against the edges of the door (I), then attach 1 1/2-inch utility hinges, knob, and bar latch to I, as shown in Detail C. Attach the door hinges to H with the screws that come with the hinges. Attach the same-sized hinges to the

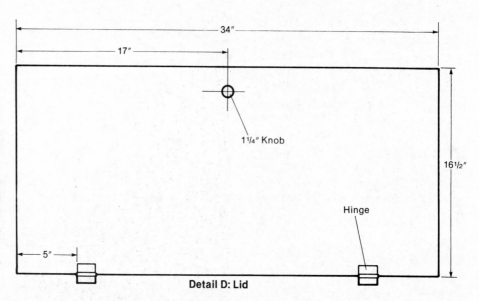

Detail D: Lid

top (S) along with the knob, as shown in Detail D. Outline the decoration on the sides of the wagon according to the drawing in the Side View and paint with acrylic latex high-gloss enamel, following the color code.

Open-Back Dollhouse

Materials List

Base (1), $3/4 \times 14 \times 24^1/2''$, plywood
Base sides (2), $1/4 \times 2^1/4 \times 14''$, plywood
Base front and back (2), $1/4 \times 2^1/2 \times 25''$, plywood
Casters (4), #C1-Comet "Shepherd" casters
House front (1), $1/4 \times 15^1/2 \times 20^1/2''$, plywood
House sides (2), $1/4 \times 10 \times 15^1/2''$, plywood
Base molding, sides (2), $10^1/2 \times 1/2''$, quarter-round molding
Base molding, front left (1), $16^1/2 \times 1/2''$, quarter-round molding
Base molding, front right (1), $2^1/4 \times 1/2''$, quarter-round molding
Bottom step (1), $3/4 \times 1^1/2 \times 4''$, pine or other softwood
Top step (1), $3/4 \times 3/4 \times 4''$, pine or other softwood
Balcony (1), $3/4 \times 3 \times 7^1/2''$, softwood or plywood
Second floor (1), $1/4 \times 10 \times 20''$, plywood
Third floor (1), $1/4 \times 10 \times 20''$, plywood
Top molding, front (1), 22", ornamental or quarter-round molding
Top molding, sides (2), 11", ornamental or quarter-round molding
Corner molding, house (2), 14", pine corner molding
Roof top (1), $3/4 \times 7 \times 13^7/8''$, plywood
Roof sides (2), $1/4 \times 11^1/4 \times 9''$, plywood
Roof front (1), $1/4 \times 22^1/4 \times 9''$, plywood
Chimney (1), $2 \times 2^1/2 \times 3^1/2''$, $1/4''$ plywood border, paint-can tops or thread spools
Corner molding, roof (2), 11", pine corner molding
Railings (4), $1/2''$ plywood (see Detail A)
Railing uprights, $1/8'' \times 10'$, fence wire or comparable aluminum wire
First- and second-floor room dividers (2), $1/4 \times 7^1/2 \times 7^1/2''$, plywood
Top-floor room divider (1), $1/4''$ plywood (see Detail H)
Shutters (12), $1/4 \times 1 \times 3^1/4''$, plywood
Windows (6), posterboard (see Detail G)
Doors (2), $1/4 \times 2^3/4 \times 5^7/8''$, plywood
Decorative lintels (2), $1/4''$ plywood (see Detail I)
Butt hinges, $5/8 \times 3/4''$
Wood putty
Glue
No. $6 \times 3/4''$ flathead wood screws
Brads, 1", $3/4''$
Paint

Tools

Band saw, coping saw, or saber saw
Hammer
Screwdriver
Drill
Sander or sandpaper
Mat knife

Level of Difficulty

Moderate

Length of Time Required

All day

Safety Precautions

Safety goggles

To obtain a full-sized traceable pattern for this project, use the order form at the back of this book and order pattern number 411.

A dollhouse is a classic children's toy. This one is roomy and detailed, and it rolls about on casters hidden in the base. This project has more pieces than most, but it is one of the

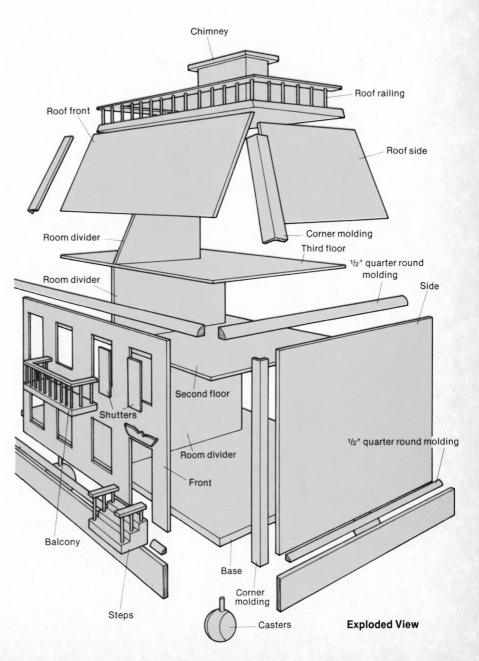

Chimney
Roof railing
Roof front
Roof side
Room divider
Corner molding
Third floor
Room divider
$1/2''$ quarter round molding
Side
Room divider
Second floor
$1/2''$ quarter round molding
Shutters
Room divider
Front
Balcony
Base
Corner molding
Steps
Casters

Exploded View

easier construction jobs in this book. Most of your effort goes into cutting—make your measurements accurately and cut the pieces to fit exactly so the house will be solid. The railings on the roof, balcony, and front steps are easy to install if you drill their anchor holes precisely. Finish the inside of the house with bits of wallpaper and paint the floors. If you want to do a first-class decorating job, paint the inside parts in detail—with rugs, pictures on the wall, a fireplace—before assembling the house.

STEP 1
Making the Base
Cut the base to the given dimensions from ¾-inch plywood and sand the top side and top edges smooth. Cut the base sides and base front and back to the given dimensions, sand, and attach to the base (sides first) with glue and 1-inch brads so that the top edges of the sides and the front and back are flush with the top of the base. Finally, install #C1-Comet "Shepherd" casters at each corner inside the base, leaving room for them to swivel without rubbing against its sides.

STEP 2
Cutting the House Front and Sides and Assembling the Shell
Cut the house sides to the given dimensions, sand, and fill any holes with wood putty. Cut the house front to the given dimensions; then mark the positions of the windows and doors, as shown on the Front View. Drill pilot holes inside the corners of each window, and the balcony door, and the upper corner of the front door. Use a saber saw to cut out the openings. After making the cuts on the front, attach the sides, as indicated in the Front View, with glue and ¾-inch brads.

STEP 3
Attaching the House Shell to the Base
Cut the molding for the base of the house to the given dimensions. Lay out the pieces as they will fit around the house and mark for 45° miter cuts at the corners of the house and at the doorway. (Mark the cuts to angle away from the door.) Make the cuts, sand the molding lightly, and then attach to the house shell with glue and ¾-inch brads. Position the

house shell so that the edge of the molding on the front is 1 inch from the front of the base and the house is centered on the base from side to side (1¾ inches from the sides). Attach the house shell to the base with glue and 1-inch brads driven through the molding.

STEP 4
Attaching the Steps and Balcony and Drilling for Railings
Cut the step pieces to the given dimensions, sand lightly, and glue and nail them together with 1-inch brads. Center the steps in front of the front door, and attach them to the base with glue and ¾-inch brads driven from inside the base. The uprights for the step and balcony railings are made of whatever thick wire you have on hand (⅛-inch fench wire or comparable aluminum wire is best), and the holes you drill to hold them should be the same width as the wire you choose. All holes—to hold the uprights, in the steps and balcony, and in the railings—should be ¼ inch deep. Drill holes for the uprights on a line ⅜ inch in from the edge on either side of the steps in the center and also ⅝ inch back from the edge of the base. Cut the balcony to the given dimensions and sand smooth. Mark the balcony for upright holes ¾ inch apart along the front edge, ⅜ inch in from the edge, and ⅜ inch in from either side (ten holes), and for two more upright holes an

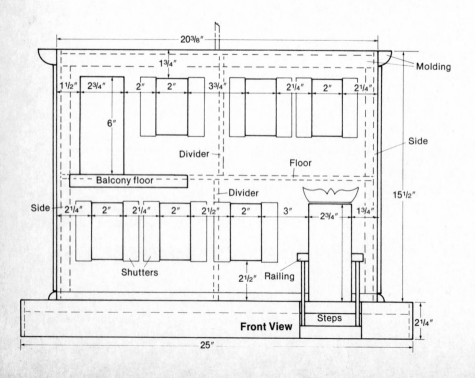

Front View

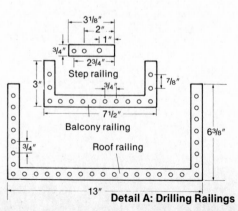

Detail A: Drilling Railings

inch apart along the side, 3/8 inch in from the side edges, see Detail A. Drill the holes 1/4 inch deep. Attach the balcony to the house shell in the position indicated in the Front View with glue and No. 6 × 3/4-inch flat-head wood screws.

STEP 5
Installing the Second and Third Floors and Molding

Cut the second and third floors to the given dimensions, sand the edges, and install them in the house shell with glue and 3/4-inch brads, as indicated in the Front View. Cut the pieces of molding for the top of the house to the given dimensions and miter the corners at the front to a 45° angle. Install around the top edge of the house, flush with the third floor, with glue and 3/4-inch brads. Cut two pieces of corner molding to the given dimensions and install with glue and 3/4-inch brads to the two front corners of the house between the top molding and the base molding.

STEP 6
Building the Roof

The roof is made up of four pieces: top, two sides, and front. Cut the pieces to the dimensions given in Details B, C, and D. Mark the roof top for upright holes 3/4 inch apart, 3/8 inch in from the edge all the way around the front and two sides (as shown in Detail B); drill the holes 1/4 inch deep. Attach the roof front and sides with glue and 3/4-inch brads. When the glue is dry, fill the gap along the top edge, where the roof

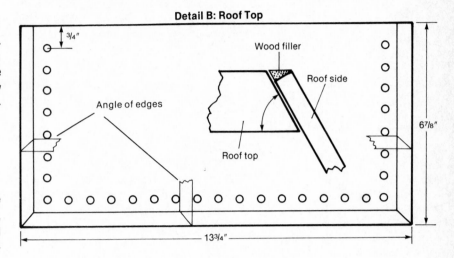

Detail B: Roof Top

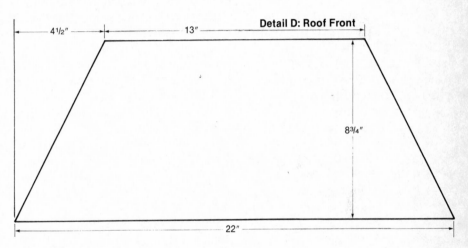

Detail D: Roof Front

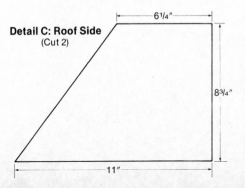

Detail C: Roof Side
(Cut 2)

pieces meet the roof top, with wood putty. When the putty is dry, sand smooth.

STEP 7
Making the Chimney and Installing the Roof and Roof Molding

To make the chimney, cut a piece of 2 × 4 about 2½ inches long, make a border around the top with 1-inch-wide strips of 1/4-inch plywood, and decorate the top with spray-can tops or thread spools, as shown in Detail E. Before gluing on the decorative tops of spools, attach the chimney to the roof, in the center of the roof top, flush with the back edge, with glue and 1-inch brads. When the chimney is attached, seat the roof on the house and nail the front and sides to the molding at the top of the house and nail the front and sides to the

molding at the top of the house with 3/4-inch brads, as shown in Detail F. When the roof is attached, cut the roof-corner molding to the given dimensions and hold it against the roof corners. Mark it at the top and bottom for cutting the angles; cut to fit. Install with glue and 3/4-inch brads.

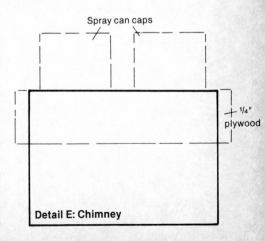

Detail E: Chimney

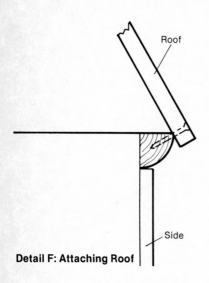

Detail F: Attaching Roof

Roof

Side

STEP 8
Cutting and Drilling the Roof, Balcony, and Step Railings; Cutting the Uprights

Cut the roof, balcony, and step railings to the dimensions shown in Detail A. Mark them for drilling the upright holes as shown, and drill the holes 1/4 inch deep. Cut the uprights 2½ inches long for the roof and balcony (45 pieces altogether), and two each 2½, 3¼, and 4 inches long for the steps.

STEP 9
Cutting and Installing the Room Dividers

Cut the two lower-floor room dividers to the given dimensions, and cut the top floor room divider to the dimen-

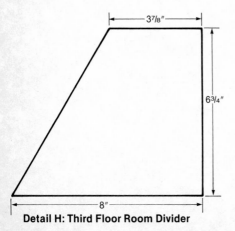

Detail H: Third Floor Room Divider

3⅞"

6¾"

8"

sions shown in Detail H. Sand the pieces lightly and install with glue and 3/4-inch brads in the center of the house; set the second floor slightly to the side of the first floor so you can nail all the dividers from both top and bottom.

STEP 10
Cutting the Shutters, Windows, Doors, and Decorative Lintels; Painting

Cut the 12 shutters to the given dimensions and sand lightly. Cut the windows from posterboard with a mat knife to the size and shape given in Detail G. Trace the shape in Detail I, transfer the pattern to 1/4-inch plywood, and cut the decorative lintels for the two doorways. Finally, cut the two doors to the given dimensions. At this point, you should decide on a decorative painting scheme, and paint the house and loose pieces; see the picture of the finished house for suggestions, and decorate however you wish.

STEP 11
Finishing the House

Attach the shutters with glue. Attach the front door and balcony door with

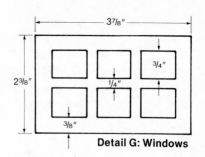

Detail G: Windows

3⅞"

2⅜"

¾"

¼"

⅜"

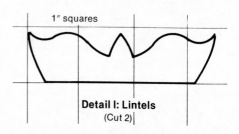

1" squares

Detail I: Lintels
(Cut 2)

5/8 × 3/4-inch butt hinges. Attach the decorative lintels over the doors with glue. Attach the windows from the inside with glue. Finally, glue the roof, balcony, and step uprights into the holes in the railings; then glue the uprights into the holes in the roof, balcony, and steps. The house is now ready to move into. You can furnish and decorate the interior as you please (try wallpaper).

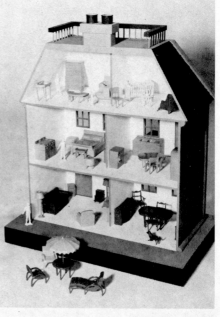

Dollhouse Furniture

Materials List
Scrap wood
Fabric
Buttons
Thread spools
Indoor paneling
India ink
Paint
Glue

Tools
Table saw, band saw, or coping saw
Sandpaper

Length of Time Required
Afternoon

Level of Difficulty
Easy

Safety Precautions
Safety goggles

Sofas and other items can be wooden blocks covered with bits of fabric. Just let your imagination roam. The drawings shown below are for some of the more typical furniture pieces with the appropriate sizes to match the dollhouse.

Use scraps of wallpaper to brighten up the walls of some rooms and paint the walls and floors in other rooms. You can cut area rugs, or wall-to-wall carpeting from pieces of felt and glue them to the floors. All of the additions to the dollhouse can be left loose, or glued in: If they are glued in, they won't shift out of place when the dollhouse is jostled, but, of course, your child won't be able to move them around to suit a change of taste. As with all other toys, be sure to sand all the pieces thoroughly before finishing.

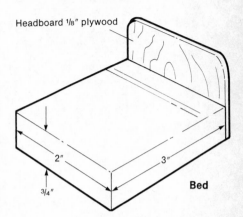
Headboard 1/8" plywood
2"
3"
3/4"
Bed

Furnishings for the dollhouse are limited only by your imagination, and the following are meant only as suggestions. The kitchen cabinets, stove, refrigerator, and such things as dressers and wardrobes can be nothing more than small blocks of wood, cut to the correct size, painted or stained appropriately and such things as stove oven doors or burners merely marked in place with India ink.

To make a dining table, simply cut a wooden thread spool in half and glue a piece of thin room paneling cut in a circle in place. Mirror and picture frames can be made simply by using buttons with a decorative outer edge.

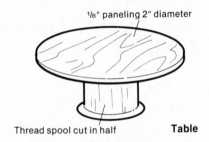
1/8" paneling 2" diameter
Thread spool cut in half   **Table**

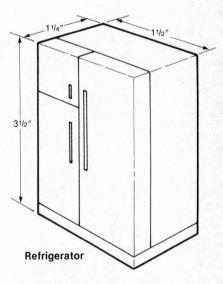
1 1/4"   1 1/2"
3 1/2"
Refrigerator

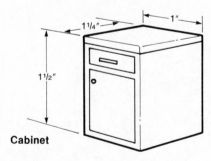
1 1/4"   1"
1 1/2"
Cabinet

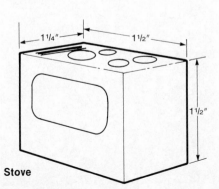
1 1/4"   1 1/2"
1 1/2"
Stove

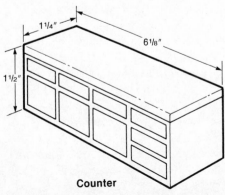
1 1/4"   6 1/8"
1 1/2"
Counter

Trophy or Model Case

Materials List

Case, top and bottom (2), ¾ × 23½ × 4″, any stock
Case, ends (2), ¾ × 8 × 4″, any stock
Back (1), 7 × 23½″, ¼″ hardboard or ¾″ stock
Front retaining strips, top and bottom (2), ¼ × ¼ × 23½″
Front retaining strips, ends (2), ¼ × ¼ × 7″
Glass, 7 × 23½″
Glue
½″ roundhead brass screws
Stain and finish, or paint

Tools

Table saw or radial arm saw
Router (optional)
Sandpaper
Screwdriver
C-clamps

Level of Difficulty

Moderate

Length of Time Required

Afternoon

Safety Precautions

Safety goggles

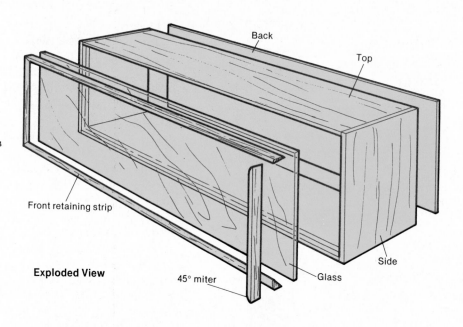

Exploded View

Back
Top
Front retaining strip
45° miter
Glass
Side

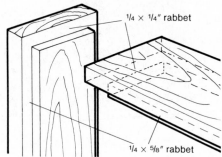

Detail A: Joining Frame

¼ × ¼″ rabbet
¼ × ⅝″ rabbet

Youngsters often have models or trophies that merit special display. To house these items, this project is the answer. It is a larger, freestanding version of the Collection Display Case, and it is somewhat sturdier in construction, so it can bear a reasonable amount of weight on top. The case shown here was made of solid walnut and finished to highlight the wood, but any stock, finished any way, will be fine for this job.

STEP 1
Cutting the Case Sides

Cut the top, bottom, and ends to the given dimensions from any ¾-inch stock. Then cut or rout a ¼ × ⅝-inch rabbet in the front edge of each piece (see Detail A) and cut a ¼ × ¼-inch rabbet into the remaining three edges.

STEP 2
Assembling the Case

Attach the top and bottom to the sides with glue, making sure that the ⅝-inch-deep rabbet is at the front on all four pieces. Clamp and allow to set overnight. When dry, cut the back to the given dimensions from ¼-inch hardboard or, for a stronger case, from ¾-inch plywood. If you use a ¾-inch back, cut a ¼ × ¼-inch rabbet around all sides so that it will fit snugly into the rabbet on the back of the case. Attach the back to the case with four ½-inch roundhead brass screws so it can be removed easily when you want to change the display. When the case is assembled, sand it all over.

STEP 3
Installing the Glass Front

Cut the ¼ × ¼-inch front retaining strips to size, miter the corners at a 45° angle, and check to see that they fit inside the rabbeted front of the case; correct the cuts if necessary. Then stain and finish, or paint, the case and front retaining strips however you like. After the finish or paint is dry, insert the glass in the rabbeted front, glue the front retaining strips in place, and clamp with C-clamps until set.

These wooden toys are easy to build and young children are sure to love them. They are designed like the classically simple wooden toys that parents played with when they were children.

This crayon holder makes an ideal gift. It is quick and easy to make and children love it.

Here's a way to make brushing teeth fun. This friendly bear holds toothbrushes and cup, a project that will help encourage good habits.

Puzzles are an excellent way to stimulate young minds. After you have made the ones in this book, you can design your own and make them more complicated as they get more adept at putting these together.

Baseballs and bats are hard things to keep out from under foot. With this simple rack, an afternoon's work, your kids will always have a place to put them away.

A coat and cap rack made of a child's name will get more use than a simple row of pegs. This project calls for careful cutting, but otherwise it's quick and easy.

The initial letter of your child's name can be designed as brightly-colored bookends or a handsome wall plaque.

For hauling anything—from rocks to dolls or other favorite playthings—this sturdy wagon will be a long lasting hit. Building the wagon does not require special skills.

All children love riding toys and ones made at home are the most fun. Youngsters who haven't graduated to a tricycle will get good mileage out of this project.

Imitating Mom and Dad in the garden is a happy pastime for children. You can give them a special garden plaything with this wheelbarrow.

This intermediate size rocker is for graduates from the toddler's rocker on the opposite page. Plans for this project include an elephant's head that can be substituted for the horse's head.

Make this low rocking horse as smooth as satin. With lots of sanding you'll have a safe exercise toy for the toddler in the house. The construction is simple and durable.

Older riders will get a lot of action from this traditional rocking horse. A suspension system of bent metal rods allows the horse's body to rock back and forth.

Left: Children who play with dolls will want a scaled down cradle for putting them to bed. The project is a good one for sharpening your skill at dowelling joints.

Below: A hanging cradle swings easily to lull a baby to sleep and the spindle sides let the infant look through when awake. The cradle can be locked in place when you want it to stay still.

Right: A classic cradle, this one is rocked by foot to help an infant drift off to sleep. The design is centuries old, but easy to build in a modern workshop.

Below: Handsome wood stained to show off its beauty can make the traditional cradle a children's room showpiece.

A double easel is a perfect play station for two children. The drawing pad holder is designed to hold large size paper, the kind kids like best.

The blackboard, a good skill builder, is painted hardboard so you won't need to find a piece of slate for constructing this project.

This desk will start a preschool child in the right direction. Because
the height can be adjusted, the desk can grow with the youngster.

For children not yet old enough for a full-sized sled, this toddler's one is a great way to get pulled through the snow.

If you live where it snows, your older children will want this full-sized sled. It is an easy project that can stand up to the pounding it will get.

78

Children love to have toy boxes that are toys themselves. With the big rig toy box, you can make tidying-up a game.

The stick pony is probably one of the oldest toys known to children. A few minutes of
time in the shop making this project will give a child hour after hour of imaginative play.

Little Red Barn

Materials List
Base (1), ¾ × 8¼ × 12″, any stock
Ends (2), ¾ × 7 × 9¼″, any stock
Front (1), ¾ × 6 × 11″, any stock
Loft floor (1), ¾ × 7 × 9½″, any stock
Upper roof piece (1), ⅛ × 2½ × 12″, hardboard
Lower roof piece (1), ⅛ × 3½ × 12″, hardboard
Stall and ladder supports, ¼ × ¼″, cut as needed
Ladder rungs and stall rails, Popsicle sticks, cut as needed
Paint
No. 6 finishing nails
No. 4 flathead cement-coated nails
Glue
Wood putty

Tools
Saber saw or coping saw
Hammer
Nailset
Sander or sandpaper
Vise

Level of Difficulty
Easy

Length of Time Required
Afternoon

Safety Precautions
Safety goggles

This simple, rugged project will delight any young farmer, whether in the city, suburbs, or country. It is cut from any ¾-inch stock you happen to have around and roofed with ⅛-inch hardboard. The directions given here will make you the barn I made for my children, but they invite variation. If you enjoy this project, use the same basic methods to build some other outbuildings and create a scaled-down farm. To populate the farm, get a few animals, and maybe a tractor, from your local toy store.

STEP 1
Cutting the Pieces
Cut the base to size from any ¾-inch solid stock. Mark the outline of the end pieces on ¾-inch stock, following the dimensions and angles given in the Side View, and cut out two ends. Mark the dimensions of the front piece, cut it from ¾-inch stock, and cut one edge to the angle shown in the Side View. Use a saber saw or coping saw to cut out the door as shown in the Front View. Finally, mark off the loft floor piece, cut it from ¾-inch stock, and cut a 1½ × 1½-inch notch in one corner. This will be the opening for a ladder into the loft. Sand the pieces thoroughly. Paint the outside and the edges of the front and sides red—leave the inside of the barn natural to give it a realistic look, or paint it as you like.

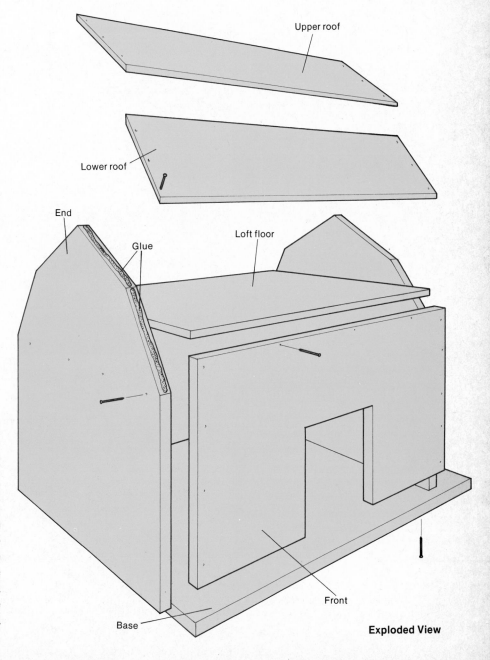

Upper roof

Lower roof

End

Glue

Loft floor

Base

Front

Exploded View

Side View

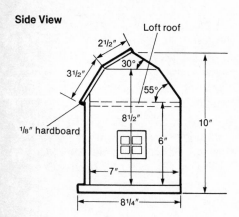

2½"

Loft roof

3½"

30°

55°

8½"

10"

6"

⅛" hardboard

7"

8¼"

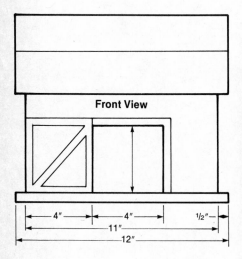

Front View

4"   4"   ½"

11"

12"

STEP 2
Assembling the Frame

Use glue and No. 6 finishing nails to attach the ends to the base; the ends should be set in ½ inch from the sides of the base and flush with the back of the base (see Front View and photos). To attach the base, clamp one of the end pieces in a vise, bottom up, and position the base; then nail down through it. Use a nailset to countersink the nails, and fill the holes with wood putty. When the ends are attached, glue and nail the front to both the ends and the base, standing the barn on its back to nail into the ends and clamping the front piece in a vise to nail through the base. Use the same size nails and countersink and finish as you did the ends. Finally, glue and nail the loft

floor in place at the base of the first roof angle, as shown in the Side View, with the notched corner at the back.

STEP 3
Adding the Roof

Cut the roof pieces to size from ⅛-inch hardboard, paint them white, let paint dry, and fasten them in place with glue and No. 4 flathead cement-coated nails.

STEP 4
Making and Installing Interior Details

Cut ¼ × ¼-inch wood strips to make up the posts of the ladder and stall(s). Glue pieces of Popsicle sticks in place to form the rungs of the ladder and rails on the stalls. Look at the photo for inspiration; then follow your own imagination for placing the stalls. When finished, install the ladder and stalls with glue.

Toy Chest

Materials List
Sides (2), ¾ × 14 × 19½", glued-up
   stock
Front and back (2), ¾ × 14 × 30"
   glued-up stock
Bottom (1), ¾ × 18 × 28½" plywood
Top (1), ¾ × 20½ × 31" glued-up stock
Cross braces (2), 1 × 3 × 18"
Corner blocks (4), 1 × 1 × 12¾"
Flat-bottomed casters (4), with screws
Blanket hinges (2), with screws
Glue
No. 8 × 1¼", No. 8 × 1½" flathead
   wood screws
No. 8 finishing nails
Stain or clear finish

Tools
Handsaw, table saw, or radial arm saw
Hand drill or power drill
Doweling jig
Bar clamps
Screwdriver
Hammer
Sander or sanding block, sandpaper

Level of Difficulty
Moderate

Length of Time Required
Overnight

Safety Precautions
Safety goggles

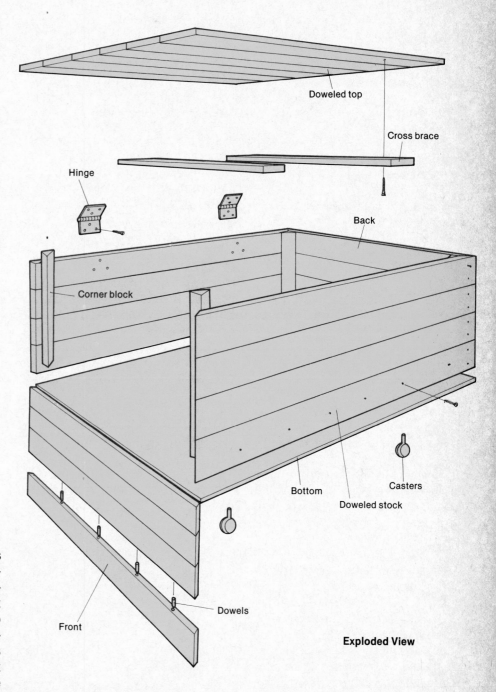

Doweled top

Cross brace

Hinge

Back

Corner block

Bottom

Casters

Doweled stock

Front

Dowels

Exploded View

A large, sturdy box with a lid is something every crafts-oriented parent should build for his or her children. Kids like to have a place to put away toys, and parents like them to have one, too. This chest is also useful outside the playroom or children's bedroom; it makes an excellent place to store blankets or linens. The one shown here was made from red cedar stock, a fragrant wood that imparts a fresh odor to blankets and linens. Cedar is also reputed to repel moths, so it is good for storing woolen items. Kids aren't much interested in blanket storage, but if you make one chest for them and another for yourself, they won't mind.

The chest shown here happens to be one I made entirely with hand tools, and I recommend it for polishing handwork skills. I completed the chest with a handsaw, hand drill, doweling jig, bar clamp, hammer, and screwdriver.

STEP 1
Doweling the Top and Sides
The dimensions for the chest are arbitrary; you can vary them to build a chest whose size depends on your needs or the materials you have on hand. If you use your own dimensions, just make sure that the opposing sides are exactly the same size, and when the box is assembled, measure its inside dimensions for fitting the bottom, and its outside dimensions for fitting the lid. The

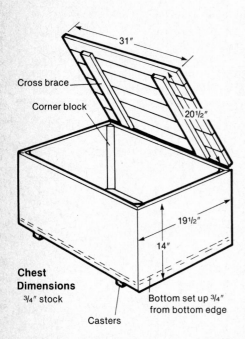

Chest Dimensions
3/4" stock

Cross brace
Corner block
31"
20½"
19½"
14"
Casters
Bottom set up 3/4" from bottom edge

chest sides and lid are made of glued and doweled stock; the bottom is 3/4-inch plywood.

To glue and dowel the stock for each side and the lid, lay out pieces of 3/4-inch stock, alternating the direction of the grain in every other piece to minimize warpage, until you have enough stock to make a side. Smooth the butted edges of the stock with a jointer (or a hand plane) until the pieces fit perfectly against each other. Mark four parallel lines across the width of the pieces (at a right angle to the butted edges) so that they divide the stock into five equal parts. Use a doweling jig to drill a 1-inch-deep hole at the four marks in each facing edge. Squeeze glue into the holes along the edge of one piece of stock and drive in 1⅜-inch spiral dowels; glue along the facing edge of the next piece and drive it onto the dowels. Repeat the procedure until you have glued and doweled all the stock for the piece you are making, then fix the stock in a bar clamp and tighten the clamp until the glue squeezes out of the joint lines. Wipe the glue away with a warm, damp cloth. Allow to dry over-

night. Use this same procedure for making the other sides and lid.

STEP 2
Cutting the Sides and Assembling the Box
When the pieces are dry, cut each side to the proper size and miter each end at 45°. Use glue and No. 8 finishing nails set below the surface, or countersunk No. 8 × 1½-inch wood screws, to attach the sides. Check to see that the box is squared as you assemble the pieces.

STEP 3
Cutting and Fitting the Corner Blocks and Bottom
Cut the bottom from 3/4-inch plywood to the inside dimensions of the box you are building. Rip 45° corner blocks 1¼ inches shorter than the depth of the box and miter the tops at 45°. Install them with glue. Attach the bottom with glue and No. 8 × 1½-inch wood screws driven in through the sides.

STEP 4
Building the Lid
Cut the stock you've glued and the dowel for the lid to 1 inch larger than the outside dimensions of your toy chest. Cut the cross braces to about 2 inches shorter than the inside width of the box; they must clear the edges for the lid to close. Attach the braces across the lid with countersunk No. 8 × 1¼-inch flathead wood screws.

STEP 5
Finishing the Chest
Position the lid so that it overlaps the edges by the same distance on all sides. Attach it with standard blanket chest hinges, which are available at hardware stores or home centers. Attach flat-bottomed casters to the bottom of the box at the corners. Finish the chest however you like, inside and out. If you use cedar stock, as I did, don't finish the inside: if you do, you will seal in the oils that give the wood its pleasant smell.

Animal Chairs

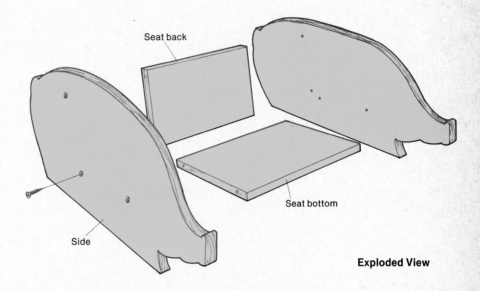

Seat back

Seat bottom

Side

Exploded View

Materials List
Sides (2), $^3/_4 \times 25 \times 24''$,
    hardwood-faced core board or any
    plywood
Seat bottom (1), $^3/_4 \times 9 \times 12''$,
    hardwood-faced core board or any
    plywood
Seat back (1), $^3/_4 \times 9 \times 12''$,
    hardwood-faced core board or any
    plywood
No. 8 $\times$ 1$^1/_4''$ flathead wood screws
Metal runners
Wood putty
Sealer or paint
India ink, paint, or felt-tip pen

Tools
Coping saw or saber saw
Belt sander or wood rasp
Sandpaper
Screwdriver

Level of Difficulty
Easy

Length of Time Required
Afternoon

Safety Precautions
Safety goggles, filter mask

These whimsical-looking but practical chairs will delight the young and amuse the old. They are extremely easy to build and, if made of hardwood-faced plywood, they can be given a natural finish and be presentable in any room of the house. If they are to be used only in the playroom or children's bedroom, they can be made of any plywood and painted in bright colors. No matter what material you use, the most important part of this project is to sand all the edges absolutely smooth—the child who gets a scrape, a scratch, or a splinter from a sharp edge won't soon sit in the chair again. The two animal patterns given here are by no

means the only ones that make appealing chairs. Try one of these; then try drawing your own. Just follow the directions below, and your own animal will turn out as well as either of these.

STEP 1
Cutting the Pieces
Enlarge the squared drawing and transfer the pattern to $^3/_4$-inch hardwood-faced plywood. If the stock you are using has only one

good side, flop the pattern when you draw the second piece so the good sides can both face outward. Use a saber saw or a coping saw to cut out the sides.

STEP 2
Sanding the Sides
Tack-nail the two sides together at the spots marked for the screws that hold the seat and seat back; clamp the piece in a vise. Use a belt sander, wood file, or other appropriate tool to

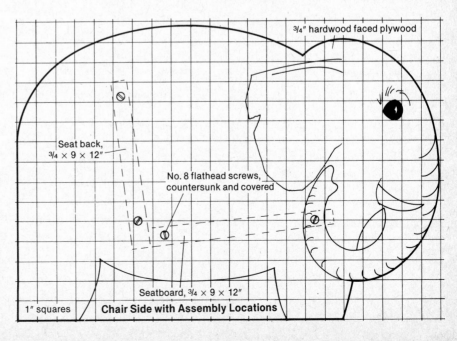

$^3/_4''$ hardwood faced plywood

Seat back,
$^3/_4 \times 9 \times 12''$

No. 8 flathead screws,
countersunk and covered

Seatboard, $^3/_4 \times 9 \times 12''$

1" squares   **Chair Side with Assembly Locations**

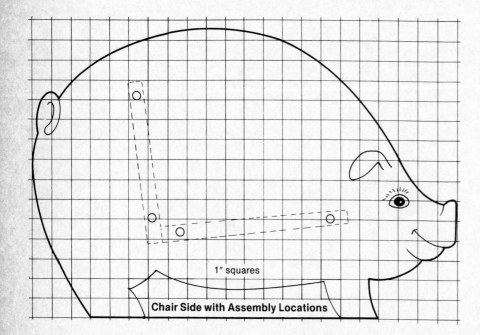

1" squares

Chair Side with Assembly Locations

STEP 4
Finishing the Chairs
Transfer the pattern for the animal's features to the sides. Then apply a sealing coat of finish and allow to dry. Apply the features with a small brush and India ink, paint, or a waterproof felt-tip pen. When the features are dry, apply several more coats of finish. If you are painting the chairs, paint at least two coats and apply the features last. To protect your rugs, tack metal runners along the bottom edges of the chair.

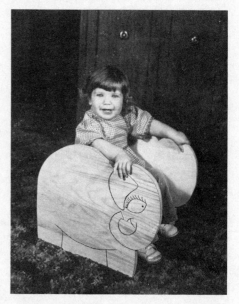

smooth the edges—tacking the sides together ensures that both sides will be finished identically. When thoroughly smooth, take the sides apart and sand each one all over again.

STEP 3
Installing the Seat
Cut the seat bottom and seat back to the given dimensions and sand these pieces thoroughly. Then mark the locations for the seat bottom and seat back on the inside of the sides, and mark the locations of the screw holes on the outside. Glue the edges of the seat bottom and attach to the sides with countersunk No. 8 × 1¼-inch flathead screws. Position the seat back and attach in the same manner. You can leave screws exposed (just be sure that they are well countersunk and have no burrs sticking up), or you can cover them with wood plugs or wood putty.

Giraffe Clothing Rack

Materials List

Heads (2), 1 × 10 × 12″, clear pine stock
Neck (1), 2 × 4 × 31½″
Body (1), 2 × 6 × 17″
Front legs (2), 2 × 2 × 20⅝″
Back legs (2), 2 × 2 × 18″
Clothes pegs (4), 7 × ⅝″ dowel
Antlers (2), 6 × ½″ dowel
Antler tops (2), 1″ wooden or rubber balls
Whisk broom
No. 8 × 1¾″ flathead wood screws
No. 8 × 1½″ flathead wood screws
No. 8 × 1″ flathead wood screws
No. 10 × 3″ flathead wood screws
Glue
Paint, two colors

Tools

Table saw, band saw and coping saw, or saber saw
Drill
Screwdriver
Sander or sandpaper

Level of Difficulty

Easy

Length of Time Required

Afternoon

Safety Precautions

Safety goggles

To obtain a full-sized traceable pattern for this project, use the order form at the back of this book and order pattern number 113.

The kids will think neatness is a game with this friendly giraffe to help them keep their clothes organized. Standing 44 inches high, it has pegs for clothes hangers in its neck, at just the right height for someone learning to hang up his or her coat. The con-struction is easy as long as you cut the angled sides and ends of the legs accurately for a tight fit against the body and a flat stance on the floor. The giraffe has a whisk broom tail that is both decorative and useful: it pulls out to be used as a clothes brush. After you have cut out the pieces, but before assembly, mark them for whatever decorations you like. I recommend black or dark brown spots painted over a yellow, tan, or beige body. To decorate the rack, paint it with a few undercoats

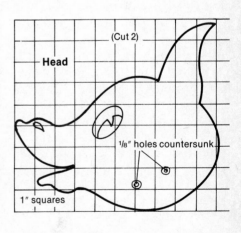

Ball
Head
Whisk broom
Dowel
Neck
Body
Back leg
Front leg

Exploded View

(Cut 2)
Head
⅛″ holes countersunk
1″ squares

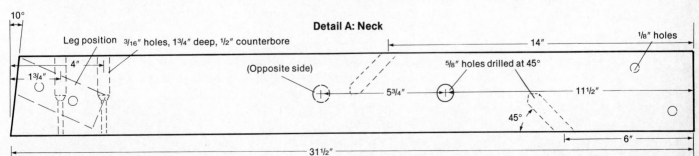

10°
Leg position
3/16″ holes, 1¾″ deep, ½″ counterbore
Detail A: Neck
14″
⅛″ holes
4″
(Opposite side)
⅝″ holes drilled at 45°
1¾″
5¾″
11½″
45°
31½″
6″

87

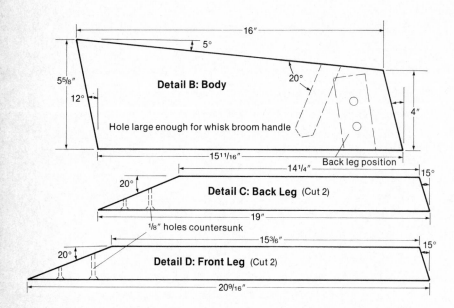

Detail B: Body

16"

5°

5⁵/₈"

12°

Hole large enough for whisk broom handle

20°

4"

15¹¹/₁₆"

Back leg position

14¹/₄"

15°

20°

Detail C: Back Leg (Cut 2)

19"

¹/₈" holes countersunk

15³/₆"

15°

20°

Detail D: Front Leg (Cut 2)

20⁹/₁₆"

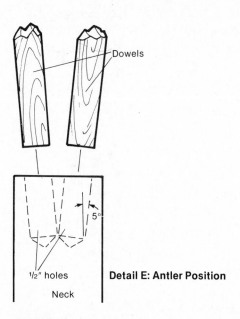

Dowels

5°

¹/₂" holes

Neck

Detail E: Antler Position

of a bright solid color (yellow or tan is the most lifelike). Then draw on the spots as you like or using the picture of the finished project as a guide. Fill these in with black or another dark color. Paint on the facial features, and the giraffe is ready for a useful life.

STEP 1
Cutting the Pieces
Enlarge the squared drawing of the head, transfer the pattern for two heads onto 1 × 10-inch clear pine stock, and cut out the heads with a band saw or saber saw. Mark off the dimensions for the neck given in Detail A, on a piece of 2 × 4 and make the cut for the angled end. Mark off the dimensions for the body given in Detail B, on a piece of 2 × 6 and cut it out. Mark off the dimensions for the front and back legs given in details C and D, and cut two of each to fit. Finally, cut two 6-inch pieces of ¹/₂-inch dowel and four 7-inch pieces of ⁵/₈-inch dowel.

STEP 2
Drilling the Pieces
Drill ¹/₈-inch countersunk holes from the outside of both parts of the head at the points indicated in the squared drawing. Drill ⁵/₈-inch holes at a 45° angle in the front, back, and sides of the neck as indicated in Detail A—

these are for the dowel clothes pegs. Also, drill two ³/₁₆-inch holes through the neck from the front at the points indicated in Detail A and then counterbore the holes to a ¹/₂-inch diameter 1³/₄-inches into the neck from the front—these are screw holes for attaching the neck to the body. Drill and countersink ¹/₈-inch holes on the center lines of the legs at the points indicated in Details C and D. Finally, bore a 1-inch hole (or larger as needed) in the center line of the body, at the point indicated in Detail B, to hold a whisk broom that doubles as the giraffe's tail and a clothes brush. Measure the diameter of the handle of the whisk broom you will use, and bore a hole slightly larger than it so that the brush can be removed easily.

STEP 3
Assembling the Clothing Rack
Attach the neck to the body with glue and No. 10 × 3-inch flathead wood screws driven through the predrilled screw holes. Attach the back legs to the body with glue and No. 8 × 1-inch and No. 8 × 1³/₄-inch flathead wood screws, as shown in Detail B. Attach the front legs to the neck in the same manner in the position indicated in Detail A. Finally, attach the two pieces of the head on either side of the neck with glue and No. 8 × 1¹/₂-inch flathead wood screws.

STEP 4
Finishing the Rack
Bore two ¹/₂-inch holes 1 inch deep in the end of the neck between the heads as shown in Detail E. Glue the two 6-inch dowels into these holes. Bore a ¹/₂-inch hole ¹/₂ inch deep in two 1-inch wooden balls, or cut holes in two rubber balls, and glue these onto the ends of the dowels. Glue the ⁵/₈-inch dowels into the four holes in the neck.

Toddler's Rocking Horse

Materials List

Seatboard (1), 3/4 × 5 × 15″, any stock or hardwood-faced plywood

Rockers (2), 3/4 × 4 × 16″, any stock or hardwood-faced plywood

Head (1), 3/4 × 9 × 11″, any stock or hardwood-faced plywood

Seat brace (1), 3/4 × 2 × 3 1/2″, any stock or hardwood-faced plywood

Handle (1), 3/8 × 5″ dowel

Sealer

Wood finish

India ink and brush, or other marker

No. 8 × 1 1/4, No. 8 × 1″ flathead wood screws

Glue

Wood plugs or wood putty

Tools

Coping saw, band saw, or saber saw

Hand drill or electric drill

Several grades of sandpaper

Level of Difficulty

Easy

Length of Time Required

Afternoon

Safety Precautions

Safety goggles

Hand-built wooden toys are a blessing in more ways than one. Not only do they give a lot of pleasure to the builder, but their sturdy simplicity can be enjoyed by generations of children as the toys are passed down, rich with fond memories. This project is one of the classic examples of such a keepsake. To a child, of course, it is simply fun.

The toddler's rocking horse can be made entirely with hand tools, and it takes only a few hours' work and a little time for paint and glue to dry. It can be constructed of almost any wood—hardwood, softwood, or hardwood-faced plywood—you happen to have left over from some cabinet or furniture building. No matter what wood or mix of woods you choose, be sure to follow the instructions regarding the direction of the grain so as to ensure the rocking horse's durability. Choose close-grained wood that won't splinter for this toy.

STEP 1
Cutting the Pieces

Enlarge the squared drawings of the rocker, seat, and head, and transfer the patterns to 3/4-inch stock. Mark the rocker and seat patterns so that the grain of the wood runs along their length. If you are using solid stock for the head, mark the pattern so that the grain runs up and down the head; if you are using softwood stock for the seat and rockers, use hardwood-faced plywood for the head. When the pieces are marked, cut them to shape with a hand coping saw, saber saw, or band saw. Mark the positions of the screw holes on the two rockers and bore them with a hand drill. Then countersink the screw holes with a countersink bit. (Of course, you can use an electric drill here.) Also bore a 3/8-inch hole through the head, as indicated on the drawing. Cut the seat brace and handle dowel to the given dimensions.

STEP 2
Sanding the Pieces

The rocking horse deserves to be sanded as smooth as silk—there is probably no square inch on the toy

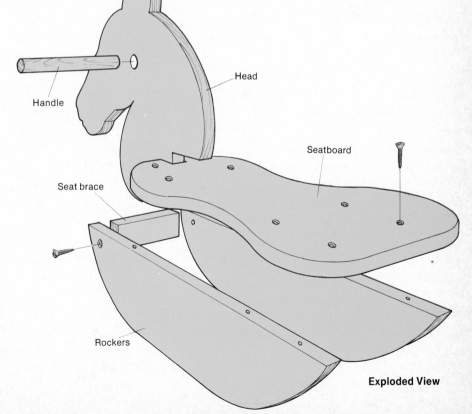

Handle

Head

Seatboard

Seat brace

Rockers

Exploded View

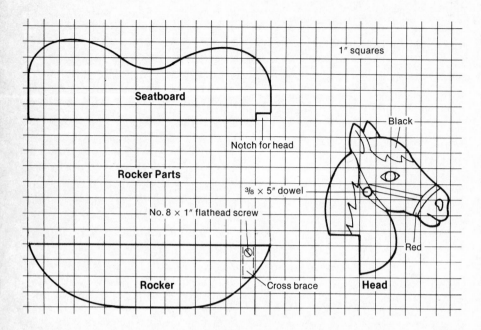

1" squares

Seatboard

Notch for head

Rocker Parts

3/8 × 5" dowel

No. 8 × 1" flathead screw

Rocker

Cross brace

Black

Red

Head

STEP 5
Mounting the Head and Handle
Fasten the head in place in the notch in the seatboard with glue and No. 8 × 1¼-inch screws driven up from under the seat and through the back of the seat brace. Smear glue on the inside of the hole in the horse's head and drive the handle dowel through until it is in place. Wipe away the glue that the dowel squeezes out, and allow the head and handle to set.

STEP 6
Finishing the Rocking Horse
When the entire horse is assembled and dry, apply several more coats of finish, sanding with very fine sandpaper, after each application has dried, to give a perfectly smooth finish.

that won't be handled, if not licked and chewed on. Sand all the pieces using progressively finer grades of sandpaper. Spend as much time sanding as you spend on all the building; you, and your toddler, will be well satisfied with the result.

STEP 3
Assembling the Body
Mark the location of the rockers on the bottom of the seat board by centering them with the brace between them and attach them with glue and countersunk No. 8 × 1-inch flathead wood screws driven through the seat. Wipe away any excess glue with a damp cloth so you won't have any extra sanding to do when it dries. You can leave the screws exposed, as they are in the model shown here—just be sure that they are countersunk well below the surface of the seat and that there are no burrs sticking up—or your can fill the screw holes with wood plugs or

putty. If you use plugs or putty, sand the filling smooth (after it is well set, if you use putty). Fasten the seat brace between the rockers with 1-inch screws through the holes bored in the rockers and with the same-sized screws driven down through the top of the seat. Again, be sure that all screws are safely smooth.

STEP 4
Finishing the Head and Body
Give both the head and body of the rocking horse a coat of sealing finish. Remember that the riders are likely to chew on the horse, so check the label to be sure that the finish is nontoxic. After the sealer coat on the head is dry, mark the details, as shown in the drawing, and paint them in with a small brush and India ink, or use a colorfast felt-tip pen. Paint the halter red (or whatever color you like) and allow the head to dry; then apply a second coat of finish and allow it to dry.

Toddler's Horse-Chair Rocker

Materials List
Sides (2), ³⁄₄ × 20 × 35″, hardwood-faced plywood
Seat back (1), ¹⁄₂ × 7 × 12″, any stock
Footboard (1), ¹⁄₂ × 7 × 12″, any stock
Handlebar (1), ³⁄₄ × 13¹⁄₂″, dowel
Stretcher dowels (2), ¹⁄₂ × 13¹⁄₂″, dowel
Red, white, and black paint
Glue
Wood putty
No. 8 × 1¹⁄₄″, No. 8 × 1″ flathead wood screws

Tools
Band saw or saber saw
Drill
Screwdriver
Sander or sandpaper

Level of Difficulty
Easy

Length of Time Required
Afternoon

Safety Precautions
Safety goggles, filter mask

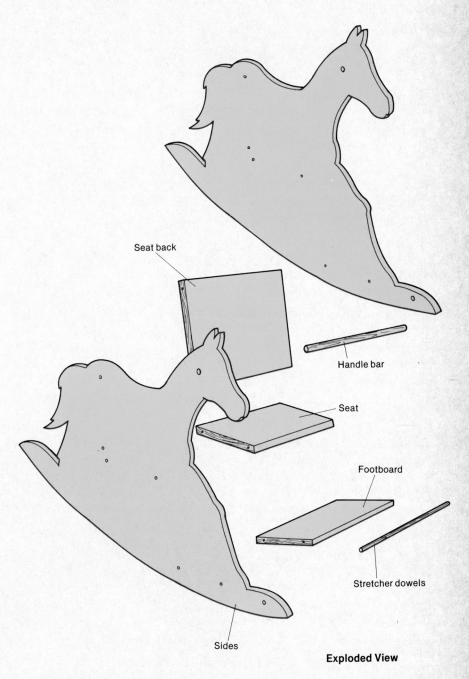

Seat back

Handle bar

Seat

Footboard

Stretcher dowels

Sides

Exploded View

The very youngest buckaroo can ride in this horse-chair rocker before graduating to the toddler's rocking horse. The design is safe for small children because the horse is just a seat with rockers and with a dowel across the front that serves as both a handhold and a safety bar. A strap running from the dowel to the underside of the seat keeps the child from sliding forward off the seat and under the dowel. The sides of the chair are made from ³⁄₄-inch hardwood plywood, and the seat and footboard from ³⁄₄- and ¹⁄₂-inch scrap stock.

STEP 1
Cutting and Drilling the Sides
Enlarge the squared drawing for the sides and transfer the pattern to ³⁄₄-inch hardwood-faced plywood for both sides. Mark the locations of the dowel holes for both the bottom stretcher dowels and the handlebar dowel. Cut out the sides and mark them with the position of the seat, seat back, and footboard. Use an electric drill to bore stopped holes (which do not go through) ¹⁄₄ inch deep on the inside of the sides to hold the bottom stretcher dowels and the handlebar dowel, as shown in the Side View. Bore screw holes through from the outside of the sides into the stopped holes, using a countersinking bit. Sand all the edges

91

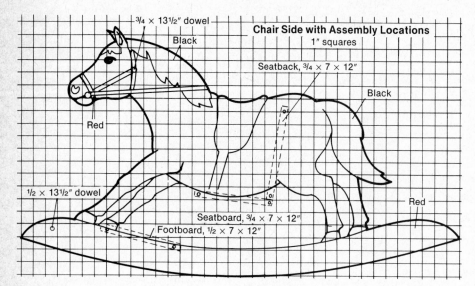

Chair Side with Assembly Locations
1" squares

¾ × 13½" dowel
Black
Red
½ × 13½" dowel
Seatback, ¾ × 7 × 12"
Black
Seatboard, ¾ × 7 × 12"
Footboard, ½ × 7 × 12"
Red

smooth, fill any gaps with wood putty, let the sides set and do a final, thorough sanding. Finish both sides with two coats of white paint.

STEP 2
Making the Seat
While the paint on the sides is drying, cut the seat back and footboard to the given dimensions from ½-inch stock. Round the edges and sand smooth. Cut the seat to the given dimensions, round the edges, and sand smooth. Then attach the seat back to the seat with No. 8 × 1-inch screws and glue, as shown in the Side View.

STEP 3
Preparing the Seat and Dowels
Cut the handlebar dowel from ¾-inch dowel rod to the width of the seat and footboards, plus ½ inch. Cut the two ½-inch bottom stretcher dowels to the same length. Paint the bottom dowels, the seat assembly, and the footboard bright red. Don't paint the handlebar dowel. Children have a tendency to chew on everything, and this dowel is a prime target for them. Leave the dowel unfinished, but make sure that it is made of a good, solid, tight-grain wood, and that it is sanded as smooth as possible.

While the red paint is drying on the inside assembly pieces, draw the horse pattern on the sides and paint. Use red for the rockers, saddle, and bridle; use black for the mane, tail, eyes, and trim.

STEP 4
Assembling the Rocker
Putting all the pieces together is no trouble if you have four hands, so get some help with the assembly. Place one side face down on clean newspaper and use the pattern to mark the location of the seat assembly and footboard. Glue the top ends of the stretcher dowels and handlebar dowel and fit the other ends into the stopped holes on the side. Then smear glue along the top edge of the seat assembly and position the bottom edge in place. Set the other side onto the glued dowels and seat, position correctly, and fasten with countersunk No. 8 × 1¼-inch flathead wood screws. When the pieces are secure, turn the top over (with your helper) and repeat the procedure to attach the other side with glue and screws. Wipe away any excess glue and touch up any smeared paint.

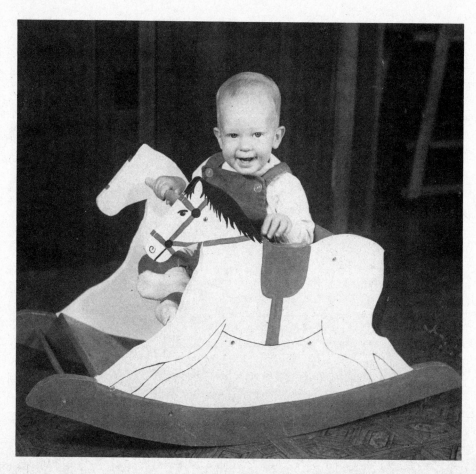

Elephant Rocker

Materials List

Head (1), $3/4 \times 15 \times 18"$, plywood
Sides (2), $3/4 \times 6^{3/4} \times 16^{1/2}"$, plywood
Spacer (1), $3/4 \times 6 \times 10"$, plywood
Legs (4), $3/4 \times 4^{1/4} \times 9^{3/4}"$, solid stock
Wedges (4), $3/4 \times 3^{1/4} \times 5^{1/4}"$, solid stock
Rockers (2), $3/4 \times 5^{1/4} \times 31"$, solid stock
Seat (1), $3/4 \times 6^{1/4} \times 9^{3/4}"$, plywood or solid stock
Platforms (2), $1 \times 3^{7/8} \times 12"$, plywood or solid stock
Handle (1), $1/2 \times 6"$, dowel
Glue
Wood putty
No. $10 \times 1^{3/4}"$ flathead wood screws
No. $10 \times 1^{1/2}"$ flathead wood screws
Short piece of rope
Gray paint and other bright colors

Tools

Band saw, coping saw, or saber saw
Drill
Rasp
Screwdriver
Sander or sandpaper
C-clamps

Level of Difficulty

Easy

Length of Time Required

Afternoon

Safety Precautions

Safety goggles

To obtain a full-sized traceable pattern for this project, use the order form at the back of this book and order pattern number 56.

This rocker is for the middle-sized riders. Measure your child to see if his or her feet will reach the platform. Take extra care to cut and sand the rockers to ensure the smoothest rocking action. This project should be sanded very smooth because it will get a lot of use from bare legs. Paint the elephant's head, body, and legs light gray, then decorate the rockers with bright colors.

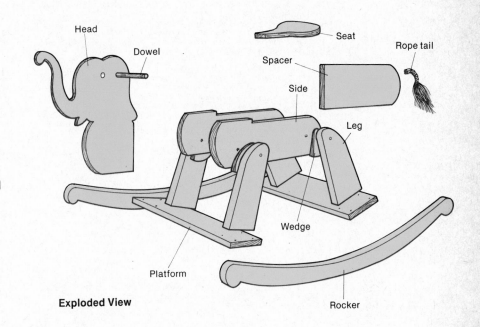

Exploded View

Except for the shape of the head and a few finishing and painting details, this elephant rocker is the same project as the one featured on the cover of this book. If you would like to build either version, a full-sized pattern is available which can be ordered by filling out the form at the back of this book.

STEP 1
Cutting the Parts

Enlarge the squared drawing of the head, in Details A-1 or A-2, and trans-

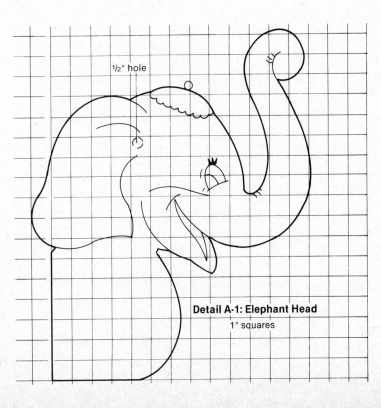

Detail A-1: Elephant Head
1" squares

Detail A-2: Horse Head

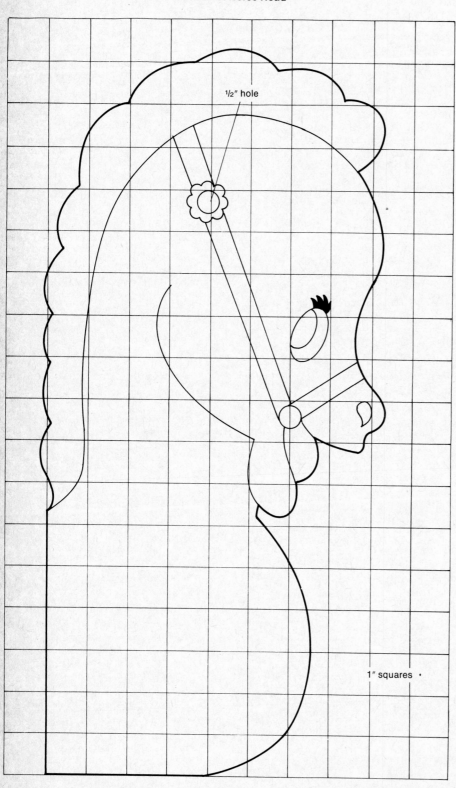

½" hole

1" squares

fer the pattern to a piece of ¾-inch plywood. Cut out the head with a band saw, coping saw, or saber saw, drill a ½-inch hole where indicated, and sand the head smooth rounding the edges with sandpaper. Enlarge the squared drawings for the two sides and the spacer in Detail B, the four legs in Detail C, the four wedges in Detail D, the two rockers in Detail E, and the seat in Detail F. Cut out all the pieces from 1 × 12-inch clear

Detail B: Side and Spacer

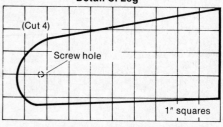

Spacer
(Cut 1)

1" squares

Position of back leg   Position of front leg

Side (Cut 2)

Detail C: Leg

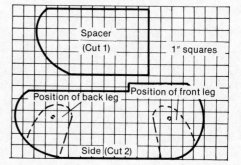

(Cut 4)

Screw hole

1" squares

Detail D: Wedge   (Cut 4)

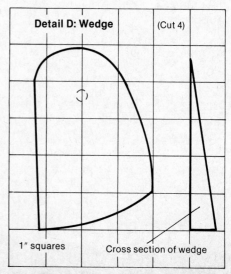

1" squares   Cross section of wedge

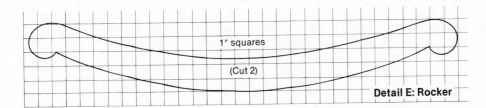

1" squares

(Cut 2)

Detail E: Rocker

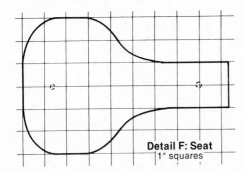

Detail F: Seat
1" squares

pine or other suitable stock. Cut the two platform pieces to the given dimensions. Sand these pieces, except the wedges, and round the top edge of the seat with a rasp.

STEP 2
Assembling the Body
Lay one side piece down (outside down) on a flat surface, coat it with carpenter's glue, and seat the spacer and head on it making sure that all edges are flush (see Exploded View). Coat the inside of the other side piece with glue and seat it on the head and spacer so that all edges are flush; clamp the assembly with C-clamps. Wipe away any glue that squeezes out and allow to dry.

STEP 3
Attaching the Legs
Use the enlarged squared drawing of the sides, in Detail B, to mark the position of the legs on the body. Glue the wedges to the tops of the legs (be sure they are on the inside of the legs), clamp, and allow to dry. When dry, drill 3/16-inch holes and countersink in the legs, as indicated in Detail C. Attach the legs to the body, as shown, with glue and No. 10 × 1³/4-inch flathead wood screws.

STEP 4
Attaching the Body to the Rockers
Mark the position of the legs on the platform pieces, with the outside edge of each leg 2¹/2 inches from the edge of the platform. Drill and countersink two 3/16-inch holes in the platform in each position where the legs attach; fasten the platforms to the legs with glue and No. 10 × 1¹/2-inch flathead wood screws. Drill and

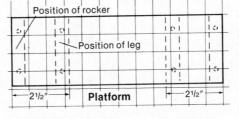

Position of rocker

Position of leg

2¹/2" **Platform** 2¹/2"

countersink two 3/16-inch holes at the ends of the platform pieces and attach the platforms to the rockers with glue and No. 10 × 1¹/2-inch flathead wood screws.

STEP 5
Finishing the Rocker
Drill and countersink two 3/16-inch holes in the seat, as indicated in Detail F, and attach the seat to the body with glue and No. 10 × 1¹/2-inch wood screws driven into the spacer. Drill a 3/8-inch hole about 3/4 inch deep in the center of the spacer at the back, just below the seat, and glue in a 5- or 6-inch rope or yarn tail. Cover all the countersunk screw heads with wood putty, allow to dry, and touch up with paint. Finally, cut a 6-inch length of ¹/2-inch dowel and glue it, centered, in the hole in the head; this will serve as a handle. Paint on the facial features, as shown in the squared drawing (Details A-1 or A-2), and, if you like, a blanket on the elephant's back.

Old Charlie Rocking Horse

Materials List

Horse's body, seat, and seat braces, ³/₄ × 15 × 30", hardboard plywood

Uprights (4), ³/₄ × 3 × 15", oak stock

Bottom end pieces (2), ³/₄ × 2¹/₂ × 13", oak stock

Bottom side pieces (2), ³/₄ × 2¹/₂ × 32", oak stock

Footboard (1), ³/₄ × 5³/₄ × 22", oak stock

Footboard cleats (2), 1 × 1³/₈ × 5³/₄", oak stock

Suspension rods (2), ¹/₂" diameter steel rod × 30"

Brackets (4), ¹/₈" steel flat × 1 × 10"

Spacers (4), ¹/₂" pipe × 2" long

Handle (1), 6 × ³/₄" dowel

¹/₄" bolts and nuts

1¹/₄" flathead wood screws

2¹/₂" ovalhead wood screws

Wood putty

Paint and stain, varnish, or other finish

Tools

Saber saw
Band saw
Radial arm saw with dado blade
Router
Torch
Drill
Screwdriver
Sander or sandpaper
File
Chisel

Level of Difficulty

Moderate

Length of Time Required

Overnight

Safety Precautions

Safety goggles, filter mask, full face protection, leather gloves

weather had reduced Old Charlie to a pile of rotted pieces. There was enough left, fortunately, to reconstruct patterns for all the pieces, so now he can ride again in any house. Hardwood plywood and oak lumber were used for the original and for this reproduction.

This project takes a real pounding from children, so sturdy joints and rugged construction are absolutely necessary. Be sure to cut all the angles exactly because a tight fit makes a sound joint. If you don't have a torch, or if you don't want to try heating and bending the steel rods and straps that hold up the horse, check around with local welders for one who might do that part of the job for you.

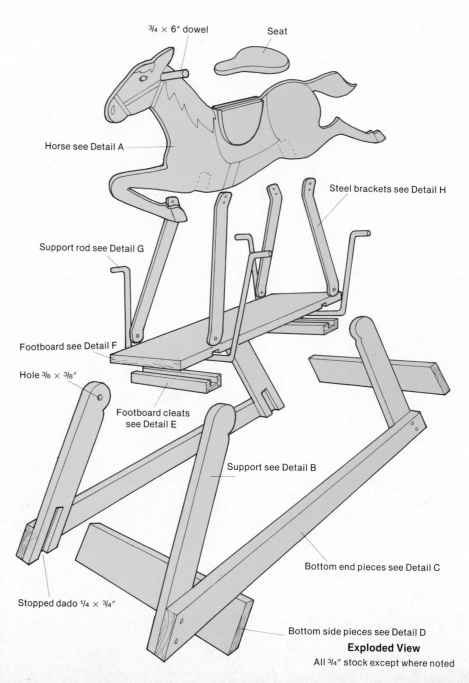

³/₄ × 6" dowel

Seat

Horse see Detail A

Steel brackets see Detail H

Support rod see Detail G

Footboard see Detail F

Hole ³/₈ × ³/₈"

Footboard cleats see Detail E

Support see Detail B

Bottom end pieces see Detail C

Stopped dado ¹/₄ × ³/₄"

Bottom side pieces see Detail D

Exploded View
All ³/₄" stock except where noted

When I was a boy my Dad made a rocking horse, and we called him "Old Charlie." Thirty years after my last ride, I found him in the loft of an old barn with a leaky roof, but the

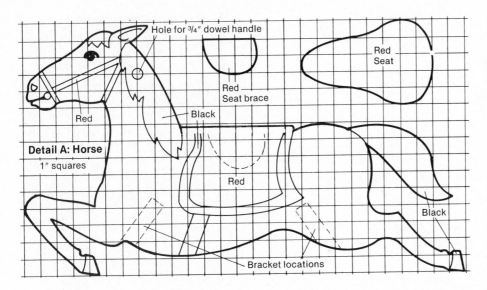

Hole for ¾″ dowel handle

Red
Seat

Red
Seat brace

Black

Red

Detail A: Horse
1″ squares

Black

Bracket locations

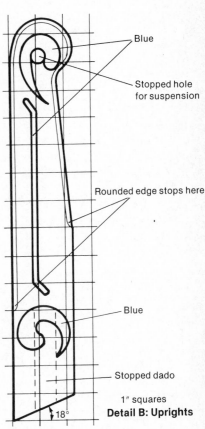

Blue

Stopped hole
for suspension

Rounded edge stops here

Blue

Stopped dado

1″ squares
Detail B: Uprights

18°

STEP 1
Cutting the Horse's Body, Seat, and Seat Braces

Enlarge the squared drawings for body, seat, and seat braces (Detail A) and make patterns for the pieces. Cut out the body from hardwood plywood with a saber saw; you can use a band saw to cut the seat and two braces. Drill a ¾-inch hole at the back of the horse's head as indicated for the dowel handle. Fill any holes on the body with wood putty, and sand these areas when the putty is set. Sand the body thoroughly and round the edges with a file and sandpaper. Sand the seat smooth and round the edges; a file and sandpaper can be used for this, too, but a rounding-over bit on a router is preferable. When these surfaces are smooth, paint the body white and the seat and its braces bright red. Apply at least two coats. When the undercoats are dry, paint details as indicated on Detail A, or create a design of your own.

STEP 2
Cutting and Shaping the Uprights

Enlarge the squared drawing of the uprights (Detail B) and make a pattern. The bottom edge should be angled inward 18°, so check the exact angle on the pattern and correct if necessary. Cut four uprights from oak stock and shape the edges on both sides of the pieces, as marked on the drawing, with a router or shaper.

Use a saber saw to cut the horse's body from a piece of plywood.

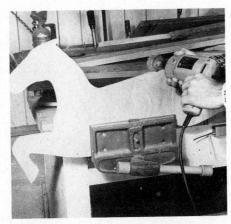

Smooth all the edges of the horse's body and then go over them again.

Take care to cut the bottom frame pieces to the exact angles.

STEP 3
Cutting Bottom End Pieces, Side Pieces, and Footboard

Cut bottom end pieces (Detail C) from ³/₄-inch stock to the dimensions given in the materials list, then cut an 18° angle along one of the long edges of each, as shown. Cut the bottom side pieces from ³/₄-inch stock to the given dimensions, then cut each end of both pieces in at an 18° angle (see Detail D and Exploded View). Cut the footboard from ³/₄-inch stock to the given dimensions. Sand all the pieces smooth, and decorate as illustrated or as you please.

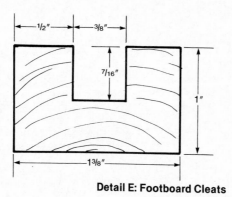

Detail E: Footboard Cleats

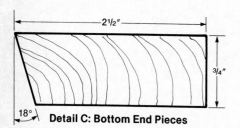

Detail C: Bottom End Pieces

Detail D: Bottom Side Pieces

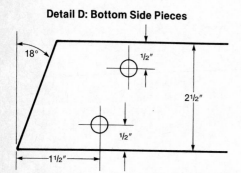

Steel bracket screw hole

Detail F: Footboard

A dado blade on a radial arm saw makes cutting the stopped dadoes easy.

STEP 5
Cutting Stopped Dadoes and Blind Holes in the Uprights

Stopped dadoes—dadoes that are stopped before they reach the top of the posts—hold the bottom end pieces. They are cut into the center of the uprights at the angled bottom, ³/₄ inch wide and ¼ inch deep (see Detail B). Make the cuts with the dado blade on a radial arm saw or on the table saw, finishing the cut with a chisel. As you cut the dadoes, stop and check their fit with one of the bottom end pieces. Make sure that the fit is snug. After cutting the stopped dadoes, drill ³/₈ × ³/₈-inch blind holes on the same side at the top end, as indicated in Detail B and the Exploded View. These will hold the suspension system.

STEP 4
Cutting and Notching the Footboard Cleats and Notching the Footboard

Cut the footboard cleats from 1-inch stock to the dimensions given. Then cut a ³/₈ × ⁷/₁₆-inch notch down the center of each cleat's full length (see Detail E) with a dado blade on a radial arm saw. Cut ³/₈ × ¼-inch notches at either end of the footboard following the dimensions given in Detail F. The grooved footboard cleats will later be fastened over the grooves in the footboard to hold the steel support rods. Sand the cleats.

Be careful not to drill all the way through the upright when boring the holes for the suspension rods; use a drill press if you have one.

STEP 6
Shaping the Suspension System

The suspension system is made of two ½-inch steel rods, each holding two 2-inch pieces of pipe as spacers (see Detail G) and four brackets of ⅛ × 1-inch steel flat (see Detail H). Heat these with a torch and bend to fit the given dimensions. Before starting to heat the steel, slip two pipe spacers onto each rod: you won't be able to get the spacers on after the rods are bent, so don't forget to put them on first. Lay out a pattern for the rods and brackets on a piece of plywood to serve as a guide for bending the metal to the correct shape. Clamp the rods in a vise and heat them with the torch at the points of the bends until the steel is red hot, but do not heat past bright red. Bend them against the pattern. Use leather gloves. While the rods and steel flats may vary slightly from the pattern, make sure that the rods match each other exactly and that the steel flats match each other. Also make sure that the suspension pieces are not twisted: the steel rods should have all the bends in the same plane, and the ends of the steel flats must be parallel. If they are not, the horse will be difficult to move. When cool, all the metal parts should be sprayed with rust-inhibiting paint. My choice is bright yellow.

Make sure the support frame is securely fastened together.

STEP 7
Assembling the Frame

Fit the bottom end pieces into the stopped dadoes on the uprights, making sure that the bottom edges of the end pieces are flush with the bottom edges of the uprights. Mark the bottom side pieces for screws at each end, as indicated in Detail D, and fasten them to the uprights and end pieces with glue and 2½-inch ovalhead wood screws. Work on a flat surface and check to be sure that the frame is sitting flat as you fasten each corner.

STEP 8
Attaching the Suspension System and Footboard

Spring the suspension rods (pull them out slightly) and fit the ends into the blind holes at the tops of the uprights. You may need a helper for this task. Set the footboard over the suspension rods, with a spacer on either side of both ends; then attach the cleats over the rods on the underside of the footboard with 1¼-inch wood screws.

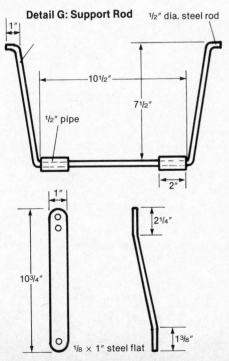

Detail G: Support Rod   ½" dia. steel rod

1"

10½"

7½"

½" pipe

2"

1"

2¼"

10¾"

⅛ × 1" steel flat   1⅜"

Detail H: Steel Brackets

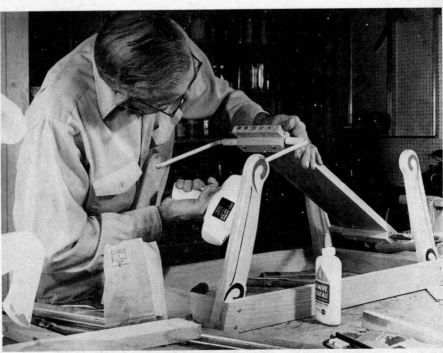

The cleats on the bottom of the footboard hold the suspension rods in place; a power screwdriver makes attaching them easy.

STEP 9
Attaching the Seat and Handle to the Body

Cut a ³⁄₄-inch dowel to 6 inches and glue it in place in the hole at the back of the horse's head. Glue and screw the seat braces to either side of the body, as shown in the Exploded View, and, after the glue has set, glue and screw the seat down onto the body with countersunk 1¹⁄₄-inch flathead wood screws, one in each brace and one into the body at each end of the seat.

STEP 10
Attaching the Body

Drill ¹⁄₄-inch holes in the steel flats as indicated in Detail H. Screw the lower ends of the flats onto the footboard ⁷⁄₈ inch from either end, as indi-

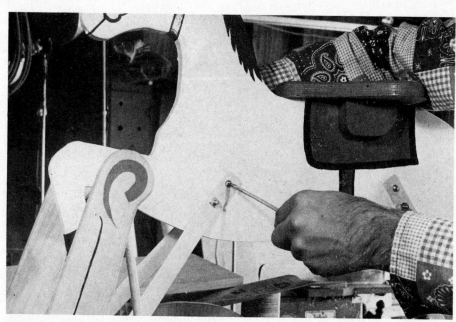

After attaching the horse's body to the suspension system, smooth the ends of the bolts so there will be no sharp edges to cause a scratch.

cated in Detail F. Then ask someone to help you to hold the body and, with the body in place between the upper ends of the steel flats, as indicated in Detail A, mark through the holes in the steel and drill ¹⁄₄-inch holes to accept ¹⁄₄-inch bolts. Attach the body with nuts and bolts and file the exposed nuts and bolt ends smooth so that small-fry riders won't get scratched.

STEP 11
Finishing the Rocking Horse

The hardwood frame can be given a coat of stain and varnish or simply left unfinished. A wipe-on penetrating stain-sealer is a good finish to use because it leaves no surface finish. Cleaning the frame is always easier if it has a finish of some sort.

Wooden Red Wagon

Materials List

Ends (2), $3/4 \times 4 \times 14^{1}/_{2}''$
Sides (2), $3/4 \times 4 \times 33''$
Bottom pieces (4), $3/4 \times 3^{15}/_{16} \times 33''$
Inside front brace (1), $1/2 \times 3 \times 14^{1}/_{2}''$
Axle yokes (2), $3/4 \times 5 \times 16''$
Axle yoke braces (8), $3/4 \times 3^{1}/_{2} \times 5''$
Bottom axle braces (2), $3/4 \times 2^{1}/_{4} \times 16''$
Axles, $1/2''$ threaded rod (2), $21''$ long
$1/2''$ nuts, $1/2''$ washers (4)
Back braces (2), $3/4 \times 4 \times 5''$
Front axle yoke top piece (1), $3/4 \times 5^{1}/_{2}''$
    diameter
Tongue (1), $3/4 \times 1^{1}/_{2} \times 24''$
Handle (1), $4 \times 1/2''$, dowel
Outside tongue supports (2), $3/4 \times 4 \times$
    $3''$
Inside tongue support (1), $3/4 \times 1^{1}/_{2} \times$
    $3''$
Outside back brace (1), $3/4 \times 1^{1}/_{2} \times 15''$
Wheels (4), $8''$ lawn mower wheels
Front support bolt (1), $2 \times 5^{1}/_{2}''$
Tongue bolt (1), $1/2 \times 3''$
Metal brace (1), $1/8 \times 1''$ steel flat, $12''$
    long
No. $8 \times 1^{1}/_{4}''$, No. $8 \times 1''$ flathead wood
    screws
Glue
Wood plugs

Tools

Band saw
Clamps
Electric drill or drill press
Drum sander
Sandpaper

Level of Difficulty

Moderate

Length of Time Required

Overnight

Safety Precautions

Safety goggles, filter mask,
    leather gloves

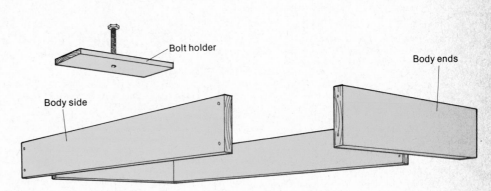

Bolt holder
Body ends
Body side

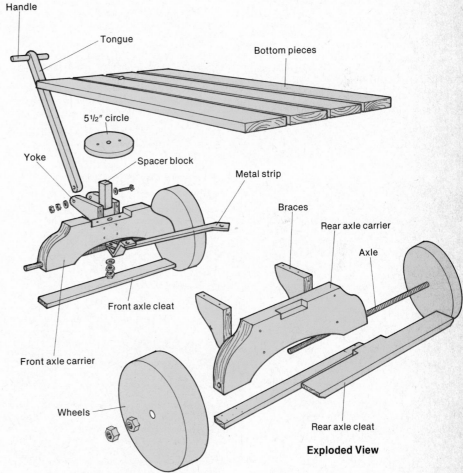

Handle
Tongue
Bottom pieces
$5^{1}/_{2}''$ circle
Spacer block
Metal strip
Yoke
Braces
Rear axle carrier
Axle
Front axle cleat
Front axle carrier
Wheels
Rear axle cleat

Exploded View

A wooden wagon is a popular toy for both the builder and the ultimate owner. Every youngster should have one around the yard, and one made at home gives everyone involved a satisfaction that can't be bought ready-made. There are no special tricks or complicated techniques for building the wagon, but two matters are very important: because a wagon gets rough use, it must be built to stand the punishment, with all pieces joined strongly enough to take a pounding; and the basic materials must be solid and rugged. The wagon shown here was built entirely of $3/4$-inch oak stock.

Building the wagon is a moderately easy job, but it will take a few days because of the time required for the glue between surfaces to dry. For this project, a drill press makes a few of the steps much easier to complete than would a hand-held electric drill. If you use a vise to grip the pieces you are drilling, however, a portable drill will get the job done. The project proceeds from the ground up—starting with building the axle carriers and the rest of the undercarriage,

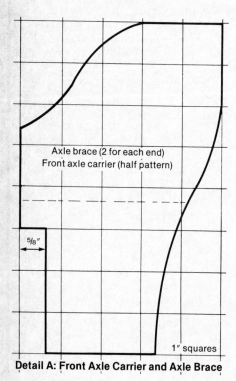

Axle brace (2 for each end)
Front axle carrier (half pattern)

5/8"

1" squares

Detail A: Front Axle Carrier and Axle Brace

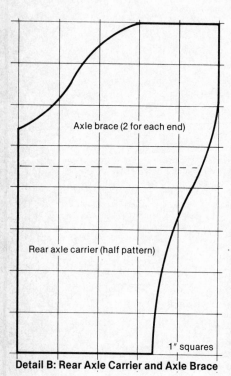

Axle brace (2 for each end)

Rear axle carrier (half pattern)

1" squares

Detail B: Rear Axle Carrier and Axle Brace

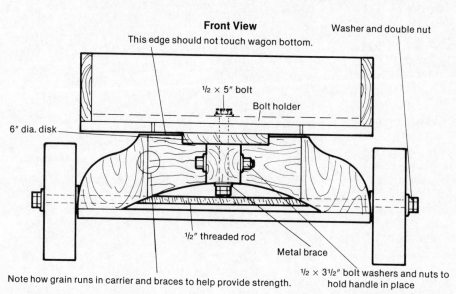

Front View
This edge should not touch wagon bottom.

Washer and double nut

$1/2 \times 5''$ bolt

Bolt holder

6" dia. disk

$1/2''$ threaded rod

Metal brace

$1/2 \times 3^1/2''$ bolt washers and nuts to hold handle in place

Note how grain runs in carrier and braces to help provide strength.

then building the body, and finally putting it all together.

STEP 1
Assembling the Axle Carriers

Enlarge the squared drawings shown in Details A and B, double the drawings as indicated to make a pattern, and transfer this to ¾-inch oak stock. Also enlarge the pattern for the axle braces shown in Detail A and transfer to the stock. Use a band saw to cut both axle carriers to size. Take care to make the upper notch in the front axle carrier exactly ⅝ inch deep. This notch accommodates a disk of stock that serves as a large washer allowing the front wheels to turn. Cut the eight braces from the stock with the grain turned 90° to that of the axle carriers (see detail in Front View); this will give the axle carriers greater strength. Attach the braces, with glue and No. 8 × 1¼-inch wood screws, to both sides of both ends of the axle carriers. Clamp tightly and allow to dry overnight.

STEP 2
Drilling the Axle Holes

When the axle carriers are set, use a ½-inch paddle bit or forstner bit to bore the axle holes through the center of each end of the carriers ½ inch from the bottom as in the Front View. A drill press makes this job easy, but a portable drill will do if the pieces are fixed tightly in a vise. Make sure that you keep the drill bit square both up and down and side to side or the axles won't align properly. Use a drum sander to sand the glued ends of the carriers.

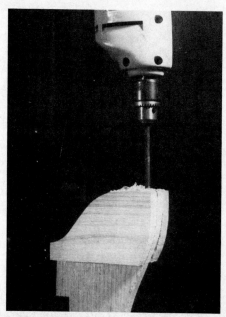

Be sure that you bore the axle holes in the axle carriers straight through.

Smooth the glued pieces of the axle carriers with a drum sander or by hand.

Be sure to attach the wheels before cutting off the excess length of the threaded axle, then turn the wheels back off.

STEP 3
Fitting the Axles

Slip the 1/2-inch threaded rods through the axle holes; if they stick, you may have to rebore the holes slightly. Position the axle so that one end protrudes from the carriers just enough to accept the washer, wheel, and nut; fasten the wheel in position. Then slip the other washer and wheel over the long end and screw on the nut. With both wheels now in place, cut off the long end of the axle just outside the nut with a hacksaw. You must fit the wheels in place before you cut the axle because it may be impossible to thread the nut onto the cut end; removing the nut over the cut rethreads the axle. When the axles are cut, remove the nuts, wheels, and washers.

STEP 4
Completing the Front Axle Carrier and Building the Yoke

Cut a 6-inch disk from 3/4-inch oak stock with a band saw and sand it smooth. Check to be sure that the disk fits in the notch on the front axle carrier. Enlarge the squared drawing for the yoke and spacer block (Detail C), transfer the pattern to the stock, and cut out the two yoke pieces and

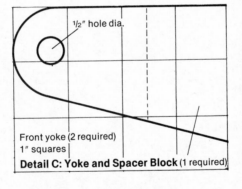

1/2" hole dia.

Front yoke (2 required)
1" squares
Detail C: Yoke and Spacer Block (1 required)

the spacer. Use glue and No. 8 × 1¼-inch wood screws to attach the yoke pieces with the spacer between them. Clamp and dry overnight. When set, cut 1/2-inch holes for the

handle bolt where marked. Then attach the yoke to the center of the axle carrier with the top edge flush with the bottom of the notch; use glue and No. 8 × 1¼-inch wood screws driven in from the back of the carrier. When the glue is dry, use glue and the same-sized screws to attach the center disk to the axle carrier and yoke. The disk should be centered on the middle of the carrier. Countersink the screws so that they will not rub against the wagon body.

STEP 5
Boring the Center Bolt Hole

When the disk is set, bore a 1/2-inch hole through the center of the disk and down through the axle carrier. Be sure to drill straight down; otherwise you may bore through the side of the carrier. Again, use a drill press for this task if possible.

STEP 6
Making the Tongue and Handle

Cut the tongue to size from 3/4-inch stock. Round both ends and sand thoroughly; then bore 1/2-inch holes through the tongue 3/4 inch from either end, as shown in the Side View. Glue a 1/2-inch dowel, 5 inches long, through one end.

STEP 7
Building the Body

Cut the side and end pieces to size from 3/4-inch stock. Fasten the end pieces between the sides with glue and No. 8 × 1¼-inch flathead wood

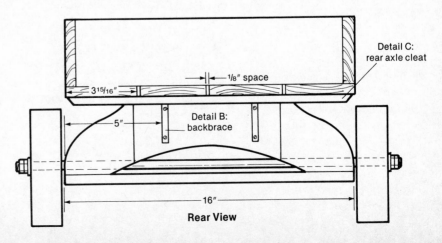

Detail C:
rear axle cleat

1/8" space

3¹⁵/₁₆"

5"

Detail B:
backbrace

16"

Rear View

screws counterbored and covered with wood plugs. Glue the plugs in place; then cut them flush and sand them off. Cut the bottom pieces to size, sand them, and fasten them to the frame with flathead wood screws, leaving 1/8-inch gaps between the bottom pieces as shown in the Rear View. Countersink these screws, but don't bother to plug them. Check to make sure that the body is squared up as you install the bottom.

STEP 8
Installing the Bolt Holder
Cut the front bolt holder to size and glue and screw it in place inside the

STEP 9
Installing the Rear Axle Carrier
Transfer the pattern for the rear axle cleat in Detail D to a piece of 3/4-inch stock, cut it out, and sand smooth. Use glue and 1 1/4-inch flathead wood screws to install the cleat on the underside of the wagon body, 2 inches from the back of the wagon, with the notches on the ends facing forward. Then fit the rear axle carrier up against the cleat as shown in the Side View and fasten it with glue and 1 1/4-inch flathead wood screws to the cleat and to the wagon body, driving the screws down through the floor-boards from the inside. Countersink

these screws and be sure that no sharp points remain on the screw heads to scratch a passenger. Enlarge the squared drawing for the braces that fit on the front of the rear carrier (Detail E), transfer the pattern to 3/4-inch stock, and cut the two pieces. Fasten them in place as shown in the Side View with glue and 1 1/4-inch flathead wood screws driven down through the body and in from the back of the axle carrier. Again, countersink the screws and be especially careful about sharp edges in the wagon bed.

STEP 10
Installing the Front Carrier
Position the front carrier over the hole in the front of the body and insert the holding bolt with a large washer in place from inside the wagon bed up through the front carrier. Fasten the bolt in place with a washer and nut; then cut the metal brace shown in Detail F, bend it to shape, bore the holes for the bolt, and screw and fasten one end in place to the wagon bed. Slip the other end over the bolt and fasten in place with the two nuts tightened together. This provides plenty of brace, but allows the axle carrier to turn freely.

STEP 11
Painting the Wagon
With the wheels removed, paint the entire wagon bright red, giving it several coats of a good sturdy enamel. Then reinstall the wheels, insert the tongue between the holders, and bolt in place.

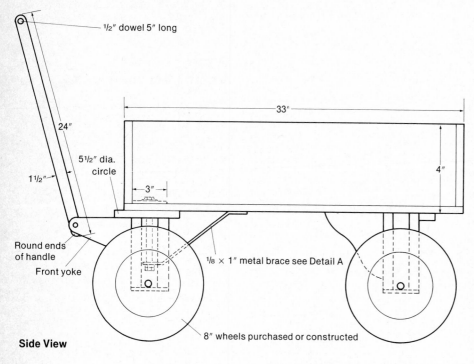

Side View

- 1/2" dowel 5" long
- 24"
- 5 1/2" dia. circle
- 1 1/2"
- 3"
- 33"
- 4"
- Round ends of handle
- Front yoke
- 1/8 × 1" metal brace see Detail A
- 8" wheels purchased or constructed

wagon body at the front, with countersunk 1-inch flathead wood screws as shown in the Side View. Bore a 1/2-inch hole down through the bolt holder exactly in the center. Sand the entire wagon body smooth, especially around all the edges and corners, and be sure to sand the wooden plugs flush with surrounding surfaces.

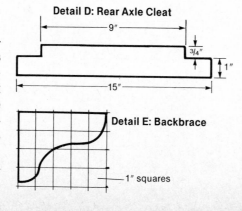

Detail D: Rear Axle Cleat
- 9"
- 3/4"
- 1"
- 15"

Detail E: Backbrace
- 1" squares

STEP 12
Adding Side Racks
You can construct an enclosing rack of 3/4 × 3/4-inch stakes held in place with angle iron straps bent to shape and screwed to the inside of the wagon body. The racks themselves are constructed of 1/2-inch oak stock fastened to the stakes with 3/4-inch roundhead brass screws.

Attach the axle cleats across the axle carriers with glue and screws.

The front axle carrier must move freely on its large wooden washer.

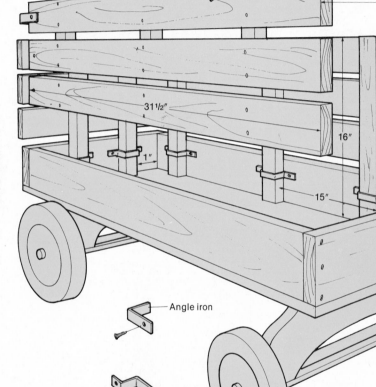

³/₄″ stock

2″

½″ side stock

14½″

3″

3″

1″

31½″

16″

1″

15″

Angle iron

1″ flat iron bent to shape

Sides

1″

8″

1″

Detail F: Metal Brace

Riding Toy

Materials List

Seat (1), $3/4 \times 10 \times 24''$ plywood or solid stock

Rear sides (2), $3/4 \times 8 \times 10''$

Side strengtheners (2), $3/4 \times 3 \times 5''$

Top inside cleats (2), $3/4 \times 1 \times 8''$

Back (1), $3/4 \times 6 \times 8''$

Front wheel yoke sides (2), $3/4 \times 1^1/2 \times 5^3/4''$

Front wheel yoke spacer (1), $3/4 \times 7/8 \times 1^1/2''$

Front wheel yoke turning block (1), $3/4 \cdot \times 3''$ diameter

Handlebar post (1), $8^1/2 \times 1''$ dowel

Handlebar holder (1), $1^1/2 \times 2 \times 4''$

Handlebars (2), $3^3/4 \times 1''$ dowel

Front wheel axle (1), $2^1/2 \times 1/2''$ dowel

Rear axle (1), $14 \times 1/2''$ threaded steel rod

Washers and nuts to fit $1/2''$ rod

Paint

Glue

No. $8 \times 1^1/2$, No. $8 \times 1^1/4$, No. $8 \times 1''$ flathead wood screws

No. 6 finishing nails

Tools

Band saw, coping saw, or saber saw

Table saw or radial arm saw

Drum sander and sandpaper

Drill

Doweling jig

Screwdriver

Hammer

Clamps

Level of Difficulty

Moderate

Length of Time Required

Overnight

Safety Precautions

Safety goggles, filter mask

This little riding toy is patterned on the traditional riding toys that have been popular with children for countless generations.

STEP 1
Cutting the Pieces

Enlarge the squared drawings for the sides and side strengtheners (see grid portion of Side View) and for the seat (see Detail A). Cut two sides (the whole pattern) and two side strengtheners (lower portion of the pattern);

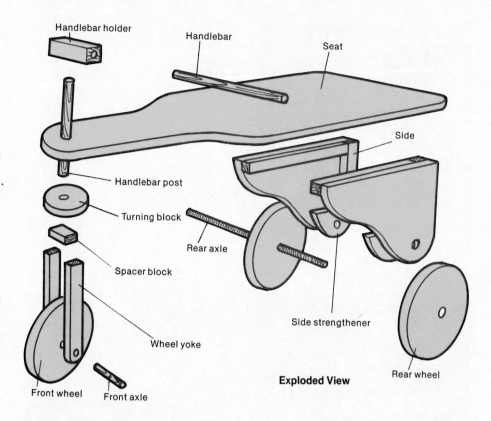

Exploded View

make the cuts with a band saw, coping saw, or saber saw. Sand all the edges with a drum sander and then sand by hand until they are perfectly

Detail A: Seat

1" squares

smooth. After sanding the seat, bore a 1-inch hole in the front end, $2^1/2$ inches in from the end on the center line.

STEP 2
Assembling the Sides

Glue the side strengtheners to the bottom of the sides (edges flush) and clamp; allow to dry overnight. Also, cut the top inside cleats to the dimensions given and glue these to

Side View

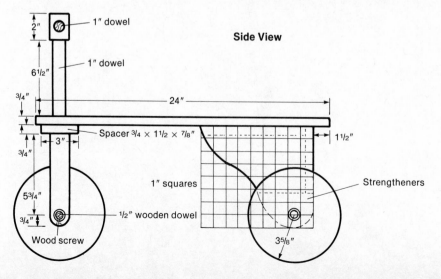

the inside of the tops of the side, flush with the top edge. Clamp and let dry overnight. When these assemblies are dry, drill ½-inch holes through the bottoms of the sides for the axle at the point indicated in the Side View.

STEP 3
Making the Wheels
Glue and dowel enough stock for three wheels from two pieces of ¾-inch stock. Position the grain of the wood in the two pieces at opposite angles to provide more strength and prevent the wood from splitting apart. Clamp it solidly and allow the glue to dry overnight. Then mark the circumference of the wheels with a compass and cut to shape. Sand the edges thoroughly and round the outside edges with a shaper. Bore the ½-inch holes for the axles in the centers of the wheels and paint the wheels the color desired.

STEP 4
Assembling the Body
Mark the bottom side of the seat for the position of the side pieces as shown in the Side and Back Views. They should be set in 1 inch from

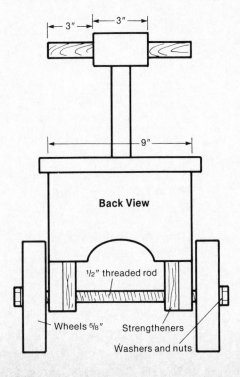

either side and 1½ inches from the back of the seat. Turn the seat over and drill counterbored holes for screws to attach the sides. Install the sides with glue and No. 8 × 1½-inch flathead wood screws. Cut the back to the given dimensions and cut out the semicircular shape (as shown in the Back View). Install the back flush against the bottom of the seat and flush with the edges of the sides with countersunk No. 8 × 1-inch flathead wood screws. Paint or finish the seat and sides as you wish.

STEP 5
Making the Wheel Yoke
Cut the pieces for the front wheel holder to the given dimensions and shape as shown in the Side View and Detail B. Use No. 6 finishing nails and glue to attach the front between the yoke sides flush with the top as shown in Detail B. Bore a 1-inch hole in the center of the turning block and use glue and countersunk No. 8 × 1¼-inch flathead wood screws to attach it, centered, on top of the yoke. Finally, bore ½-inch holes through the ends of the yoke sides, at the point indicated in the Side View.

STEP 6
Installing the Wheels
Put the wheel in the yoke and drive a 2½-inch length of ½-inch dowel through the axle holes and the wheel. Cut off the dowel flush with the side of the yoke and pin the dowel in place with a countersunk No. 8 × 1-inch flathead wood screw driven in from the bottom of one of the yoke sides (see the Side View). Slip the threaded rod through the back axle holes and fit a wheel on either end. Secure each wheel with three washers and two nuts and cut off any excess axle rod, smoothing off any sharpness from the ends.

STEP 7
Making and Attaching the Handlebar
Cut the handlebar holder to the given

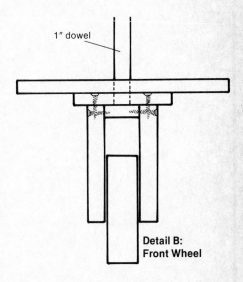

Detail B:
Front Wheel

dimensions, sand it, and bore stopped 1-inch holes 1 inch deep in the center of either end and in the center of the bottom side (see the Back View for location). Glue 3¾-inch lengths of 1-inch dowel into both ends and allow to dry. Cut the handlebar post to the given dimension and glue it into the bottom of the handlebar holder. When the glue is set, paint the assembly and the yoke. When dry, stick the handlebar post through the hole in the seat and glue it into the hole at the top of the yoke—put a piece of wax paper over the top of the yoke (with a hole through it to let the handlebar post pass) and take extra care not to get glue on the top of the yoke. Allow the glue to dry overnight, and the toy is ready to ride.

Wheelbarrow

Materials List
Sides (2), $3/4 \times 8^{1}/_2 \times 19''$, softwood
  stock
Front (1), $3/4 \times 8^{3}/_4 \times 9''$, softwood
  stock
Bottom (1) $3/4 \times 15 \times 14^{3}/_4''$, softwood
  stock
Handles (2), $5/4 \times 1^{3}/_4 \times 25''$, softwood
  stock
Wheel (1), $5/4 \times 6^{1}/_2 \times 6^{1}/_2''$, softwood
  stock
Supports (2), $5/4 \times 5 \times 5^{1}/_2''$, softwood
  stock
Axle (1), $4 \times 1/2''$ dowel
No. $8 \times 2''$ flathead wood screws
No. $8 \times 1^{1}/_4''$ flathead wood screws
No. $8 \times 1^{1}/_4''$, No. $8 \times 1/2''$ roundhead
  brass wood screws
Washers
Glue

Tools
Band saw or saber saw
Radial arm saw or table saw
Router with quarter-round cutter or
  radius-ease cutter
Shaper
Screwdriver
Drill
Wood rasp
Sandpaper and sander

Level of Difficulty
Moderate

Length of Time Required
Afternoon

Safety Precautions
Safety goggles

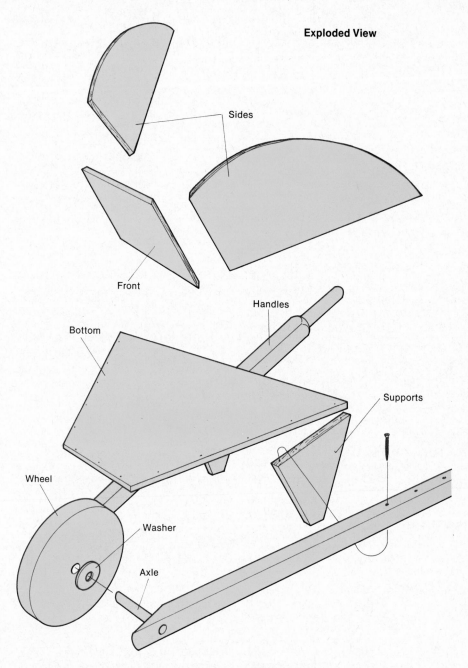

Exploded View

Sides

Front

Bottom

Handles

Supports

Wheel

Washer

Axle

A sturdy toy wheelbarrow is an item that seems to delight all youngsters. They can use it to carry everything from dolls to puppies to rocks—and for that reason it must be well constructed to stand hard knocks. The one shown here is made of white pine, with $3/4$-inch stock for the sides, front, and bottom, and $5/4$-inch stock for the handles, wheel, and supports. The $5/4$-inch stock is available at many building-supply yards, but you may have to order some. You can also use $1^{1}/_2$-inch stock—such as 2 × 4's for the handles or 2 × 6's for the wheel and supports—and run it

down on a planer to the required thickness. The supports and wheel can also be made of $3/4$-inch stock in a pinch, but this thickness will not be as sturdy.

The only difficult parts of this project are cutting the angles on the sides and front and the curved edge of the sides. A band saw does the quickest job on the curved edge of the sides, and a table saw or radial arm saw is best for cutting the angled edges.

STEP 1
Cutting the Pieces
Enlarge the squared drawing for the sides and transfer the pattern to pieces of $3/4$-inch stock—check to be sure that the pattern is correct for the bottom dimension and front angle shown in the squared drawing. Cut out the sides with a band saw or a saber saw. Cut the front piece to the dimensions and angles shown in Detail A. Cut the bottom to the dimensions given in Detail C. Sand

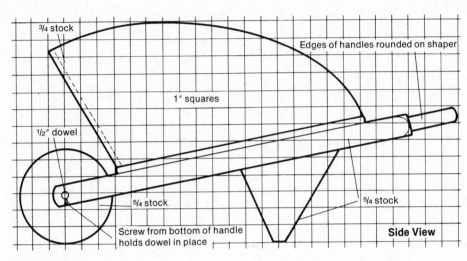

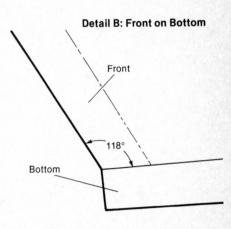

Detail B: Front on Bottom

Front

118°

Bottom

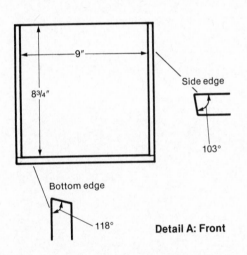

9″

8³/₄″

Side edge

103°

Bottom edge

118°

Detail A: Front

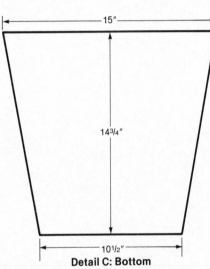

15″

14³/₄″

10¹/₂″

Detail C: Bottom

all the pieces thoroughly, taking care that the edges on the bottom, the upper edge of the front piece, and the top and curved edge of the side pieces are smooth.

STEP 2
Assembling the Barrow
Fasten the front piece between the sides with glue and countersunk No. 8 × 1¹/₄-inch flathead wood screws. Then fasten this assembly to the bottom in the same manner. Cover the countersunk screws with wood plugs and sand them down. Sand the entire barrow and set it aside.

STEP 3
Cutting the Handles
Cut the handles to the given dimensions; then mark for the angled ends, as shown in Detail D, and make the cuts. Position each handle as shown in Detail E, and bore a ¹/₂-inch hole straight through the center, 1 inch from the end. Round the front ends of the handle pieces with a band saw, as shown on the squared drawing. Use a quarter-round cutter or a radius-ease cutter in a router or shaper to cut a 4-inch rounded portion for the handle end of the handle pieces.

STEP 4
Cutting the Wheel and Supports
Use a compass to mark a 5³/₄-inch circle on ⁵/₄-inch stock and cut it out with a band saw. Smooth the saw cuts with a belt sander or disc sander so that the wheel is round and rolls smoothly. Then use a rounding cutter on a shaper or wood rasp and sandpaper, and round both edges of the wheel. Sand it thoroughly. Enlarge the squared drawing for the supports, transfer the pattern to ⁵/₄-inch stock, cut out the supports, and sand them smooth.

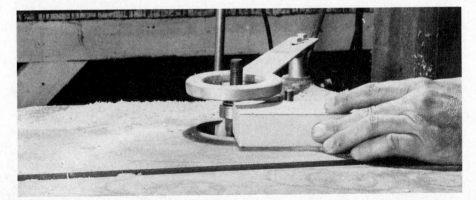

Use a shaper to cut stock down for the handles; if you don't have a shaper try a hand plane. Sand them smooth afterward.

Detail D: Axle Assembly

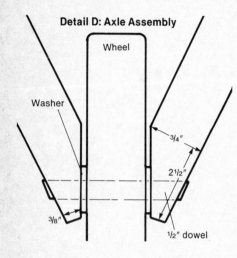

Wheel

Washer

3/4"

2 1/2"

3/8"

1/2" dowel

Drill at right angle to flat surface.

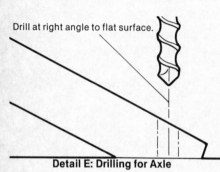

Detail E: Drilling for Axle

STEP 5
Assembling the Handles, Wheel, and Supports

Fasten the supports to the handles, as shown on the squared drawing, with glue and No. 8 × 2-inch flathead wood screws, countersunk and driven down through the top edge of the handle pieces. Bore a 1/2-inch hole exactly in the center of the wheel and sand it out with sandpaper wrapped around a 3/8-inch dowel until a 1/2-inch dowel will turn easily in the hole. Cut a 4-inch length of 1/2-inch dowel; then put the wheel between the angled handle ends and drive the dowel through one handle,

the wheel with a washer on either side, and the other handle. Turn the assembly on its back and drive a No. 8 × 1 1/4-inch wood screw through one of the handle ends into the dowel to secure it in place. Work the handles apart or together so that there is room enough for the washers to turn easily. Then cut the dowel ends flush with the edges of the handle pieces.

STEP 6
Finishing the Handle and Wheel Assembly

Sand the assembly thoroughly. If you plan to paint the barrow, handle, and wheel assembly in contrasting colors, do it now. If you plan to paint the entire project in one color or use a single finish over the whole piece, proceed with final assembly first.

STEP 7
Final Assembly

Lay the handles on a flat, smooth surface and fit the body in place for marking positions. The outside edge of the back of the body should be flush with the outside edges of the handles when the front of the wheelbarrow body is 1 inch away from the back edge of the wheel and is centered over the front of the handle assembly. After marking the location of the handles on the underside of the body, use glue and countersunk No. 8 × 1 1/4-inch flathead wood screws to fasten on the handles, driving the screws down through the body. Cover the screws with wood plugs, sand them smooth, and touch up the plugs with paint to match the rest of the body.

Toddler's Wooden Sled

Materials List

Sides (2), $\frac{1}{2} \times 7\frac{1}{2} \times 10''$, hardwood stock

Seat back (1), $\frac{1}{2} \times 7 \times 10\frac{3}{4}''$, hardwood stock

Runners (2), $\frac{1}{2} \times 3\frac{1}{2} \times 24''$, hardwood stock

Inside slats (2), $\frac{1}{2} \times 3\frac{3}{8} \times 22''$, hardwood stock

Outside slats (2), $\frac{1}{2} \times 2 \times 20\frac{1}{2}''$, hardwood stock

Cleats (3), $\frac{3}{4} \times 1 \times 11''$, hardwood stock

No. 8 $\times$ 1$\frac{1}{4}''$, No. 8 $\times$ 1$\frac{1}{2}''$ roundhead brass screws

Large screw eye

Pull rope

Spar varnish

Tools

Coping saw
Sander or sandpaper
Screwdriver

Level of Difficulty

Easy

Length of Time Required

Afternoon

Safety Precautions

Safety goggles

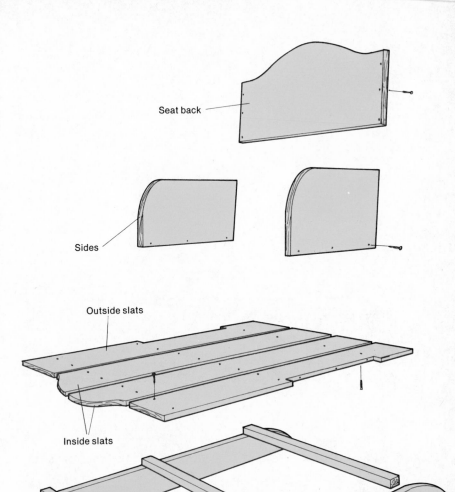

Seat back

Sides

Outside slats

Inside slats

Screw eye

Cleats

Runners

Exploded View

Since their invention, wooden sleds have been popular with children of all ages, and this toddler's version will be a hit with both the youngsters who use it and the craftsman who puts it together and gives them their first thrilling rides through the snow. The high sides and back provide both safety and comfort. This is another project that can be completed with hand tools and another of the handmade playthings that will be handed down lovingly from generation to generation.

In order that it can last through the years, the sled should be made of tough, durable wood such as ash, hickory, or oak, and the stock should be $\frac{3}{8}$- to $\frac{1}{2}$-inch thick. This unusual thickness may be hard to find at a lumberyard; however, since you don't need much, it might be practical to order the wood from a mail-order supplier.

STEP 1
Cutting and Varnishing the Pieces

Enlarge the squared drawings for the sides, seat back, runners, and slats. Mark the given dimensions of the two sizes of slats, transfer the pattern for the ends of the middle slats to the stock, and mark the notches in the outside slats. Mark the dimen-

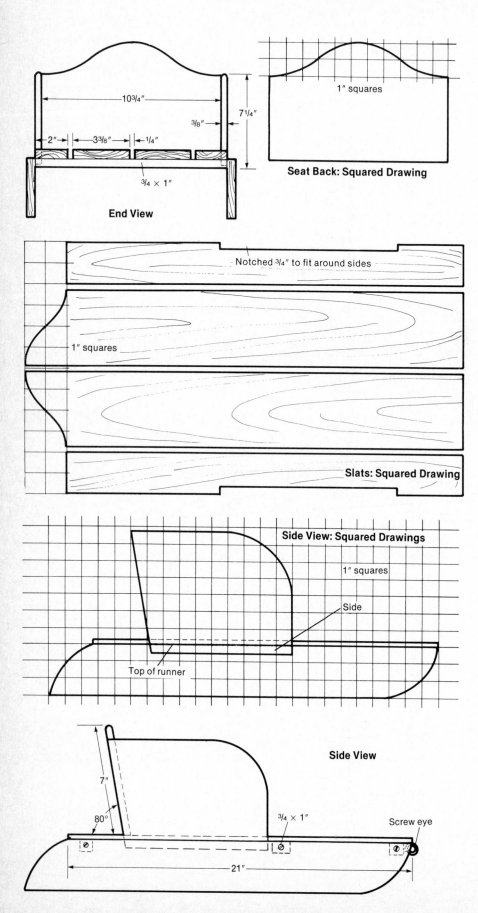

10³/₄"

7¹/₄"

³/₈"

2" 3³/₈" ¹/₄"

³/₄ × 1"

End View

1" squares

Seat Back: Squared Drawing

Notched ³/₄" to fit around sides

1" squares

Slats: Squared Drawing

Side View: Squared Drawings

1" squares

Side

Top of runner

Side View

7"

80°

³/₄ × 1"

Screw eye

21"

sions for the seat back and transfer the pattern for the curved top. Transfer the patterns for the runners and sides. Cut out all the pieces with a sharp coping saw. Cut the three cleats to the given dimensions. Sand all the pieces thoroughly and finish with several coats of spar varnish.

STEP 2
Assembling the Sled

Fasten the cleats between the runners with No. 8 × 1½-inch roundhead brass screws flush against the top edges, as shown in the Side View. Use one screw at each end of each cleat. Fasten the slats to the cleats using No. 8 × 1¼-inch countersunk screws, two screws at each cleat. Position the slats as shown in the End View leaving a ¼-inch space between them. Then slip the sides of the seat into the notches in the outside slats and fasten 1 inch deep, as shown in the Side View, with 1-inch brass wood screws driven from the inside into the runners. Finally, fasten the seat back between the sides with 1-inch brass wood screws. Screw a large screw eye into the front cleat, tie on a pull rope, and the sled is ready to go.

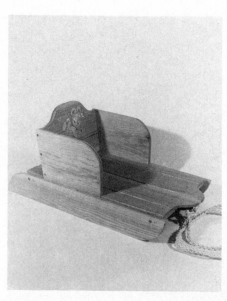

Full-Sized Sled

Materials List
Runners (2), $3/4 \times 4 \times 44''$, any
   hardwood stock
Inside slats (2), $1/2 \times 3^{1}/4 \times 46''$, any
   hardwood stock
Outside slats (2), $1/2 \times 3^{1}/4 \times 43''$, any
   hardwood stock
Handle (1), $3/4 \times 2^{1}/2 \times 25''$, any
   hardwood stock
Cleats (2), $3/4 \times 1^{3}/4 \times 11^{1}/2''$, any
   hardwood stock
No. 8 $\times$ 1$^{1}/2''$ roundhead wood screws
No. 8 $\times$ 1$^{1}/2''$ flathead wood screws
No. 8 $\times$ 1$''$ flathead wood screws
Pull rope
Implement or exterior paint
Exterior varnish

Tools
Band saw, saber saw, or coping saw
Drill
Power screwdriver
Sander or sandpaper

Level of Difficulty
Easy

Length of Time Required
Afternoon

Safety Precautions
Safety goggles

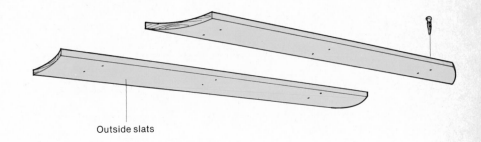

Outside slats

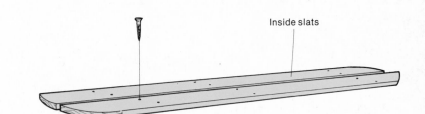

Inside slats

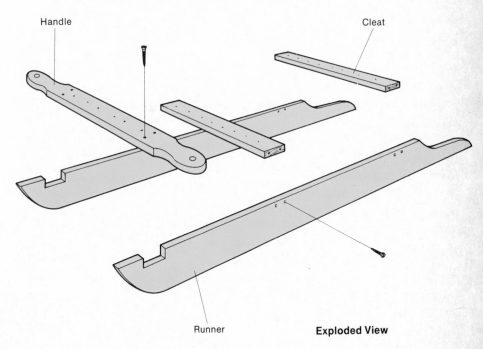

Handle

Cleat

Runner   **Exploded View**

This is a sled for graduates of the toddler size. It can carry one teenager or several smaller riders together. It naturally gets rougher use than the toddlers' sled, but if it is solidly constructed and well painted, it should last a long time. The project is simple if you have a band saw to cut out the patterns for the runners and slats; also, a power screwdriver makes the job go much faster. The sled shown here was built of oak for greatest strength and resilience, but any hardwood stock will do. The runners are cut from 3/4-inch stock and the slats from 1/2-inch stock.

STEP 1
Cutting the Pieces
Enlarge the squared drawings for the runners, the slats, and the handle. Make full-size patterns for both ends. Cut the stock for the runners to the given dimensions; then lay out the patterns on either end and cut to shape with a band saw, saber saw, or coping saw. Using a saber saw, cut the notch in the top front of each runner for the handle, as shown in the Side View. Cut the slats to the given dimensions, separate the patterns for the ends, transfer them to the stock, and cut them out. Follow the same procedure for cutting out the handle. Cut the cleats to the given dimensions.

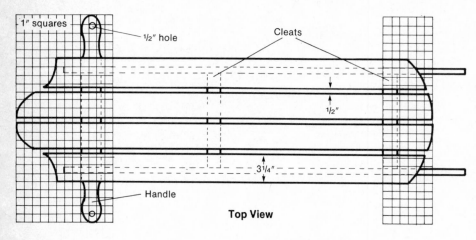

Top View

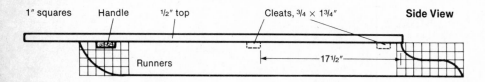

Side View

STEP 2
Assembling the Sled Frame
Use No. 8 × 1½-inch roundhead wood screws to attach the cleats between the runners, as shown in the Side View; drive the screws into the ends of the cleats from the outsides of the runners. Sand the entire assembly smooth and paint it with several coats of implement or exterior paint.

STEP 3
Attaching the Handle
Bore ½-inch rope holes in the ends of the handle with a paddle or spur bit, stopping just when the point of the bit starts to come through the other side. Then turn the handle over and finish the hole from the opposite

side—this prevents the drill bit from splintering the stock as it goes through. Sand the handle, sanding the edges of the rope holes with a piece of sandpaper wrapped around a dowel. Attach the handle, centered, in the notches at the front of the run-

ners with No. 8 × 1½-inch flathead wood screws counterbored to be flush with the handle.

STEP 4
Finishing the Sled
Sand the slats thoroughly. Mark the exact center of the sled on the handle and the back cleat; then position the two inside slats ¼ inch from either side of the center, as shown in the Top View. Using a countersink bit in an electric drill, bore each slat for two small wood screws at the handle and two cleats and fasten the slats down, driving in No. 8 × 1-inch flathead wood screws from the top. The screwheads should be just slightly below the surface of the wood. Check to make sure that there are no burrs sticking up from the screwheads—they can tear clothes and give nasty scratches. Position the outside slats ½ inch away from the inside slats and attach in the same manner, also driving screws down into the tops of the runners. Finish the unpainted parts with several coats of exterior varnish, allow to dry completely, and then put a pull rope on the handle.

Baby Cradle

Materials List

Rockers (2), ⁵/₄ × 4 × 28″, any stock
Bottom (1), ³/₄ × 14 × 28¹/₂″, glued-up
    stock
Sides (2), ³/₄ × 21¹/₄ × 34″, glued-up
    stock
Back (1), ³/₄ × 22 × 16″, any stock
End (1), ³/₄ × 11 × 14″, any stock
Roof facer (1), ³/₄ × 5 × 14″, any stock
Roof (3), ¹/₂ × 7¹/₂ × 10³/₄″, any stock
Cleats (2), ³/₄ × 1¹/₂ × 12″, any stock
No. 8 × 1¹/₄″ flathead wood screws
Glue
1¹/₂ × ³/₈″ dowels
No. 8 × 2″ roundhead wood screws
No. 4 finishing nails
Wood putty

Tools

Band saw, saber saw, or coping saw
Radial arm saw
Drill, doweling jig
Sander
Jointer or hand plane
Bar clamps
Table saw
Wood rasp

Level of Difficulty

Moderate

Length of Time Required

Overnight

Safety Precautions

Safety goggles, filter mask

To obtain a full-sized traceable pattern
for this project, use the order form at the
back of this book and order pattern
number 666.

A baby's cradle is probably the first
thing a woodworker will think to
build when there is a first child or
grandchild on the way. Cradles must
date back as far as woodworking,
and they never go out of fashion.
Build yours well and it can be handed
from one generation to the next. This
one was designed in a traditional,
early American style in the manner of
the Pennsylvania Dutch. It was made
of white pine stock glued and doweled together to make up pieces wide
enough for the body; it was finished
with several coats of paint. To build

your cradle, you can use any solid
stock you like. For the most traditional look, use white pine and finish
with a light tan stain. The project is
somewhat complicated by the many
angled cuts you must make in the
end, back, rockers, sides, and roof
facing. Be sure to keep the pieces
properly oriented as you make the
angled cuts shown in the Front and
Side views.

STEP 1
Making Up the Stock

To make up the stock for the sides,
bottom, and back, lay out enough
stock to make up a piece from which
you can cut one of the parts. Use a
jointer or hand plane to get the edges
as smooth as possible for the best fit.
Butt the edges of the stock together
and mark lines across the pieces as
guides for the dowel holes—mark

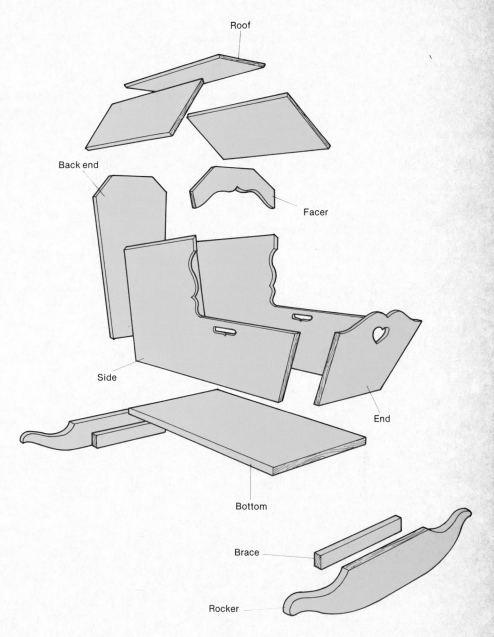

Roof

Back end

Facer

Side

End

Bottom

Brace

Rocker

Exploded View

three lines for the sides and bottom (dividing the pieces into four equal parts), and two lines for the back (dividing it into equal thirds). Use a doweling jig to drill ³⁄₈-inch holes slightly more than ³⁄₄ inch deep into each facing edge where the lines you have drawn cross it. Squeeze glue into the holes along one edge, drive in standard 1¹⁄₂-inch doweling pegs, glue the opposite edge, and drive it onto the dowels. When the stock is made up to size, clamp it in a bar clamp, tighten the clamp until glue squeezes out of the joint, and wipe the glue away with a damp cloth. Allow to dry overnight. Make up enough stock for all the large pieces in this manner.

STEP 2
Cutting the Pieces

While the glued and doweled stock is setting, enlarge the squared drawings for the sides, end, back, rockers, and roof facer. Make patterns for all the pieces and, when the stock is set up, mark the straight dimensions of the pieces, measuring the angles given in the End and Side views.

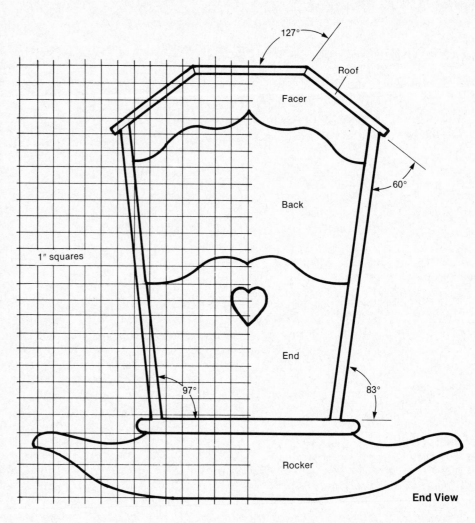

End View

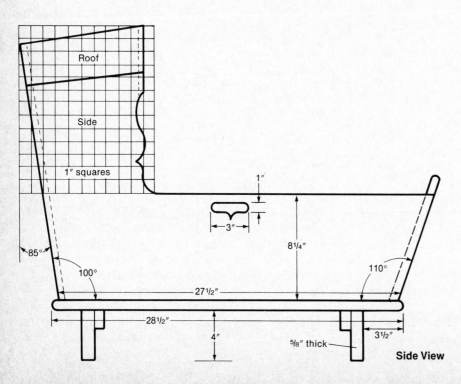

Side View

then lay down the patterns for the curved edges and mark them. Cut out the pieces with a band saw, saber saw, or coping saw. Sand all surfaces with a drum sander in a radial arm saw or drill press. Be especially careful to sand the bottoms of the rockers smooth where saw cuts start and stop to enhance easy rocking. Try the rockers on a flat surface as you work. Use a table saw to cut the bottom of the sides to the angle given in the End View. Then use a radial arm saw to cut the bottoms of the end and the back to the angles given in the Side View. Cut the bottom and the three roof pieces to the given dimensions and sand them thoroughly. Round all edges and corners on all pieces using a wood rasp and a sander.

STEP 3
Assembling the Bottom

Cut the cleats to the given dimensions, sand, and fasten to the bottom of the cradle, as shown in the Side View, with glue and No. 8 × 2-inch roundhead wood screws. After the glue has set, fasten the rockers to the cleats and to the bottom using glue and countersunk No. 8 × 1¼-inch flathead wood screws driven down through the cradle bottom into the tops of the rockers and through the cleats into the rockers. After you have installed one rocker (taking care that it is squared), try the cradle with the other rocker in position to be sure that it rocks smoothly. If it doesn't, you can sand a little off one of the rockers to produce smooth movement.

STEP 4
Assembling the Cradle Body

Fasten the sides to the ends with glue and countersunk No. 8 × 1¼-inch flathead wood screws. If you are working with white pine or other softwoods, you can use No. 8 finishing nails; if you are working with hardwood, drill pilot holes before driving in the screws so as to prevent splitting the wood. Assemble the body on a flat surface so you can be sure it sits square and is not twisted in any direction.

STEP 5
Attaching the Roof Facer and Roof

When the body is assembled, attach the roof facer between the sides with No. 4 finishing nails and glue. When the glue is set, install the roof pieces with glue and No. 4 finishing nails set below the surface, butting the edges of the pieces tightly. Fill the nail holes with wood putty and sand smooth when dry.

STEP 6
Final Assembly

When the body is complete and entirely dry, fasten it to the bottom so that there is a 1-inch overlap all the way around. Use glue and countersunk No. 8 × 1¼-inch flathead wood screws driven up through the bottom. Fill all countersunk screw holes with wood plugs and sand them smooth. Give the entire assembly a last sanding and finish as you wish.

Doll Cradle

Materials List
Uprights (4), $1^3/8 \times 1^3/8 \times 9''$, any clear stock
Rockers (2), $1^3/8 \times 4 \times 14''$
Center ends (2), $3/4 \times 7^5/8 \times 9^3/8''$
Sides (2), $3/4 \times 7^5/8 \times 21^1/4''$
Bottom (1), $3/4 \times 4 \times 22''$
Standard $3/8 \times 1^1/2''$ spiral dowels
Paint or other finish
Glue

Tools
Band saw, coping saw, or saber saw
Wood lathe
Drill
Doweling jig or drill press
Screwdriver
Clamps
Sander or sandpaper

Level of Difficulty
Moderate

Length of Time Required
Afternoon

Safety Precautions
Safety goggles, filter mask

This old-fashioned looking, scaled-down cradle can be made to serve more than one function around the house. It obviously is suited to be a delightful toy cradle; but, with the rockers slightly flattened on the bottom, it can make an unusual chair-side storage piece for magazines or knitting.

The cradle shown here was made from scraps of white pine left over from shelving projects—all standard $3/4$-inch stock—except for the end posts and rockers, which were made from $1^1/4$-inch white pine. The cradle shown was embellished with motifs taken from designs found in tole

painting (decorative painting on tinware), but you can decorate the cradle any way your imagination suggests—with paint, decals, or even decoupage. Patterns for different painted designs are available in craft shops. The construction of the cradle is fairly easy, although it involves cutting some angled pieces accurately. The one moderately difficult part of the project is doweling the pieces together. If your first try doesn't come out right, cut some new pieces and try again. You will master the technique pretty quickly and gain the expertise necessary for more complicated projects.

STEP 1
Cutting the End Pieces and Sides
Enlarge the squared drawing for the end pieces (rocker, two end posts, and center end). Transfer the pattern

for the rocker to $1^1/4$-inch stock and cut out the two rockers with a band saw, coping saw, or saber saw. Sand the edges of the rocker smooth with a small drum sander in a drill press, making sure as you work that the rockers rock back and forth smoothly on a flat surface. Then cut the four end posts from the same-sized stock, squared off at both ends, leaving about 2 inches of extra length at the top where the decorative knob shows on the pattern. Mark for the decorative knob and mount the end posts on a lathe to turn the top, sanding the posts while they are on the lathe. When the tops are finished, cut the bottoms to the proper angle, as shown on the squared drawing. Cut the center end pieces to size and sand smooth. Cut the side pieces to size; then cut angled edge as shown in the End View, and sand it smooth.

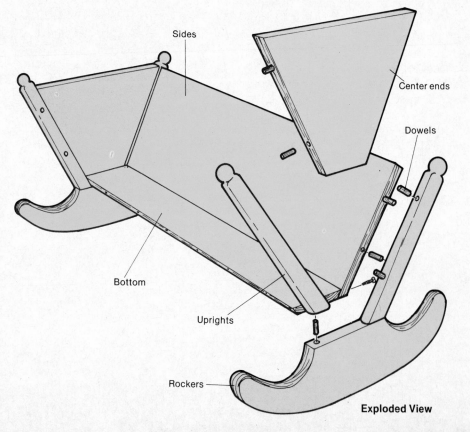

Exploded View

Sides

Center ends

Dowels

Bottom

Uprights

Rockers

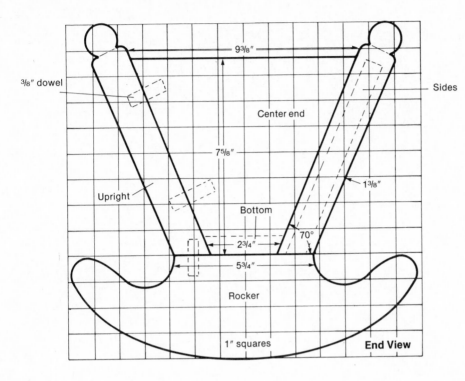

9³/₈"
³/₈" dowel
Center end
Sides
7⁵/₈"
Upright
1³/₈"
Bottom
70°
2³/₄"
5³/₄"
Rocker
1" squares
End View

and glue the edge of the piece that fits against it. Drive it on. Continue in this manner until the ends are entirely glued; then jury-rig a clamp or hold together with rubber bands, and allow to set overnight. When the end sections are dry, attach the sides to one of the end pieces; then attach the other end piece with glue and dowels. Don't attach both end pieces to one side—you won't be able to fit the other side over its dowels. Set the assembled cradle body on a flat surface and clamp with two bar clamps, making sure the body is squared. Allow to dry overnight.

STEP 4
Finishing the Cradle
When the sides have dried, give the body one more sanding. Then fasten down the bottom with glue. Decorate and finish however you like.

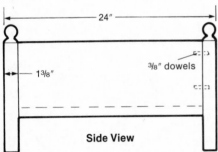

24"
1³/₈"
³/₈" dowels
Side View

STEP 2
Marking and Drilling the Cradle Body
Set out all of one set of end pieces in position on a flat surface. Mark the locations of the dowels' holes, shown in the End View, labeling each piece (A1, A2, and so on) so that you can reconstruct the assembly just as it was marked. After marking the ends, mark the sides and uprights as shown in the Side View. Drill all the holes, taking care not to drill through the uprights.

STEP 3
Assembling the Cradle Body
Squeeze glue into the holes on one of the end pieces, drive in the dowel(s),

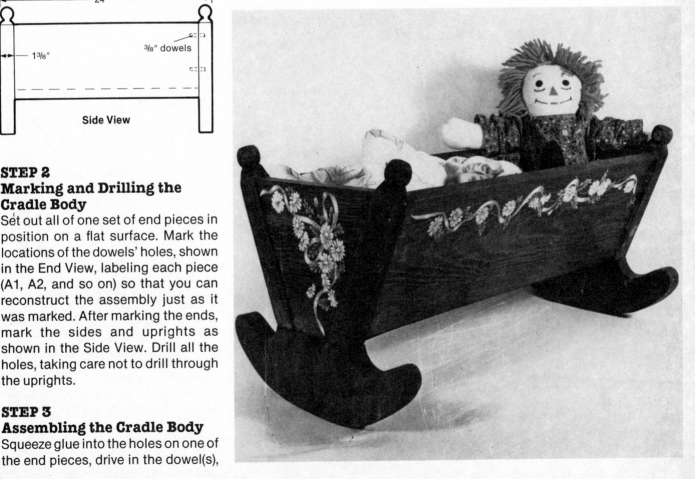

Country-Style Cradle

Materials List

End posts (2), $3/4 \times 4^1/2 \times 29''$
Bases (2), $3/4 \times 3 \times 22''$
Brackets (2), $3/4 \times 5^1/2 \times 5^1/2''$
Stretcher (1), $3/4 \times 4^1/2 \times 39^1/2''$
Key stem (1), $2 \times 3/8''$ dowel
Key ball (1), 1" wooden ball
Washer (2), $3/4 \times 2''$
Dowel pins (2), $2^1/4 \times 5/8''$ dowel
Floorboard (1), $1/4 \times 18^1/4 \times 36''$
Long floorboard supports (2), $3/4 \times 3/4$
  $\times 36''$
Short floorboard supports (2), $3/4 \times 3/4$
  $\times 16^1/2''$
Headboard and footboard (2), $3/4 \times 19$
  $\times 23^1/2''$ glued-up stock
Spindles (28), $9^1/4 \times 3/8''$ dowel
Rails (4), $3/4 \times 1^3/4 \times 37^1/2''$
Hardwood plugs (30), $3/8''$ furniture
  buttons or dowel
No. $8 \times 1''$ flathead wood screws
Glue
Paint or other finish
No. 6 finishing nails

Tools

Band saw, saber saw, or table saw
Drill
Screwdriver
Doweling jig
Carpenter's square
Clamps
Sander or sandpaper

Level of Difficulty

Moderate

Length of Time Required

Overnight

Safety Precautions

Safety goggles

**To obtain a full-sized traceable pattern
for this project, use the order form at the
back of this book and order pattern
number 599.**

There is nothing better for soothing a
baby than the gentle rocking of this
hanging cradle. The rail-and-spindle
sides, which let the baby look out,
give it a nice decorative touch, and
they are a good test of doweling
skills. The cradle is held together

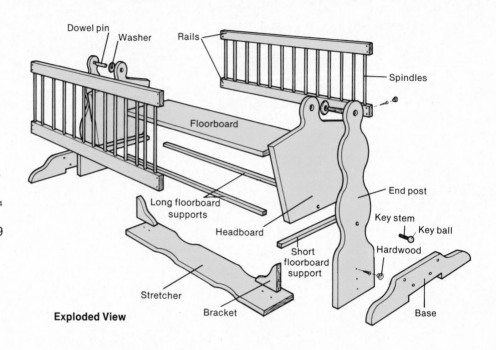

Exploded View

with screws, a few finishing nails,
and glue. To ensure that all the parts
fit properly, the body and frame
should be assembled first without
glue, then reassembled with glue.

STEP 1
Assembling the Headboards and Footboards

Enlarge the squared drawing in

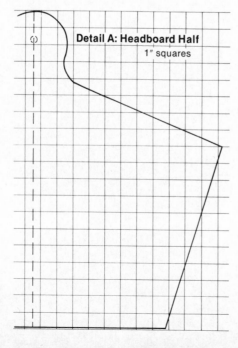

Detail A: Headboard Half

1" squares

Detail A and transfer the pattern
twice to 1×12-inch clear pine stock;
then turn the pattern over and transfer the reversed pattern twice for the
other halves of the headboard and
footboard. Cut out the parts with a
saber saw, but don't sand them yet.
To join the halves, dowel them or use
a plywood reinforcer in a slot cut in
the facing edges of the two parts. To
dowel the parts together, butt the
two halves of one board together and
mark four lines across them perpendicular to the seam, about 4 inches
apart, in the widest part of the piece.
Use a doweling jig to guide your drill
and bore $3/8$-inch holes 1 inch deep
into the edges exactly on the center
at the lines you have drawn. Run glue
along one edge and glue $1^1/2$-inch-
long, $3/8$-inch spiral dowels into the
holes in that edge. Then drive the
other half onto the dowels, clamp the
piece, wipe away any excess glue,
and allow to dry thoroughly. To use a
plywood reinforcer, cut a $1/4$-inch
groove exactly along the center line
of one edge with a table-saw blade,
as shown in Detail B. Do the same on
the facing edge. Then cut a reinforcer
to dimensions slightly smaller than
the saw cuts, as shown in Detail B,

Detail B: Joining Headboard Halves

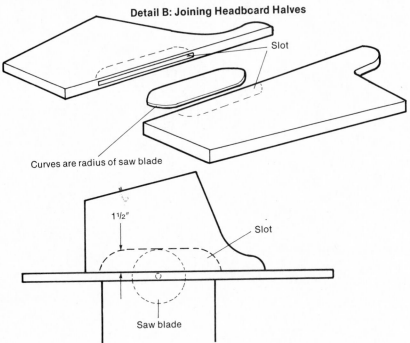

Slot

Curves are radius of saw blade

1½″

Slot

Saw blade

Measure across the edges of the two rails for spindle placement.

from ¼-inch plywood; make sure the fit is snug. Glue the reinforcer into the facing slots and clamp until the glue dries on both the headboard and the footboard. Then bore a ½-inch hole at the top of both pieces, as indicated in Detail A, and a ⅜-inch hole at the bottom of only one of the pieces at the point indicated. Sand the glued pieces and round the edges slightly.

STEP 2
Assembling the Sides
Cut the four rails to the given dimensions, sand them, and smooth the edges. Cut the twenty-eight spindles to the given dimensions. Lay out two rails with their 1¾-inch sides together and their ends squared up. Clamp the pieces so they won't shift and mark across both edges every 2½ inches with a carpenter's square. Make sure that the lines are exactly 2½ inches apart and exactly perpendicular to the seam between the pieces. Then drill ⅜-inch holes ¾ inches deep on the line, exactly in the center of each edge. Repeat the procedure for the other pair of rails.

Fit the spindles between the two rails without gluing to be sure that the holes are all drilled true. The rails should be exactly 11⅜ inches apart from inside edge to inside edge. Do not glue the rails in place until you have tested the fit of the sides with the headboard and footboard.

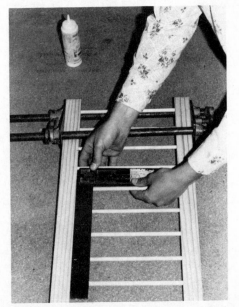

Check the rails to see that they are square before gluing.

STEP 3
Assembling the Cradle Body
Cut the short and long floorboard supports to the given dimensions, and cut the angle for the long floorboard supports as shown in Detail C. Attach the short supports to the headboard and footboard, as shown in Detail C, with glue and finishing nails. Attach the long floorboard supports to the bottom rails with glue and finishing nails; they should be centered and flush with the bottom edge, as shown in Detail C. Then

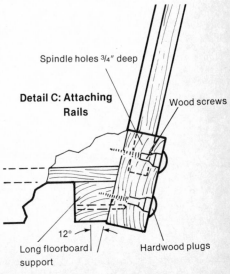

Spindle holes ¾″ deep

Detail C: Attaching Rails

Wood screws

12°

Long floorboard support

Hardwood plugs

attach the assembled sides to the headboard and footboard with glue and counterbored No. 8 × 1-inch flathead wood screws, as shown in the Side View. Finally, cut the floorboard to the given dimensions, sand it smooth, and attach it to the long and short floorboard supports with glue and finishing nails. Set the assembled cradle body inside.

STEP 4
Assembling the Cradle Base Parts

Enlarge the squared drawings for the end posts in Detail D, the stretcher in Detail E, the bases in Detail F, and the brackets in Detail G. Transfer these patterns to ¾-inch clear pine stock and make the cuts. Drill the ⅝-inch holes at the top of the end posts, as shown in Detail D. Also drill the ⅜-inch hole in the middle of one of the end posts, as indicated. Sand the pieces and smooth the edges. Using glue and counterbored No. 8 × 1-inch flathead wood screws, attach the brackets to either end of the stretcher, as shown in Detail E. Using

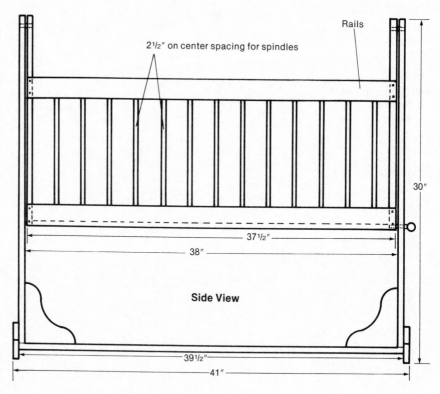

Side View

glue and the same-sized counterbored screws, attach the end posts to the stretcher and brackets, as

shown in the End View. Attach the bases in the same manner to the outsides of the end posts, as shown in the End View.

STEP 5
Hanging the Cradle

Cut two 2¼-inch lengths of ⅝-inch dowel. Fit them into the holes at the top of the end posts, and place ¾ × 2-inch washers on each dowel on the inside of the end posts. Push the

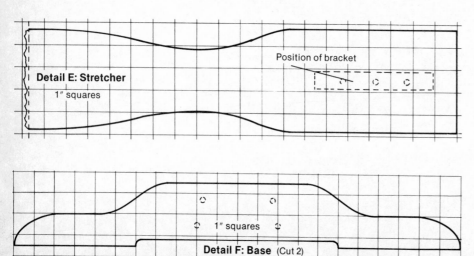

Detail D: End Post (Cut 2)

(Half pattern)   1" squares   Position of bracket

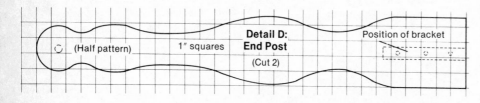

Detail E: Stretcher
1" squares

Position of bracket

1" squares

Detail F: Base (Cut 2)

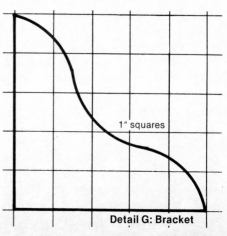

1" squares

Detail G: Bracket

End View

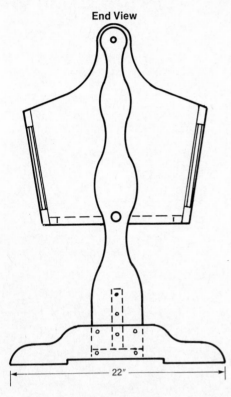

22"

STEP 6
Making the Key Stem and Ball
Drill a 1/2-inch-deep 3/8-inch hole into the center of a 1-inch wooden ball. Glue in a 2-inch length of 3/8-inch dowel. This slips into the hole in the middle of the end post and into the corresponding hole at the bottom of the cradle body to lock it in position when desired.

STEP 7
Finishing the Cradle
Fill all the counterbores with wood plugs to match the wood you are using in the cradle. Cut off the tops of the plugs and sand them level with the surrounding surface. When the plugs are installed, finish the cradle as you wish.

Copyright, U-Bild Newspaper Syndicate

dowels back to hang the cradle body, and check the fit. Make sure you hang the cradle so that the hole at the bottom of the footboard is opposite the hole in the predrilled end posts. With the cradle body hanging, drill and countersink 3/16-inch holes through the end post into the dowels as shown in Detail D. Drive in No. 8 × 1-inch wood screws to secure the dowels.

Changing Table

Materials List
Uprights (4), 1½ × 1½ × 32″, any
  stock
Sides (2), ¾ × 16 × 31″,
  hardwood-faced plywood
Back (1), ¾ × 31 × 37″,
  hardwood-faced plywood
Shelves (4), ¾ × 16 × 37″,
  hardwood-faced plywood
Facers (4), ¾ × 2 × 37″, any solid
  stock or hardwood-faced plywood
Wood tape, 8′ required
1½″ spiral dowels (24)
No. 8 finishing nails
Casters
Glue
Wood putty
Varnish or lacquer

Tools
Table saw or radial arm saw
Doweling jig
Drill
Sander or sandpaper
Hammer
Clamps

Level of Difficulty
Moderate

Length of Time Required
A few days

Safety Precautions
Safety goggles, filter mask

A changing table or dressing stand not only provides the right working height for changing and dressing a baby, but also the convenience of storage space for such things as powders, diapers, clothes, and other necessary items. This table is designed to accommodate the standard size 2 × 16 × 36-inch pad available in stores that sell baby furniture. Casters on the table make it easy to move.

If the changing table is constructed of a good hardwood-faced plywood or even solid stock doweled together, it can do double duty through the years: as your baby grows up, the table will change to a bookcase or set of storage shelves for the youngster's collections and other valuables. The changing table is moderately easy to build, with doweling the sides and back the only challenging operation.

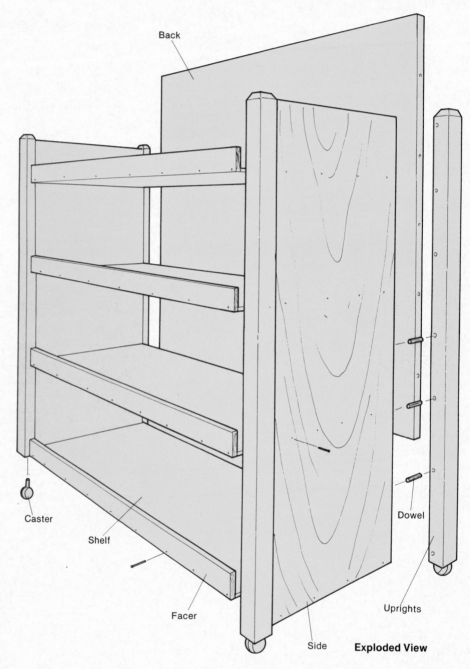

Back

Caster

Shelf

Facer

Side

Dowel

Uprights

Exploded View

STEP 1
Cutting the Uprights, Sides, Back, and Shelves
Cut the uprights from 1½-inch stock to the proper dimensions. Then use a table saw or a radial arm saw to cut a 45° chamfer around the top of each upright, as shown in the Full View. (Or cut the chamfer using a small hand plane, if you prefer.) Bore holes in the center of the bottom of the legs for the caster pins according to the dimension of the shank. Cut the back, sides, and shelves to size. Sand all the parts smooth.

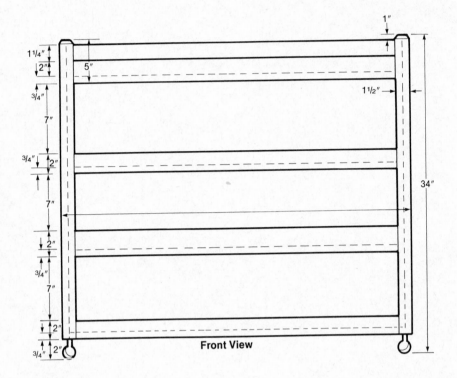

Front View

the sides are set, mark, drill, and dowel the back to the back uprights, following the same procedure.

STEP 3
Installing the Shelves
When the back joints are set, mark the location of the shelves inside the shell according to the dimensions on the Front View. Fasten the shelves in place to the back and sides using No. 8 finishing nails. Set the nailheads below the surface of the wood and fill the holes with wood putty.

STEP 4
Facing the Shelves
Cut the shelf-facer strips to the proper size and fasten them to the front edges of the shelves with No. 8 finishing nails set below the surface and puttied.

STEP 2
Making the Shell
The sides and back are fastened to the uprights with glue and dowels. (You can attach the sides and back with countersunk 2-inch wood screws and glue, but this does not provide the same sturdiness as doweling.) Lay one side next to an upright in the position shown in the Side View, and carefully mark four straight lines perpendicular to the edge of the upright across the upright and side piece as a guide for the doweling jig. Mark four locations for dowels about 6 inches apart, starting 6 inches from the bottom. When the pieces are marked, use the doweling jig to bore ⅜-inch holes 1-inch deep in the center of the edge of the side and on the center line of the uprights. Repeat the operation for the other upright and the other side of the side piece. Glue the holes and insert 1½-inch pieces of dowel into the side piece; glue the edge of the side piece; then drive an upright onto the dowels. Repeat with the other upright on the other edge of the side;

then clamp the assembly together and let it dry overnight. Assemble the other side in the same manner. When

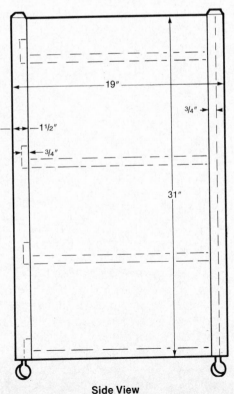

Side View

STEP 5
Finishing
Cover the top edges of the back and sides with wood finishing tape to match the wood. This kind of tape, with peel-off backing on its adhesive side, is available at lumberyards. Sand the entire project as smoothly as possible (remember that it's for a baby) and finish with several coats of varnish or lacquer. Fit the casters on the legs.

Baby's Highchair

Materials List

Legs (4), $1^{1}/_{2} \times 1^{1}/_{2} \times 24''$, hardwood stock

Foot board (1), $^{3}/_{4} \times 2^{1}/_{2} \times 14^{1}/_{2}''$

Bottom front and back braces (2), $^{3}/_{4} \times 1 \times 14''$

Bottom side braces (2), $^{3}/_{4} \times 1 \times 13^{1}/_{2}''$

Top side braces (2) $^{3}/_{4} \times 1 \times 10^{3}/_{8}''$

Top back brace (1), $^{3}/_{4} \times 1 \times 11^{7}/_{8}''$

Seat (1), $^{3}/_{4} \times 13^{3}/_{4} \times 14^{1}/_{4}''$

Lower seat support (1), $^{3}/_{4} \times 12^{1}/_{2} \times 13''$

Arms (2), $^{3}/_{4} \times 3 \times 14''$

Upper back board (1), $^{3}/_{4} \times 4 \times 11^{1}/_{2}''$

Back uprights (2), $1^{1}/_{2} \times 1^{1}/_{2} \times 17''$

Back spindles (3), $^{3}/_{4} \times 1 \times 14''$

Arm supports (4), $^{3}/_{4} \times ^{3}/_{4} \times 7''$

Tray (1), $^{1}/_{2} \times 8 \times 17^{1}/_{4}''$

Tray-support arms (2), $^{3}/_{4} \times 5 \times 13^{1}/_{2}''$

Tray lip (2), $^{1}/_{2} \times 5 \times 17^{1}/_{4}''$

Dowel spacers (2), $1^{5}/_{8} \times ^{5}/_{8}''$, dowel

Glue

No. 8 $\times 2^{5}/_{8}''$ flathead wood screws

No. 8 $\times 1^{1}/_{2}''$ flathead wood screws

No. 6 $\times 1^{1}/_{4}''$ flathead wood screws

No. 6 $\times 1''$ brass flathead wood screws

Brads

Tools

Table saw or radial arm saw

Coping saw, band saw, or saber saw

Drill, drill press, or mortise cutter

Doweling jig

Chisel

Sander and sandpaper

Screwdriver

Hammer

Router or shaper

Level of Difficulty

Skilled

Length of Time Required

Overnight

Safety Precautions

Safety goggles, filter mask

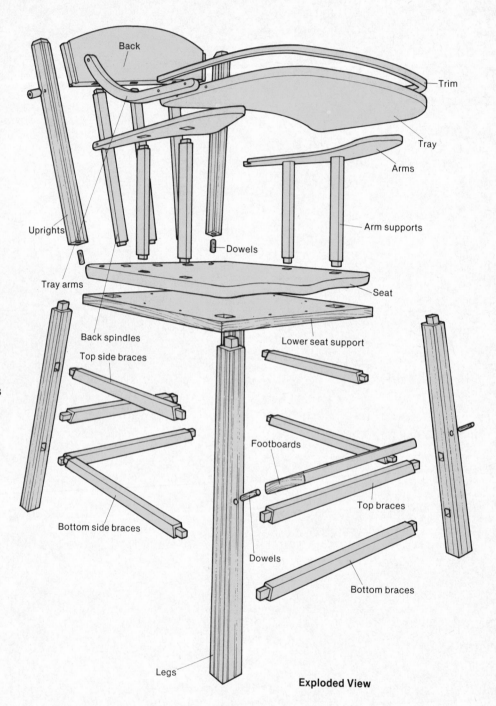

Back

Trim

Tray

Arms

Uprights

Arm supports

Dowels

Tray arms

Back spindles

Top side braces

Seat

Lower seat support

Footboards

Bottom side braces

Top braces

Dowels

Bottom braces

Legs

Exploded View

Building a highchair for a new baby is a satisfying project for the wood-working Dad, Grandad, or Mom. The finished product can be an heirloom that will be handed down from generation to generation. The chair shown here is probably the most complicated project in this book: it requires a fair amount of woodworking exper-

tise and some sophisticated tools as well. Almost all the pieces fit together with the mortise-and-tenon joints at an angle, and all angles must be cut accurately so the project will fit together tightly. Be especially sure that each angle is cut properly and that all pieces, including the tenons, are the correct length. If you

are not skilled at cutting mortises and tenons, practice on scrap wood before working with the stock for the chair. Also practice cutting and fitting mortise-and-tenon joints with scrap pieces at the angles required for the chair. You will learn what problems you might run into when you assemble the chair.

Construct the chair of a sturdy hardwood, such as oak, ash, or walnut. The chair shown here was made of red oak, stained, and finished with satin-finish varnish.

STEP 1
Cutting and Mortising the Legs and Uprights

Rip stock for the legs and back uprights to the given dimensions from 2-inch-thick oak stock. Round all four edges of the stock with a router or with a rounding or quarter-round cutter in a shaper. Use a router in a router table and a ¼-inch veining bit to cut two flutes in the length of each side of each leg and back upright, as shown in Detail A.

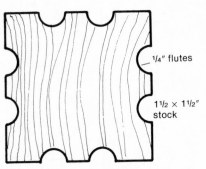

Detail A: Leg and Back Cross Section

¼" flutes

1½ × 1½" stock

The cross braces on the legs are held in place in mortises cut in the legs. Locate the position for the brace mortises in each leg (see views below) and cut ½-inch deep mortises by using a mortising attachment for a drill press or by boring holes with the drill press and finishing out the corners of the mortise with a chisel. Note that the mortises will have to be cut on an angle, as shown in the drawing. A tilting drill-press table makes this job easy. If you don't have a tilting table, you can cut the mortises using a block of wood to hold the stock at the correct angle.

STEP 2
Cutting the Braces and Tenons

After you cut all mortises on all four legs, then cut the cross braces from ¾-inch stock, round all four edges, and cut them to the correct length,

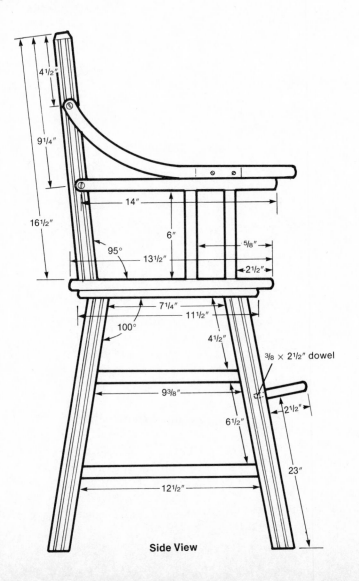

Side View

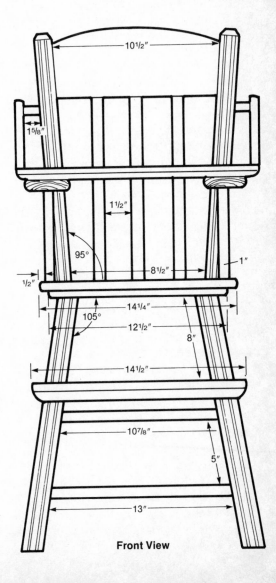

Front View

again taking care to cut the angles accurately. Then, using a dado head in a radial arm saw or table saw, cut the tenons on the ends of the braces to fit into the mortises in the legs, once again being sure to maintain the correct angle. It's a good idea to make a couple of scrap braces and try to fit them in place until you make sure you've got the correct tenon size and angle.

STEP 3
Assembling the Legs

When you have tenoned all cross braces to fit the legs properly, cut the legs to the correct length. The top and bottom cuts are both compound angle cuts, as shown in Front and Side Views. They can be cut with a radial arm saw or a table saw by setting the tools to the appropriate angles. Then cut the top tenon on each leg of the highchair.

Glue the two side leg-and-brace assemblies together, making sure that the units are square and the tenons are properly seated in the mortises. Then clamp securely and allow to dry overnight. Since a highchair can receive a lot of rough use, reinforce each cross brace with a small brass nail. Then install the cross braces on the front and back of the leg assemblies also using brass nails and clamp securely.

STEP 4
Cutting and Attaching the Lower Seat Support

Cut the lower seat support to the correct size and shape, following the drawings, and cut the mortises for legs, as indicated, in the bottom of the support, again maintaining the proper angles for the legs. You will have to tinker quite a bit to cut this compound angle correctly, so you will probably want to practice on some scraps before attempting it.

Coat the top leg tenons with glue and install them in the mortises on the lower seat support. Turn the leg

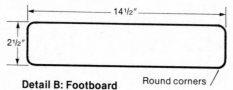

Detail B: Footboard   Round corners

assembly upright on a flat, smooth surface. Weigh down the lower seat support with plenty of weights to keep it flat and tightly over the tenons. At this time, also attach the front footboard with glue and dowels. Allow the lower seat support and front foot support to set overnight.

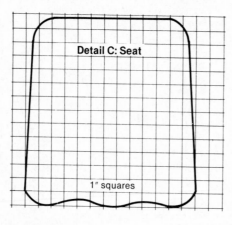

Detail C: Seat

1″ squares

STEP 5
Building the Top Section

While this portion is setting, you can build the top part. This is also assembled with mortise and tenons. Enlarge the squared drawing, Detail C, transfer to stock, and cut out the seat with a band saw or saber saw. Sand all edges as smooth as possible. Cut the upper back board and the arms in the same manner. Then cut the back mortises in the seat board, maintaining the angles shown in the

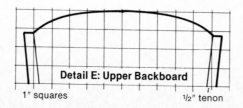

Detail E: Upper Backboard

1″ squares   ½″ tenon

Front and Side views. Cut the front arm-support mortises square with the seat board. Cut the back uprights to the proper length. Shape the upper

1″ squares   Detail D: Arms

ends of the uprights to a modified taper to provide a smooth, rounded end. Then cut the tenons on the lower parts of the uprights as well as the mortises in their inside top edges for the seat back.

Cut the mortises for the back spindles in the lower edge of the seat back. Cut the mortises for the arm supports in the underside of the arms. Then cut the spindles from ¾-inch stock, round their edges, and rout a flute in each side, as shown in Detail F. Cut the tenons on each end.

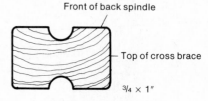

Front of back spindle

Top of cross brace

¾ × 1″

Detail F: Back Spindles

Detail G: Arm Supports

Slightly round the tops of the spindles where they fit up against the underside of the back support. Cut the arm supports to the given dimensions, cut tenons in each end, and flute as shown in Detail G. It's a good idea to sand all pieces thoroughly at this time.

Next place glue in the mortises of the seat back and insert the tenons of the spindles. Then place glue in all mortises in the seat and the uprights and insert the spindles and uprights in place. Clamp securely with bar clamps and allow to set overnight.

Glue the arm supports in place in the chair bottom and the front of the arms. Then fasten the back of the arms in place with No. 8 1½-inch brass roundhead wood screws.

STEP 6
Joining Top and Bottom
After the top assembly (seat and arms) has set thoroughly, fasten the bottom assembly (legs and seat support) to it with No. 8 × 1¼-inch roundhead brass wood screws and glue. Make sure you position them squarely with each other.

STEP 7
Making and Attaching the Tray
Enlarge the squared drawing of the tray in Detail H, transfer the pattern to ½-inch stock, and cut it out. Sand the piece thoroughly and cut the ¾-inch notches in the back corners as indicated in the drawing. Enlarge the squared drawing of the tray support arms in Detail I, transfer the pattern to ¾-inch stock, and cut out two. Round the edges with a router or shaper and sand smooth. Counterbore a screw hole at the upper end at the point indicated in Detail I and countersink screw holes at the points indicated along the lower end. Attach the arms to the tray with

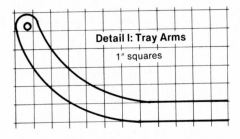

Detail I: Tray Arms
1" squares

No. 6 × 1¼-inch brass flathead wood screws. Enlarge the squared drawing of the tray lips in Detail H, transfer the pattern to ¾-inch stock,

and cut out the pieces. Round the top edges with a shaper or a router and sand the pieces smooth. Countersink screw holes in the lips at the points indicated in the drawing and attach to the tray with No. 6 × 1-inch brass flathead wood screws. Bore a screw hole through the length of the spacer dowels and install the tray as shown in the Front View with No. 8 × 2⅝-inch flathead wood screws. Finish the highchair as you would any piece of fine furniture.

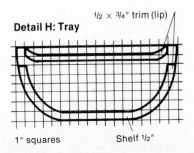

Detail H: Tray
½ × ¾" trim (lip)
1" squares   Shelf ½"

Booster Chair

Materials List

Sides (2), 3/4 × 73/4 × 10", hardwood
    stock
Back (1), 3/4 × 101/2 × 10", hardwood
    stock
Seat (1), 3/4 × 101/2 × 7", hardwood
    stock
No. 8 × 11/4" flathead wood screws
Wood plugs (8)
Glue
Stain

Tools

Table saw or radial arm saw and band
    saw
Drill
Sander or sandpaper

Level of Difficulty

Easy

Length of Time Required

Afternoon

Safety Precautions

Safety goggles

Booster Chair Dimensions

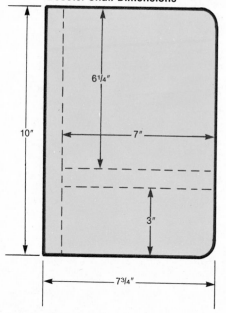

STEP 1
Cutting the Pieces

Mark the dimensions for the sides, seat, and back on 3/4-inch hardwood stock. Cut them to size and round the corners on the top and bottom of the front edge. Sand very thoroughly. Cut the back and seat to size and sand as smooth as possible.

STEP 2
Assembling the Booster

Fasten the back between the sides using glue and counterbored No. 8 × 11/4-inch flathead wood screws. Cover the screw heads with wood plugs and sand them flush with the sides and just as smooth. Install the seat in the position shown in the drawing with glue and countersunk wood screws covered with plugs. Let the glue dry; then stain and finish.

There comes a time (and often more than once) in every family when the youngest member graduates from a highchair but is still too small to sit up at the table unassisted. This is the moment to make the very practical booster chair described here. Placed on a regular chair, the booster gets the youngster's chin over the edge of the table. This is actually a two-way seat: in the high position it gives a small child a big boost; turned over to the low position it gives a larger child a smaller lift. It is designed as simply as possible both for sturdiness and for ease of cleaning. The one shown is made of red oak fastened together with glue and screws. The finish is bar varnish, which provides a durable, easy-to-clean surface safe to use.

Child's Step-Stool

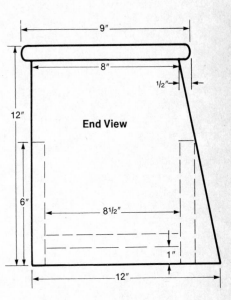

End View

9"
8"
12"
6"
8½"
1"
½"
12"

Materials List

Ends (2), ¾ × 12 × 12", any hardwood stock

Front and back (2), ¾ × 5¾ × 14½", any hardwood stock

Bottom (1), ¾ × 8½ × 14½", any hardwood stock

Top (1), ¾ × 9 × 17", any hardwood stock

No. 8 × 1¼" flathead wood screws

Wood plugs

Glue

Paint, stain, or other finish

Tools

Table saw, radial arm saw, or hand saw

Drill

Jointer or hand plane

Screwdriver

Sander or sandpaper

Level of Difficulty

Easy

Length of Time Required

Afternoon

Safety Precautions

Safety goggles

A sturdy step-stool is handy for youngsters when they have to reach up to a high shelf in a closet or on a bookcase; and it's a great place to sit as well. Mom and Dad will also find it useful for reaching high places—but a little too low for sitting. In addition to its other uses, this stool has an inside compartment just right for storing shoe-polishing gear. The storage compartment is what actually gives the stool its structural strength. You can build this project from any ¾-inch hardwood stock and finish it as you like. The one shown here was made of oak and given a natural finish that makes it a handsome addition to any room.

STEP 1
Cutting the Pieces

Cut the two end pieces to the dimensions shown in the End View. Cut the front and back sides and the top and bottom to the given dimensions. Use a jointer or hand plane to make all edges absolutely smooth for the best possible fit. Then sand all the pieces as smooth as you can.

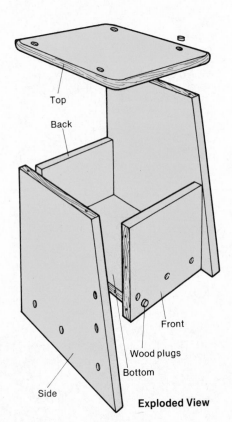

Top
Back
Front
Wood plugs
Bottom
Side

Exploded View

STEP 2
Assembling the Stool

Mark the position of the bottom piece between the front and back, as shown in the End View, and attach the pieces with glue and countersunk No. 8 × 1¼-inch flathead wood screws. In the same manner, attach the two ends to the assembled front,

back, and bottom in the position shown in the End View, driving two screws into either end of the front and back and one into either end of the bottom. Attach the top in the same manner, with an overhang of ½ inch all the way around, with one screw into each corner of the end pieces. Fill the all countersink holes with glued-in wood plugs, and sand the plugs down flush with the surfaces. Sand the whole stool again, and finish however you like.

Preschooler's Adjustable Desk

Materials List

Center support (1), 1½ × 2 × 25",
  glued oak stock
Spacer block (1), 1½ × 2 × 2", glued
  oak stock
Desk top (1), ¾ × 14 × 22", glued and
  doweled oak stock
Desk bottom (1), ¾ × 16 × 22", glued
  and doweled oak stock
Desk sides (2), ¾ × 4½ × 16" oak
  stock throughout
Desk front (1), ¾ × 1¾ × 20½"
Desk back (1), ¾ × 4½ × 20½"
Desk top back (1), ¾ × 2¾ × 22"
Front legs (2), ¾ × 2 × 26½"
Front leg braces (2), ¾ × 2 × 23½"
Back legs (2), ¾ × 2 × 15"
Bottom support (1), ¾ × 1½ × 25¾"
Seat (1), ¾ × 9 × 7"
Decorative hinges (2)
No. 8 × 1", No. 8 × 1¼", No. 8 × 2"
  flathead wood screws
1½ × ⅜" spiral dowels
Glue
Stain or varnish

Tools

Table saw, band saw
Power jointer
Shaper or router
Drill
Doweling jig
Bar clamps
Sander or sandpaper
Screwdriver
Vise
Rubber mallet

Level of Difficulty
Moderate

Length of Time Required
A few days

Safety Precautions
Safety goggles, filter mask

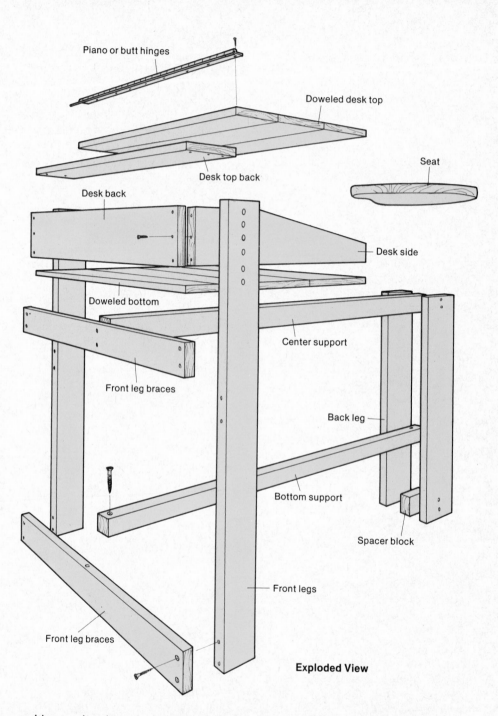

Piano or butt hinges

Doweled desk top

Desk top back

Desk back

Seat

Desk side

Doweled bottom

Center support

Front leg braces

Back leg

Bottom support

Spacer block

Front legs

Front leg braces

Exploded View

Whether you think of it as a desk or a workbench, this project will give your preschool child a place to get a head start at learning. The lid lifts for storage of paper, crayons, or whatever your youngster needs for desk-top activities. I built this desk after my children went through two ready-made desks with thin metal legs and plastic sides. My oak version will last through a family of preschool use

and be ready when the next generation appears.

The entire desk is made of ¾-inch solid oak, held together with glue and wood screws in counterbored holes, which are plugged with rounds of oak. It is an attractive piece of furniture for almost any room. In general, the construction is easy. The one challenging part of the job is doweling and gluing pieces of stock

together to make the desk top. With patience and the right tools, though, even this task is easy to master.

STEP 1
Constructing the Center Support and Spacer Block
The center support is made by gluing two ¾-inch strips together. Cut the 2 × 25-inch lengths and glue them, holding them solidly with C-clamps

spaced about 3 inches apart. Make sure the pieces are aligned on all edges. Allow to dry overnight. When dry, smooth off the glue-line edges with a jointer or sander. Round all four edges with a shaper or a router and sand smooth. Also glue up two 2 × 2-inch pieces of stock, clamp, and dry. This is the spacer block.

STEP 2
Doweling and Gluing the Desk Top and Bottom

The desk top and bottom are constructed of stock doweled and glued to make up the necessary width. For this job, you need a doweling jig like the one shown on page 12. Lay out enough stock to make the top and use a power jointer to smooth the edges that are to be glued together. Then butt the pieces on a smooth, flat surface to make sure they fit smoothly without gaps or bulges. When you have smoothed the pieces to a perfect fit, mark three equidistant parallel lines across them, perpendicular to the edges. Then clamp one piece of stock in a vise and

mount the doweling jig over the line and bore a ³/₈-inch hole 1 inch deep for the dowel. Move to the next line and repeat. Continue until you have bored all the holes marked for all edges to be doweled together. Squeeze glue into each hole in two facing edges and drive 1¹/₂-inch lengths of ³/₈-inch spiral dowel, or the same length cut from a dowel rod, into the holes along one edge. Position the next piece of stock so the protruding dowels fit into its holes, spread glue along the length of the edge, and drive it into place with a rubber mallet or wood scrap. Continue in this manner until you have enough stock doweled to make the desk top. Placed the glued-up stock in a set of bar clamps with two clamps on the bottom and one on the top in the center. Make sure the stock is square in the clamps, and tighten the clamps until glue runs out of the joints. Wipe away the excess glue with a warm damp cloth. Allow the glue to dry overnight. Make the desk bottom, following the same procedure used for the top.

STEP 3
Assembling the Desk Unit

While the glue is drying on the desk top and center support, start assembling the desk unit. Mark ³/₄-inch stock for the side pieces (see Side View) and cut the two sides. Cut the desk front and desk back to size, and cut one edge of the desk front to the proper angle (see Side View). Fasten these pieces together, front and back between the sides, with glue and counterbored No. 8 × 1¹/₄-inch flat-head wood screws, checking to be sure that the unit is squared up. Attach the desk bottom with glue and the same-sized screws. Finally, cut the top back piece and attach in the same manner.

STEP 4
Cutting and Counterboring the Legs

Cut the front legs to the proper dimensions and drill four counterbored holes an inch apart down the sides of each as indicated in the Side View. These allow for raising the desk top to fit a growing youngster or

A doweling jig is essential for boring holes when doweling stock.

After doweling and gluing stock from which to make the desk top and bottom, clamp the pieces securely and allow to dry overnight.

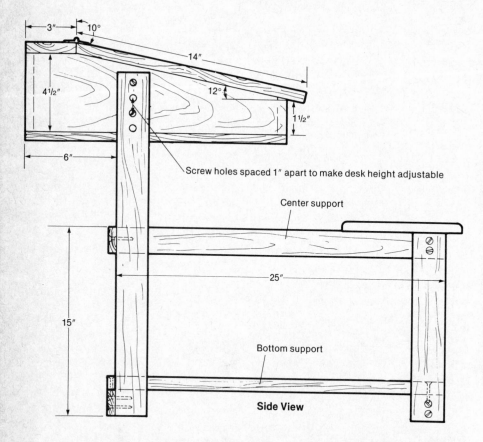

3" 10°

4½"

14"

12°

1½"

6"

Screw holes spaced 1" apart to make desk height adjustable

Center support

25"

15"

Bottom support

Side View

lowering it to fit the next in line. These holes are best cut with a drill sink—a drill bit that bores a hole in the shape of the screw to be driven in. The holes not used for attachment should be filled with wood plugs (*not* glued) or chair buttons. These can be removed when adjusting the height. Sand the legs smooth.

STEP 5
Assembling the Legs and Supports

Cut the front leg braces to the proper dimensions, sand them smooth, and fasten them to the front legs, as shown in the Side View, with glue and countersunk 1¼-inch flathead screws. Then cut the two back legs to size, sand smooth, and fasten the spacer block between them at one end, flush with the ends, with glue and same-sized screws as shown in the End View.

End View

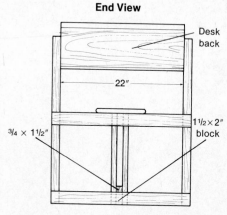

Desk back

22"

1½ × 2" block

¾ × 1½"

STEP 6
Assembling the Body

After these units have dried, attach the center support to the top front leg brace with No. 8 × 2-inch wood screws as shown in the Side View. Then fasten the center support between the top of the back legs with glue and 1¼-inch screws, as shown in the Side View. Finally, cut the bottom support to size, sand smooth, and fasten with 1¼-inch screws to the top of the spacer block between

Predrill and counterbore the screw holes on the desk legs for the screws that will hold up the desk body.

the back legs and on top of the lower front leg brace, as shown in the Side View.

STEP 7
Making and Installing the Seat

Enlarge the squared pattern for the seat and transfer to ¾-inch stock. Cut out the shape with a band saw. Round the edges on a shaper or with a router; sand smooth. Fasten it to the center support and back legs with 1¼-inch wood screws counterbored and covered with wood plugs glued in place.

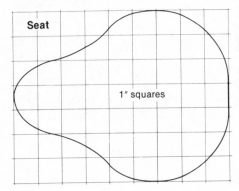

STEP 8
Completing the Desk

Cut the desk top to the correct size and cut the back edge to the angle

The back edge of the desk top must be cut to the given angle to fit properly.

Use a shaper to round the edges of the desk seat; if you don't have a shaper, use a sanding block. Sand the entire seat afterward.

Predrill screw holes to attach the desk top to the desk back with hinges. Decorative hinges like these look best.

indicated in the Side View. Attach the top to the desk body with decorative hinges. Install the completed desk body between the front legs at the desired height with No. 8 × 1-inch wood screws. Then fill all counterbored holes with wood plugs, shave the plugs flush with a wood chisel, and sand them smooth. Treat the entire desk with a natural finish that shows the beauty of the oak grain.

Fill all the counterbored screwholes with wood plugs, shave off the ends, then sand flush with the surrounding surface.

The seat is far enough away from the desk front to accommodate growing children.

Double Easel

Materials List
Blackboard back (1), $1/4 \times 14 \times 14''$, hardboard
Eraser holder (1), $3/4 \times 2^{1}/_{2} \times 17^{1}/_{2}''$ hardwood stock
Eraser-holder lip (1), $1/2 \times 1^{1}/_{2} \times 17^{1}/_{2}''$
Blackboard frame (4), $3/4 \times 2 \times 18''$
Drawing-pad holder (1), $3/4 \times 17^{1}/_{2} \times 24''$, plywood
Crayon holder (1), $3/4 \times 2 \times 18''$
Legs (4), $3/4 \times 2 \times 46''$
Butt hinges (2), $1''$
Stop latch (1), $1/2 \times 3/4 \times 9''$
Light chain, $14''$, 1 required
Miter-corner picture-frame fasteners (4)
Finishing nails
$1^{1}/_{4}''$ wood screws
$1/2''$ wood screws (2)
Small brads
Glue
Flat black latex paint
Stain or other finish

Tools
Band saw
Radial arm saw or table saw
Power shaper with beading cutter
Picture-frame clamp
Sander or sandpaper
Screwdriver
Hammer

Level of Difficulty
Moderate

Length of Time Required
Overnight

Safety Precautions
Safety goggles, filter mask

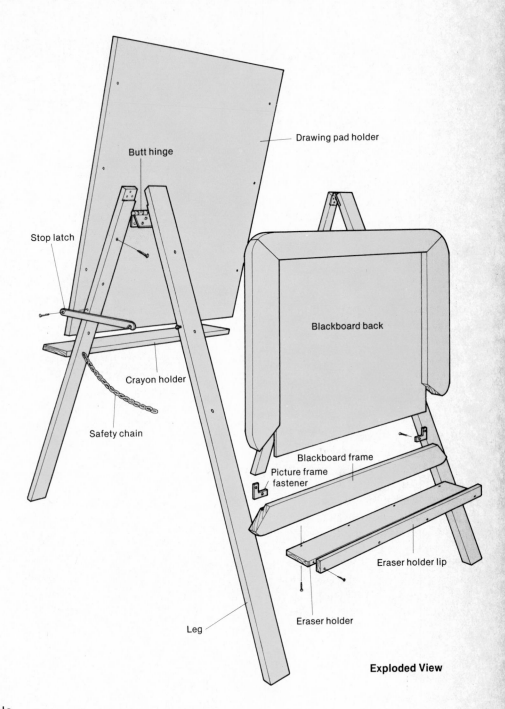

Drawing pad holder

Butt hinge

Stop latch

Crayon holder

Safety chain

Blackboard back

Blackboard frame

Picture frame fastener

Eraser holder lip

Leg

Eraser holder

Exploded View

This two-sided easel offers double fun for youngsters. One side has a blackboard (with painted wood instead of slate), and the other has a drawing-pad holder. This easel not only provides two separate skill areas, but it allows two children to work at the easel at the same time. The easel shown here was constructed of solid white oak and given a natural finish, but almost any hard-

wood will do. The easel is hinged at the top so that it can be folded up and stored away when not in use. Its legs are held apart at the proper angle by a stop block with a safety chain below to provide extra security in case a young artist accidentally knocks the stop block off its post.

The steps below are given for constructing the double easel one component at a time. Because you will have to wait for the finish on the various pieces to dry during the construction process, move along to the next step and finish the previous steps when the pieces are ready.

STEP 1
Making the Blackboard Back and Eraser-Holder Parts

Cut the hardboard back for the blackboard to fit, and paint one side with several coats of flat black latex paint. Cut the eraser holder and its lip, and round the upper corners of the lip on a band saw. Sand both pieces well and finish or stain as you wish. The easel shown here was finished with acrylic varnish.

STEP 2
Framing the Blackboard

Cut the pieces for the blackboard frame from ³⁄₄-inch stock. Lay the pieces roughly in position (they will be mitered to fit together in a moment) and lightly mark the pieces so you can tell which are the front and back sides. Now round the inside front edge of the frame pieces with a beading cutter in a shaper. Then use a table saw or a radial arm saw with a dado blade to cut a ¹⁄₄ × ¹⁄₄-inch rabbet in the inside back edges of the frame pieces; smooth the inside edge of the rabbet with sandpaper. Finally, miter the pieces at a 45° angle at the ends to the 17¹⁄₂-inch length. Glue the pieces together and clamp solidly in a picture-frame clamp, checking to be sure that the frame is square. Leave overnight to dry. When dry, use miter-corner picture-frame fasteners to give the

The four pieces of the blackboard frame are cut at a 45° angle on both ends with a radial arm saw, as shown here, or a miter box and handsaw.

frame extra strength; then round the outside edges, front and back, using a beading cutter in a shaper. Use a band saw to round the corners of the frame; then round the edge of these cuts with the shaper. Stain or finish the frame.

STEP 3
Assembling the Blackboard

Glue the blackboard back into the back of the frame and tack in two brads on each side for extra strength.

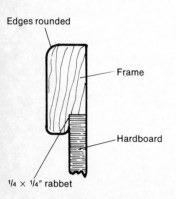

Detail A: Blackboard Frame Edge

Edges rounded
Frame
Hardboard
¹⁄₄ × ¹⁄₄" rabbet

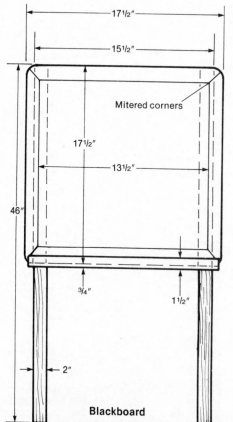

17¹⁄₂"
15¹⁄₂"
Mitered corners
17¹⁄₂"
13¹⁄₂"
46"
³⁄₄"
1¹⁄₂"
2"

Blackboard

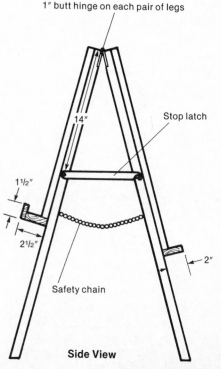

1" butt hinge on each pair of legs
14"
Stop latch
1¹⁄₂"
2¹⁄₂"
2"
Safety chain

Side View

Attach the lip to the eraser holder, as shown in the Side View of easel, with glue and finishing nails set below the surface. Attach the assembled eraser holder to the bottom of the blackboard frame with glue and countersunk wood screws.

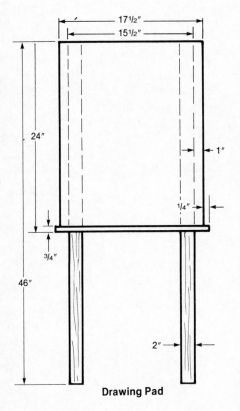

Drawing Pad

STEP 4
Making the Drawing-Pad Holder

Cut the drawing-pad holder from a piece of hardwood-faced plywood and sand well. Cut the crayon holder and round the outside corners on a band saw and sand well. Finish both the pad holder and the crayon holder with the same finish as you used for the blackboard. When dry, attach the crayon holder to the pad holder with glue and countersunk wood screws as shown in the Side View of the easel.

STEP 5
Cutting Legs and Assembling Easel

Cut the four legs to size and round all edges with a beading cutter in a shaper. Sand the legs and finish them as you did the blackboard and drawing-pad holder. When dry, attach two of the legs to the blackboard and two to the drawing-pad holder, 1 inch in from the edge of each as shown in the two head-on drawings. Use 1¼-inch wood screws, countersunk, driving them from the backs of the legs into the blackboard frame and pad holder at top, center, and bottom.

STEP 6
Stop Latch and Final Assembly

Screw two 1-inch butt hinges to the inside edges at the tops of both pairs of legs. Cut the stop latch with a band saw or saber saw from ½-inch stock to the dimensions and shape shown in the drawing. Drill a ¼-inch

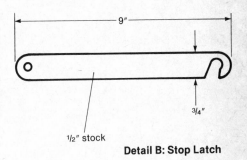

Detail B: Stop Latch

hole in the center of the rounded end and attach the stop latch on leg as shown in the Side View with a 1¼-inch roundhead wood screw. Drive in another directly opposite on the other leg (check exact position by marking with stop latch in position), allowing it to protrude slightly more than ½ inch so the stop latch will hold on the screw. Fasten a small brass safety chain with ½-inch screws about 3 inches below the stop latch to prevent the easel from falling down should the stop latch get knocked open.

Bookcase

Materials List
Sides (2), $3/4 \times 13^{1}/4 \times 54''$
Top (1), $3/4 \times 7 \times 28^{1}/4''$
Top trim, sides (2), $1/2 \times 2^{1}/4 \times 8^{1}/4''$
Top trim, front and back (2), $1/2 \times 2^{1}/4 \times 30^{5}/8''$
Back (1), $1/8 \times 28^{1}/8 \times 54''$
Front facer, top (1), $3/4 \times 2 \times 29^{3}/4''$
Side facer, top (2), $3/4 \times 2 \times 35^{1}/4''$
Shelves (3), $3/4 \times 6^{3}/4 \times 28''$
Storage top (1), $3/4 \times 14^{1}/4 \times 31''$
Facer, bottom (1), $3/4 \times 2 \times 29^{3}/4''$
Side facer, bottom (2), $3/4 \times 2 \times 11''$
Bottom door facer (1), $3/4 \times 2 \times 29^{3}/4''$
Bottom trim, front (1), $1/2 \times 2 \times 30^{3}/4''$
Bottom trim, sides (2), $1/2 \times 2 \times 14^{1}/2''$
Doors (2), $3/4 \times 11^{3}/4 \times 13^{1}/4''$
Cabinet hinges (4), $3/8''$ lip
Knobs (2)
Shelf hooks
Glue
No. 4 flathead nails
No. 6, No. 8 finishing nails
Wood putty
Magnetic catches (2)
Stain or other finish

Tools
Circular saw or table saw
Handsaw
Electric drill or drill press
Router (optional)
Hammer
Screwdriver
Sander or sandpaper
Shaper
Carpenter's square
Plane or jointer
Nail set

Level of Difficulty
Moderate

Length of Time Required
Overnight

Safety Precautions,
Safety goggles, filter mask

A bookcase is a necessity for school-age youngsters, and it is one of the pieces of furniture they are likely to take along when they go off on their own. To withstand long use, this one is designed to be as sturdy and simple as possible. The enclosed bottom section is ideal for children's games and toys; the upper section has adjustable shelves to accommodate objects of various sizes, as well as books. The height of the entire unit is just right for school children. The bookcase shown has sides, top, bottom, and doors made of 3/4-inch hardwood-faced oak plywood with the shelves, facing, and upper and lower banding made of solid oak. The back is constructed from 1/4-inch paneling that happened to be left over from another project; you can use any comparable 1/4-inch material that is handy.

STEP 1
Cutting and Boring the Sides
For the two side pieces shown in Detail A, mark off the dimensions on hardwood-faced plywood and cut them out with a circular or table saw. With both pieces, finish the inside cut in the L with a handsaw to get a perfect corner. Sand all the edges

Exploded View

Top apron, front
Top
Top apron, side
Top facer
Doors
Hinge
Shelf
Storage top
Side facer
Back
Door facer, top
Side
Door facer, side
Bottom
Bottom apron, front
Bottom apron, side

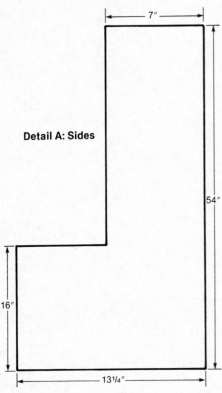

Detail A: Sides

top, and mark across the sides perpendicular to the long edge. Mark the points for the stopped holes 1½ inches in from edges. Drill ¼-inch holes ⅜ inches deep with a portable electric drill with a drill stop or use a drill press.

STEP 2
Assembling the Frame

Cut the top and bottom to size and also cut a ¼ × ¼-inch rabbet on their inside back edges. Assemble the sides and top (between the sides, flush with the top edges) and bottom (set 3 inches up from the bottom of the side), and fasten with glue and No. 8 finishing nails. Cut the back from ¼-inch leftover paneling or plywood. Square up the back with a carpenter's square and insert the back into the ¼ × ¼-inch rabbets cut in the sides and top and bottom. Glue and nail with No. 4 flathead nails.

Cut the storage top to size, making sure it fits properly into the back portion and extends out past the cabinet ½ inch on the sides and an extra ¾ inch on the front for the facing that will be added. Round the top

smooth and cut a ¼ × ¼-inch rabbet in the inside back edge of each piece (check the Exploded View for location). The shelves will sit on small metal brackets plugged into stopped holes in the upper sides as shown in Detail B: there are two at each end of each shelf and you should put them wherever else you think you might need them, or even all the way up the side, spaced at regular intervals, starting from the minimum height you want the first shelf. To mark the sides for drilling, check to make sure they are square, lay them out with the two long edges together, measure down from the

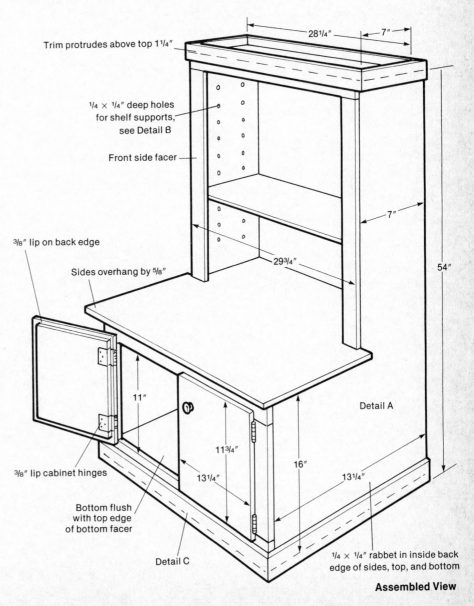

Trim protrudes above top 1¼″

¼ × ¼″ deep holes for shelf supports, see Detail B

Front side facer

⅜″ lip on back edge

Sides overhang by ⅝″

28¼″   7″

29¾″

7″

54″

Detail A

11″

⅜″ lip cabinet hinges

11¾″

13¼″

16″

13¼″

Bottom flush with top edge of bottom facer

Detail C

¼ × ¼″ rabbet in inside back edge of sides, top, and bottom

Assembled View

Detail B: Shelf Supports

Shelf

Metal shelf bracket

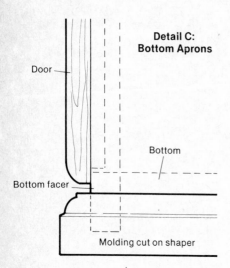

Detail C:
Bottom Aprons

Door

Bottom

Bottom facer

Molding cut on shaper

and bottom edges of the extended sides and front. Then fasten in place with glue and No. 8 finishing nails.

STEP 3
Adding the Facing
Put the case on its back. Cut the pieces of facing to the given dimensions (7 pieces in all) and joint the edges with a plane or a jointer. With glue and No. 8 finishing nails, fasten the top front facer and the bottom front facer (top flush with the top edge, bottom flush with the top edge of the storage compartment). Use the same procedure to install the top side facing in position between the storage top and the top facer, with one edge of the facer flush with the edge of the side. Install the bottom door facer flush with the top of the

bottom of the storage compartment. Finally, install the bottom side facers between the two horizontal facers on the storage compartment, edge flush with the side just as it is above.

STEP 4
Adding the Aprons
Cut the two top side aprons to the given dimensions, cutting their front corners on a 45° miter, and use No. 6 finishing nails to nail and glue in place. Then cut the front and back top aprons to fit between them and glue and nail in place. Cut the stock for the bottom aprons about 3 inches longer than needed for each piece and shape their top edges using a glass bead cutter in a shaper, or leave them plain. Then cut the side aprons to the given length with a 45° miter on each outside front edge and glue and nail in place as shown in Detail C. Cut the front piece and glue and nail it in place. Set all nails about 1/8 inch below the wood surface with a fine nail set and fill in the holes, using a wood putty of the appropriate color. Then sand the entire case thoroughly.

STEP 5
Completing the Bookcase
Cut the doors to the given dimension (3/8 inch wider and 3/4 inch higher than the opening). Then cut a 3/8-inch rabbet around the three sides of each door—leave as is the sides where the

two doors join. Then, using a radius or quarter-round cutter in a shaper, round the outside edges of the doors. Install in place, using 3/8-inch lip cabinet hinges fastened on the inside of the doors and to the outside of the cabinet facings. Bore holes for the pulls and install. Install magnetic catches on the inside of the cabinet behind to hold the doors closed. Cut the shelves to the correct size and round their front edges. Then sand and stain and finish to suit. To install the shelves in place, push in the shelf supports and drop the shelves down in place.

Child's Rocker

Materials List

Sides (2), $3/4 \times 20 \times 25^{1}/_{2}$"
Back (1), $3/4 \times 12^{1}/_{2} \times 16$"
Seat (1), $3/4 \times 12^{7}/_{8} \times 13$"
Armrests (2), $3/4 \times 2 \times 12$"
Back brace (1), $3/4 \times 3/4 \times 13$"
Front brace (1), $3/4 \times 1^{1}/_{2} \times 13^{1}/_{2}$"
No. $5 \times 1^{1}/_{2}$" flathead wood screws
No. $6 \times 1^{1}/_{4}$" flathead wood screws
5d finishing nails
Screw hole plugs
Hardwood dowels
Flexible wood trim
Semigloss wood finish

Tools

Band saw
Table saw with miter gauge or radial
    arm saw
Drill
Screwdriver
Sander or sandpaper

Level of Difficulty

Moderate

Length of Time Required

Afternoon

Safety Precautions

Safety goggles

To obtain a full-sized traceable pattern for this project, use the order form at the back of this book and order pattern number 392.

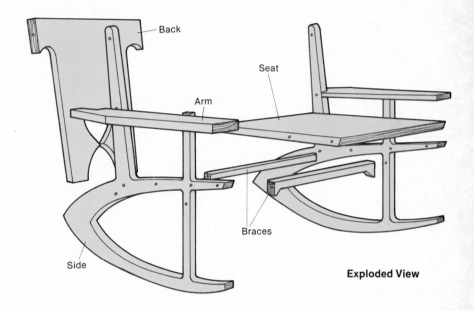

Exploded View

Children love this chair because it's their size. Parents who put it together like it for its simple design, low cost, and ease of assembly. There are no difficult joints in this project because the sides are one piece. The whole project can be made from a single 48 × 48-inch sheet of plywood. The exposed edges of the plywood are covered with matching flexible wood trim (veneer) available at any lumberyard or home center. The rocker shown here was made of birch plywood, but you can use any high-grade plywood you like; be sure to specify A-B grade or "good two

sides"—plywood that is finished on both sides. When cutting the pieces for this project, take care to measure and cut the angled edges precisely; otherwise that chair will not be sturdy.

STEP 1
Cutting the Parts

Enlarge the squared drawings in Details A and B, and transfer the patterns to ¾-inch plywood finished on

both sides. Cut two pieces from the plywood sheet, each large enough to hold one side of the rocker, tack them together so that the transferred pattern shows, and cut out the two sides at once with a band saw to ensure that the two sides are identical. Cut the back to size on a table saw or radial arm saw, then cut out the shape with a band saw. Cut the angled ends at the bottom to a 4° angle with a radial arm saw—or with

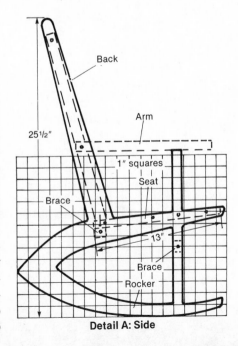

Detail A: Side

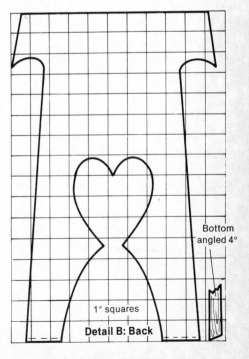

Detail B: Back

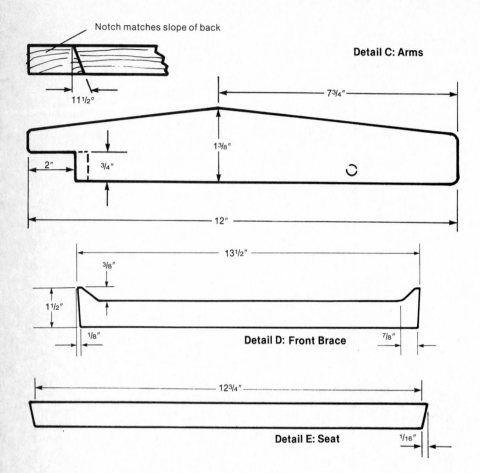

Notch matches slope of back

11½°

2″   ¾″

Detail C: Arms

7¾″

1⅜″

12″

13½″

⅜″

1½″

⅛″   **Detail D: Front Brace**   ⅞″

12¾″

Detail E: Seat   1/16″

a table saw, using a miter gauge. Lay out patterns for the two armrests (Detail C), the front brace (Detail D), and the seat (Detail E) and cut them out, taking care to cut the given angles on the notches in the arm rests, the ends of the front brace, and the sides of the seat. Finally, cut the back brace to the given dimensions and angle the ends 4° as on the front brace.

STEP 2
Drilling the Parts
Drill ⅛-inch screw holes for the armrests from the inside of both side pieces, as indicated in Detail A. Also drill for screws on each armrest at the point indicated in Detail B. Counterbore all these screw holes ⅜ inch deep to accept ½-inch wood plugs.

STEP 3
Doweling for Screws in the End Grain
For extra strength where screws are

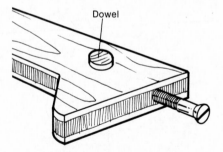

Dowel

Detail F: Screwing into End Grain

to be driven into the end grain of the plywood, you can insert a hardwood dowel plug to anchor the screw, as shown in Detail F. This procedure is not absolutely necessary, but it will extend the life of the chair. To insert the dowels, mark the location of the screw path into the end grain (the top of the back, sides of the seat, ends of the front and back braces, and front posts on the sides that support the armrests) and drill ⅜-inch or ¼-inch holes (depending on the size of the dowels you have) perpendicular to

the path of the screw. Cut dowel plugs to fit and glue them in. Sand them flush with the surface on both sides.

STEP 4
Assembling the Chair
Use glue and No. 6 × 1½-inch flathead wood screws to attach the seat and then the front brace between the sides. Use glue and No. 6 × 1½-inch flathead wood screws to attach the front of the armrests to the front posts on the sides and glue and No. 6 × 1¼-inch flathead wood screws to attach the backs of the armrests to the sides. Attach the top of the back to the sides with glue and No. 6 × 1½-inch flathead wood screws and attach it to the seat with 5d finishing nails. Finally, use glue and No. 6 × 1½-inch flathead wood screws to attach the back brace.

STEP 5
Finishing the Chair
Glue in screw-hole plugs over all screws. Apply wood trim to all exposed end grain with contact cement; follow the manufacturer's instructions for the product you choose. Then sand the chair lightly but thoroughly and finish with a clear semigloss wood finish, sanding between coats. For comfort, put a 12 × 12-inch cushion on the seat.

Small-Sized Table-and-Chair Set

Materials List
Chair backs (2), $3/4 \times 10 \times 19^{1}/_{2}''$
Chair fronts (2), $3/4 \times 9^{1}/_{2} \times 10''$
Chair seats (2), $3/4 \times 9 \times 10''$
Chair bottom braces (2), $3/4 \times 6 \times 7^{1}/_{4}''$
Chair top braces (4), $3/4 \times 1^{1}/_{2} \times 7^{1}/_{4}''$
Table top (1), $3/4 \times 14 \times 15''$
Table ends (2), $3/4 \times 14 \times 16''$
Table braces (2), $3/4 \times 2 \times 19''$
No. $6 \times 1^{1}/_{4}''$ flathead wood screws
Glue
Wood putty
Paint or other finish

Tools
Band saw
Drill
Screwdriver
Sander or sandpaper

Level of Difficulty
Easy

Length of Time Required
Afternoon

Safety Precautions
Safety goggles

To obtain a full-sized traceable pattern for this project, use the order form at the back of this book and order pattern number 103.

A small matching table-and-chair set is perfect for tea parties, games, and special dinners; your children will enjoy sitting at their own table, without booster chairs or stacks of phone books to get their chins over the dining room table. This set is very simple to put together, and all the parts for the table and two chairs can be cut from a single 48×48-inch sheet of $3/4$-inch plywood. For a handsome finish, use pine instead. Sand all the pieces thoroughly to be sure that there are no splinters or rough edges to scrape arms and knees. Paint the table and chairs, or use a clear finish. If you want to make a set of four chairs, just use double the materials listed for chairs.

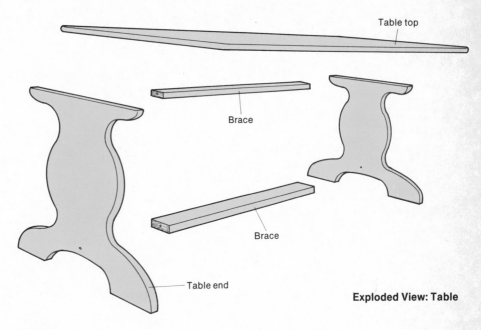

Table top

Brace

Brace

Table end

Exploded View: Table

Table

STEP 1
Cutting the Parts
Enlarge the squared drawing in the End View, transfer the pattern for two ends to $3/4$-inch plywood, and cut out the ends with a band saw. Cut the table top to the given dimensions and round the corners with a band saw as indicated in the Top View. Cut the two table braces to the given dimensions. Sand all the pieces thoroughly; you should spend far more time on sanding than on any other part of the project.

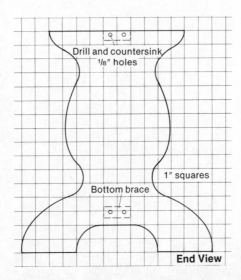

Drill and countersink $1/8''$ holes

Bottom brace

1" squares

End View

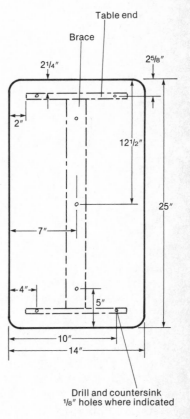

Table end

Brace

$2^{1}/_{4}''$ $2^{5}/_{8}''$

$2''$

$12^{1}/_{2}''$

$25''$

$7''$

$4''$

$5''$

$10''$

$14''$

Drill and countersink $1/8''$ holes where indicated

Top View

STEP 2
Assembling the Table Base
Mark the two ends for screw holes, as indicated in the End View, and drill and countersink $1/8$-inch holes.

Attach the two table braces between the ends with glue and No. 6 × 1¼-inch flathead wood screws. Fill the countersunk screw holes with wood putty and sand smooth when set.

STEP 3
Attaching the Table Top
Mark the table top for screw holes, as indicated in the Top View, and drill and countersink ⅛-inch holes from the top. Position the table top on the table base and attach it with glue and No. 6 × 1¼-inch flathead wood screws. When the glue has dried, finish the table with several coats of spar varnish, stain, or paint.

Chairs

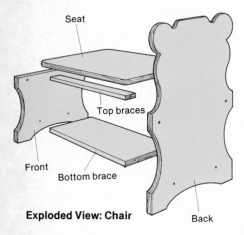

Seat

Top braces

Front

Bottom brace

Exploded View: Chair   Back

STEP 1
Cutting the Parts
Enlarge the squared drawing in the Back View, transfer the pattern for two chair backs (or however many you wish to make) to ¾-inch plywood, and cut out the chair backs with a band saw. Enlarge the squared drawing in the Front View, transfer the pattern for two (or more) chair fronts to the plywood, and cut out the pieces. Cut the chair seats to the given dimensions and round the front corners on a band saw. Finally, cut the bottom chair brace and top chair braces to the given dimensions. Sand all the pieces as thoroughly as you sanded the table parts.

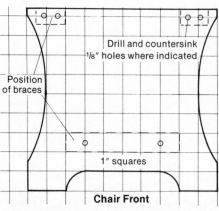

Position of seat

Position of top brace

Drill and countersink ⅛" holes where indicated

Position of bottom brace

1" squares

Back View

Drill and countersink ⅛" holes where indicated

Position of braces

1" squares

Chair Front

STEP 2
Attaching the Top Chair Braces to the Seat
Drill and countersink ⅛-inch holes 1 inch in from the ends of each top brace (drill the holes on the center line of the braces). Use glue and No. 6 × 1¼-inch flathead wood screws to attach the braces to the bottom of the seat, ½ inch in from the side edges of the seat. The ends of the braces should be flush against the back of the seat.

STEP 3
Attaching the Front and Back of the Chair
Mark the back and the front of the chair for screw holes, as indicated in the Back and Front views and drill and countersink ⅛-inch holes. Use glue and No. 6 × 1¼-inch flathead wood screws to attach the seat and braces to the chair back and front, as indicated in the Back and Front views. Finally, use glue and No. 6 × 1¼-inch flathead wood screws to attach the bottom chair brace between the chair back and chair front. When the glue is dry, finish the chairs in the same way you finished the table.

Playroom Table-and-Chair Set

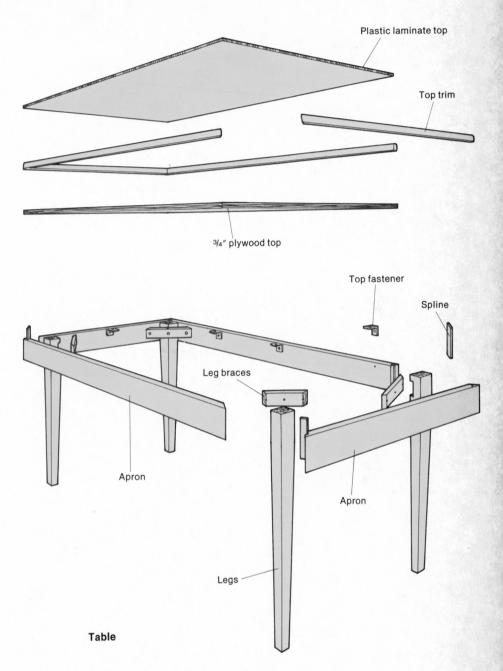

Plastic laminate top

Top trim

³⁄₄″ plywood top

Top fastener

Spline

Leg braces

Apron

Apron

Legs

Table

Materials List

Table:

Table top (1) ³⁄₄ × 22 × 30″ plywood
Top trim (2), ³⁄₈ × 1 × 23″
Top trim (2), ³⁄₈ × 1 × 31″
Apron (2), ³⁄₄ × 2³⁄₈ × 28″
Apron (2), ³⁄₄ × 2³⁄₈ × 18¹⁄₂″
Legs (4), 1¹⁄₂ × 1¹⁄₂ × 21¹⁄₂″
Plastic laminate top (1), 22 × 30″
Leg braces (4), ³⁄₄ × 1¹⁄₂ × 6″
Splines

Two Chairs:

Legs (8), 1¹⁄₂ × 1¹⁄₂ × 11³⁄₄″, any solid
stock
Front aprons (2), ³⁄₄ × 2 × 10¹⁄₂″
Back aprons (2), ³⁄₄ × 2 × 10¹⁄₂″
Side aprons (4), ³⁄₄ × 2 × 12″
Back supports (4), 1¹⁄₄ × 1¹⁄₄ × 10″
Backs (2), ³⁄₄ × 3¹⁄₂ × 13″
Seatboards (2), ³⁄₄ × 13 × 13″
Dowels (4), ⁵⁄₈ × 4″
Leg braces (8), ³⁄₄ × 1¹⁄₂ × 6″
Splines
Dowels, 1¹⁄₂ × ³⁄₈″
Glue
Plastic laminate adhesive
³⁄₄″ brads
No. 8 × 2″ roundhead wood screws
No. 8 × 1¹⁄₂″ flathead wood screws
No. 8 × 1¹⁄₂″ roundhead brass wood
screws
Stain or other finish

Tools

Table saw or radial arm saw
Band saw
Jointer (optional) or plane
Router
Drill or drill press
Doweling jig
Screwdriver
Sander or sandpaper

Level of Difficulty

Moderate

Length of Time Required

Overnight

Safety Precautions

Safety goggles, filter mask

A child-sized table-and-chair set is an ideal addition to any playroom. The one you can build with these plans suits children from about two years old until their teenage growth spurt; and it will stand up to the rough use kids can give furniture. This design has proven its sturdiness through two generations: mine is copied from a set that my father made for me, and the original set still gets a workout when my own children visit him. Children like having their own work-and-play table, and the set is especially convenient when you have guests and need a place to seat the children for meals. In fact, you will probably want to make two more chairs to seat a party of four children around the table.

The set shown here was made of native walnut, air-dried for several years, with a table top of easy-to-clean plastic laminate. You can make the set from any hardwood you choose, but it should be well-dried finish-grade wood, suitable for furniture construction, to ensure that it will not warp or shrink.

TABLE STEP 1
Making the Table Top

Cut a piece of ¾-inch plywood to the given dimensions. Cut the plastic laminate top to roughly the same dimensions (just be sure not to cut it to less than the dimensions of the plywood table top; slightly more is all right). Then use contact cement designed for plastic laminates to glue the laminate in place on the plywood. Put the glued top face down on a flat surface and load the bottom with weights to set the laminate. When it has set, rout the edges smooth and sand the cut edges of the plywood absolutely smooth by hand. Rip the top trim from walnut or whatever stock you are using to the given dimensions, miter the corners at a 45° angle, round the top edge, and sand smooth. The trim must make a perfect fit with the edge of the table top so that food and dirt won't catch between the trim and the top (see Detail A). Check the fit between the two for every edge before proceeding. Now stain the strips with the same finish you will use for the entire project—staining after the strips are attached may spoil the plastic laminate on the table top. I recommend a water-resistant lacquer; spray on at least a dozen coats. When the trim is dry, attach it to the to the top with glue and brads spaced 6 inches apart.

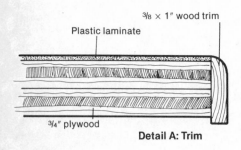

Detail A: Trim

STEP 2
Making the Apron

Cut the apron pieces to the given dimensions and then miter their corners at a 45° angle. When the miters

are cut, run the angled edges along the table of a table saw with the outside edge against the saw guard and cut ¼-inch-deep slots for splines, as shown in Detail B. Cut the splines from a tough wood such as maple (or from pieces of paneling), glue the edges of the apron and the splines, fit the apron together, slip in the splines, check to be sure the assembled unit is perfectly square, and clamp until set.

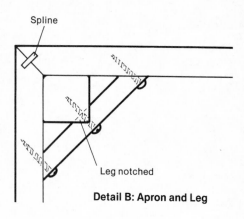

Detail B: Apron and Leg

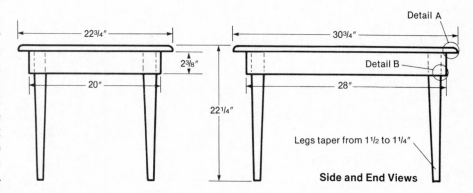

Side and End Views

STEP 3
Attaching the Apron

Use a doweling jig to drill ⅜-inch holes through the apron for countersunk 2-inch flathead wood screws. Position the apron square in the center of bottom of the table top and screw it down.

STEP 4
Making the Legs

Cut the legs to the given dimensions. You can build the table with square legs or with tapered legs, as in the version shown here. Square legs, of course, are easier to cut. If you want to cut tapers, I recommend that you practice one of the following methods on a piece of scrap before you work on the actual legs. The taper begins at the bottom of the apron, leaving the legs square inside the apron for secure attachment to the table. The legs taper from 1½ × 1½ inches (starting 2⅜ inches below

their tops) to 1¼ × 1¼ inches. You can cut the taper on a band saw along lines you have marked; you can cut them freehand, guiding the legs along a table-saw blade; or you can use a jointer. If you use a jointer, mark the straight portion of the leg (the top), and clamp a ⅜-inch-thick block on the joint so that when the leg is drawn against the cutting blade, the top of the leg will ride on the block. If you select this method, you should be especially sure to practice on scrap before trying it on the legs. Whether you taper the legs or leave them straight, round their edges.

STEP 5
Attaching the Legs

Cut the leg braces to the given dimensions and miter the corners at a 45° angle. Glue and screw the braces to the inside corners of the apron, flush against the table top,

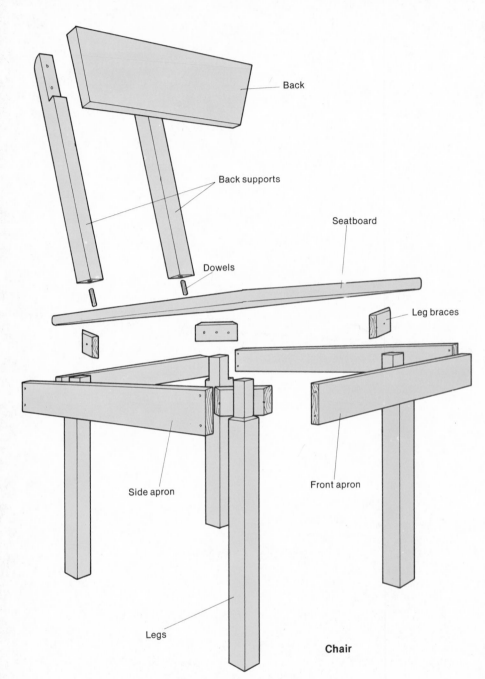

Back

Back supports

Seatboard

Dowels

Leg braces

Side apron

Front apron

Legs

Chair

CHAIRS STEP 1
Making the Chair Bottoms
The chair bottoms are made of 3/4-inch stock glued and doweled to make up the 13 × 13-inch dimensions. For each bottom, lay out stock large enough to accommodate the dimensions. Use a jointer or hand plane to smooth the butted edges so they make a perfect fit; then mark two parallel lines across the joints as guides for drilling the dowel holes. Use a doweling jig to drill 3/8-inch holes 3/4 inch deep where marked in the butted edges. Squeeze glue into the holes along one edge, drive in the dowel pegs, glue the facing edge and its dowel holes and drive it onto the dowels. Clamp in a bar clamp and allow to set overnight. When the chair bottoms are dry, cut them to the given dimensions, round the corners slightly, and sand the edges slightly round.

STEP 2
Building the Apron
Cut the apron pieces to the given dimensions and sand them. Make a frame of the pieces as shown in the Front and Side views, and attach the pieces with glue and two No. 8 × 11/2-inch brass roundhead wood screws, *not* countersunk. These can be tightened if the legs loosen after rough use. Be sure that the apron is squared as you work.

STEP 3
Installing the Apron
Position the apron in the center of the bottom of the seat, mark the position, and attach the apron with glue and 2-inch countersunk wood screws. Clamp with C-clamps and allow to set overnight.

STEP 4
Cutting and Installing the Legs
Cut the legs to the given dimensions; then notch two adjacent corners at the tops of the legs 3/8 inch in and 2

using No. 8 × 2-inch roundhead wood screws, as shown in Detail B. Then hold the legs in the position shown in Detail B, mark the portion that overlaps the apron, and cut a 11/2-inch-deep notch from one corner of each leg. Apply glue to the top edges of the legs, fit the legs in place, and fasten them to the apron, as shown in Detail B, with No. 8 × 2-inch roundhead wood screws.

STEP 6
Finishing the Table
Sand all edges thoroughly so that they are well rounded and safe. Mask the table top and apply the finish.

CHAIRS
The set shown here has only two chairs. If you wish to make more, you should cut the pieces for all of them at the same time.

Front and Side Views

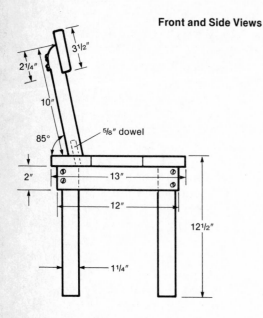

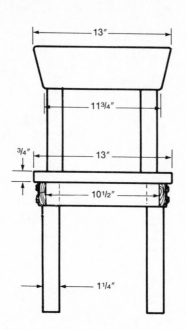

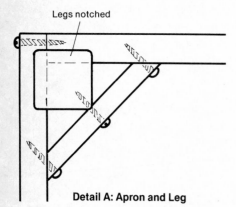

Legs notched

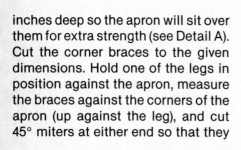

Detail A: Apron and Leg

STEP 5
Cutting and Installing the Chair Backs and Uprights

Cut the chair backs and then the uprights to the given dimensions. Cut a ½-inch notch 2¼ inches deep in the front of each upright at the top, as shown in the Side View. Cut the bottoms of the uprights to the angle shown in the Side View. Bore a ⅝-inch hole 2 inches deep in the center of the bottom of each upright and in the chair bottoms, making sure to maintain the angle shown in the Side View. Then glue and dowel the uprights in place. Position the chair backs in the notches in the uprights, bore screw holes, and then glue and screw the backs in place to the uprights with No. 8 × 1½-inch round-head wood screws driven from the back of the uprights.

Sand the chairs thoroughly; then stain and finish to match the table.

will hold the legs against the apron. Install the braces and legs, as shown in Detail A, with No. 8 × 1½-inch roundhead wood screws.

inches deep so the apron will sit over them for extra strength (see Detail A). Cut the corner braces to the given dimensions. Hold one of the legs in position against the apron, measure the braces against the corners of the apron (up against the leg), and cut 45° miters at either end so that they

Folding Game Table

Materials List
Top (1), $3/4 \times 36 \times 36''$ plywood
Plastic laminate top (1), $36\,1/8 \times 36\,1/8''$
Edging (4), $3/4 \times 1\,3/4 \times 39''$ (cut to length) hardwood stock
Legs (4), $1\,1/2 \times 1\,1/2 \times 26''$ hardwood stock
1" butt hinges (4)
Card table hinges (4)
No. $4 \times 1/2''$ flathead wood screws
Glue

Tools
Radial arm saw, table saw with plywood blade
Router
Shaper (optional)
Sandpaper
Belt sander (optional)
Screwdriver

Level of Difficulty
Easy

Length of Time Required
Afternoon

Safety Precautions
Safety goggles, filter mask

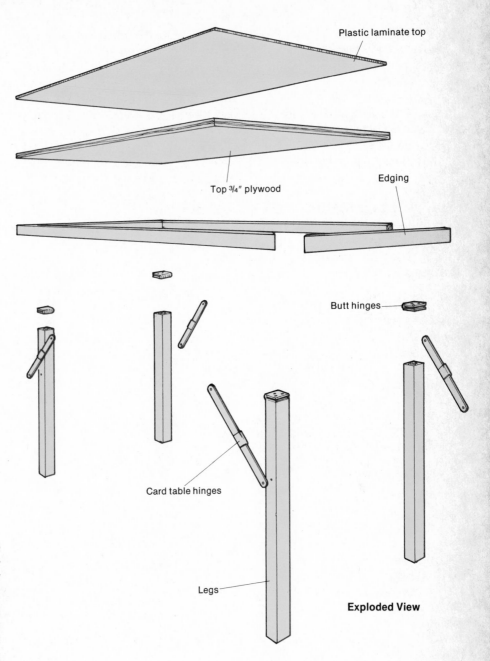

Plastic laminate top

Top 3/4" plywood

Edging

Butt hinges

Card table hinges

Legs

Exploded View

This useful folding game table is only a weekend job. In fact, the project is so simple and requires so few materials that you will probably decide to make more than one. The folding table requires very little space; several of them can easily be stored in a closet. The table is made from a ¾-inch sheet of plywood covered with plastic laminate to simplify cleaning. The laminate is bonded to solid wood with contact cement. You can, of course, make a fancier table by substituting a wood veneer for the plastic laminate, but this is harder to clean and won't stand up to children. An easy top is a piece of prefinished hardboard. However, since this material is only ¼ inch thick, you may wish to add a cross brace down the center of the table.

STEP 1
Cutting the Top and Trim
Cut the top from ¾-inch fir plywood to the given dimensions, and make sure all cut edges are square and smooth. Use a plywood blade to ensure a smooth cut. Cut the solid wood edging from ¾-inch stock and round the top edge with a shaper or router.

STEP 2
Cutting the Plastic Laminate
Cut a piece of plastic laminate about ⅛ inch larger all around than the plywood top. You can probably order the top, cut to size, from your local building-supply dealer and save yourself the work. However, if you are cutting it yourself and you are using a radial arm saw, use an old, dull ply-

wood blade and turn the laminate upside down. If you are using a table saw or saber saw, turn the laminate upright. If you use a saber saw, clamp the laminate firmly to a smooth, flat surface; the line to be cut should be fairly close to the edge of the work surface so it won't chatter from the action of the saw.

STEP 3
Gluing the Laminate
After cutting the laminate to size, brush or roll on a coat of plastic-laminate adhesive on the back of the laminate and on the top of the ply-wood, making sure that both surfaces are clean and that the plywood is smooth, without bumps or irregularities. Don't allow glue to run over the edges of the wood as it will cause problems later when trimming. Allow the adhesive to set for the amount of time specified by the manufacturer (usually until it is tacky but can be touched without coming off on your fingertip). Then place several thin wooden strips on the plywood surface and lay the laminate down on them. Make sure it is positioned correctly; then remove the strips, working from one side to the other, allowing the laminate to contact the wood surface. Roll down the laminate smooth and flat with a rolling pin, or use a soft block of wood and a hammer to seat the materials solidly together.

STEP 4
Trimming the Top
The best method of removing the excess laminate is to use a plastic laminate cutter in a router. To do this, position the top down flat and run the cutter around the edge. The wheel or guide on the cutter will keep the cutter correctly positioned. You can also remove the excess laminate with a belt sander, but this method requires a good hand and eye to avoid tilting the sander and causing dips or angles on the edge of the

stock. If you use a belt sander, place the stock in a vise, or clamp it to the edge of a sawhorse with the edges to be sanded face up so you can more easily keep the sander in the correct position. Even if you use a laminate cutter in a router, you will probably wish to do some light sanding to make sure the edge is as smooth as possible and that all excess adhesive and laminate is removed.

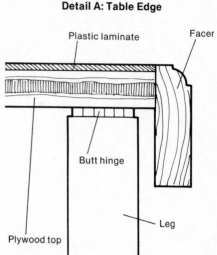

Detail A: Table Edge

Plastic laminate

Facer

Butt hinge

Plywood top

Leg

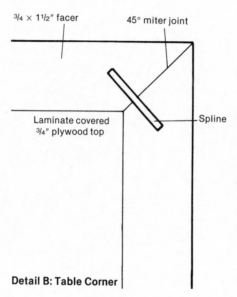

3/4 × 1 1/2" facer

45° miter joint

Laminate covered 3/4" plywood top

Spline

Detail B: Table Corner

STEP 5
Attaching the Trim
Cut the corners of the trim to a 45° miter and glue and screw the edges to the top with 1/2-inch flathead wood screws, being sure to keep the top edges of the trim flush with the top of the plastic laminate, as shown in Detail A. Wipe away all excess glue as it oozes out onto the laminate top and top edging. A stronger miter corner can be fitted with a miter spline, as shown in Detail B. To do this,

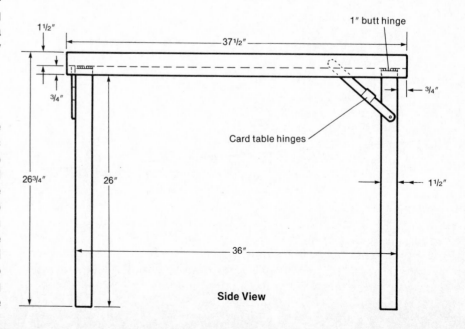

1 1/2"

1" butt hinge

37 1/2"

3/4"

3/4"

Card table hinges

26 3/4"

26"

1 1/2"

36"

Side View

make a cut across the end of the miter joint on a table saw. Then, after the joints have been completed, insert a thin wooden spline, cut it flush with the outside surfaces, and sand smooth.

STEP 6
Cutting and Installing the Legs

Cut the legs to the given dimensions from 1½ × 1½-inch stock and round their edges on a shaper or router. Then cut to length.

Sand, stain, and finish all wooden parts of the project, taking care not to get any stain or finish on the plastic laminate. Then turn the top upside down on a clean, smooth surface and fasten the legs in place with butt hinges on their top edges and special card-table hinges on the sides. These hinges are fastened to the underside of the top and the outside of the legs, as shown in the Side View. When the legs are pulled out, the hinges snap in place to hold them open securely.

Children's Patio Table

Materials List

Table-top planks (5), 1 × 4 × 35½"
Table-top cleats (2), 2 × 3 × 18¼"
Legs (4), 1 × 4 × 23"
Bench supports (2), 1 × 4 × 35⅜"
Bench planks (4), 1 × 4 × 35½"
Bench cleats (4), 2 × 3 × 6½"
Braces (2), 1 × 2 × 15¾"
No. 8 × 1", No. 8 × 1½" flathead wood screws
Carriage bolts and nuts (8), ¼ × 2"; (4), ¼ × 3½"
Paint or stain

Tools

Table saw, band saw, or radial arm saw
Drill
Wood rasp
File
Wrench
Screwdriver
Sander or sandpaper

Level of Difficulty
Easy

Length of Time Required
Afternoon

Safety Precautions
Safety goggles

To order a full-sized traceable pattern for this project, use the order form at the back of this book and order pattern number 313.

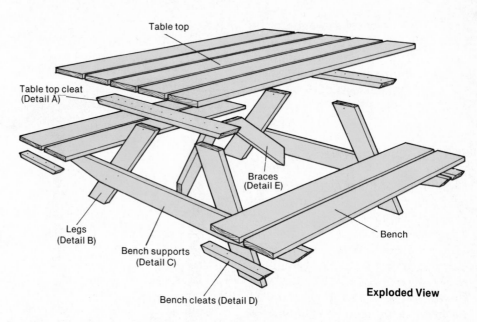

Table top
Table top cleat (Detail A)
Braces (Detail E)
Legs (Detail B)
Bench
Bench supports (Detail C)
Bench cleats (Detail D)

Exploded View

grade fir or pine, but you should avoid pieces with loose knots, holes, or cracks. If you use a softwood, finish the table to prevent weather damage; if you use redwood, you can leave the table natural. Be sure to sand all edges and corners, and be especially careful to sand away any splinters.

STEP 1
Cutting and Assembling the Table Top

Cut the 1 × 4's for the table top to the given dimensions, sand the pieces, and round their edges slightly with a wood rasp. Cut the two table top cleats to the given dimensions, cut the angles at the ends, and drill and countersink 5/32-inch screw holes along the center line of the cleats (see Detail A). Also drill two ¼-inch bolt holes in each cleat as indicated. Lay the table top planks face down on a flat surface, space them 3/8 inch apart, make sure they are perfectly square, and then use No. 8 × 1½-

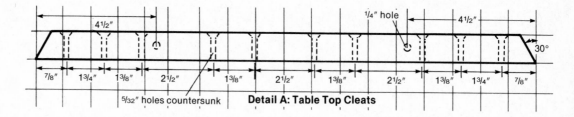

¼" hole
4½"
4½"
7/8" 1¾" 1⅜" 2½" 1⅜" 2½" 1⅜" 2½" 1⅜" 1¾" 7/8"
30°
5/32" holes countersunk
Detail A: Table Top Cleats

If your children like to picnic in the backyard or if you often eat on your porch or terrace, build a child-sized picnic table for the younger generation. This table is exactly like the classic full-sized version, and, if constructed of a durable wood like heartwood redwood that can stand up to weather, it will last until your children bring home their children. You can make the table from construction-

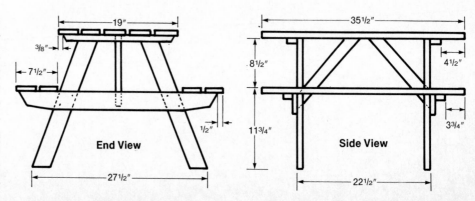

19"
3/8"
7½"
½"
End View
27½"

35½"
8½"
4½"
11¾"
3¾"
Side View
22½"

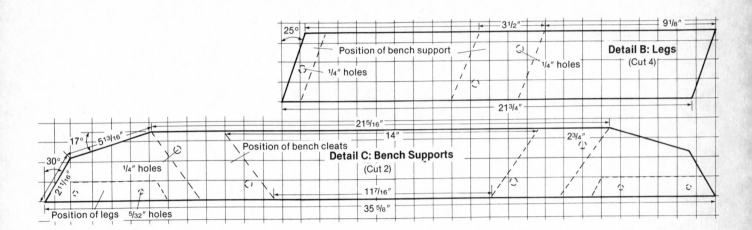

Detail B: Legs (Cut 4)

Detail C: Bench Supports (Cut 2)

inch flathead wood screws to attach a cleat at either end, 4½ inches in from the ends and ⅜ inch in from the sides (see End and Side views).

STEP 2
Cutting and Attaching the Legs
Cut the legs to the dimensions given in Detail B, sand them, and round the edges with a wood rasp. Drill ¼-inch holes, as indicated in Detail B. Attach the legs to the inside of the cleats with ¼ × 3½-inch carriage bolts. Use a file to smooth the bolts flush with the nuts.

STEP 3
Cutting and Attaching the Bench Supports
Mark out the dimensions for two bench supports, given in Detail C, and cut out the pieces. Mark the pieces for the bolt holes and screw holes, as indicated in Detail C, and drill ¼-inch holes for the bolts and

5/32-inch holes for the screws. Sand the bench supports and round the edges with a rasp. Attach the bench supports to the outside of the legs with ¼ × 2-inch carriage bolts, filing the ends of the bolts flush with the nuts.

STEP 4
Cutting and Attaching the Bench Cleats and Bench Planks
Cut the bench cleats to the given

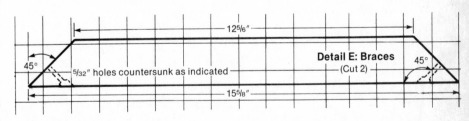

Detail E: Braces (Cut 2)

5/32" holes countersunk as indicated

dimensions and then cut angles in both ends, shown in Detail D. Drill 5/32-inch holes as indicated and sand the cleats. Cut the four bench planks to the given dimensions, sand, and round the edges with a rasp. Lay out two bench planks with a ½-inch gap between them and use No. 8 × 1½-inch flathead wood screws in the predrilled holes to attach bench cleats at either end—3¾ inches in from the ends and ½ inch from either side (see End View). Repeat the operation for the other bench.

STEP 5
Completing the Table
Attach the assembled benches to the bench supports with No. 8 × 1½-inch flathead wood screws driven through the predrilled holes from inside the bench supports. Finally, cut two braces to the dimensions given in Detail E, and drill 5/32-inch holes at either end at the indicated angle. Attach the braces to the underside of the table top and to the bench supports with No. 8 × 1-inch flathead wood screws as indicated in

the Side View. Finish with paint or stain as desired.

Detail D: Bench Cleats

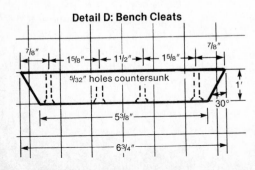

5/32" holes countersunk

Redwood Sandbox

Materials List
Sides (4), 1 × 8 × 4", redwood
Bottom boards (7), 1 × 8 × 48", redwood
Cleats (3), 1 × 4 × 48", redwood
Seat supports (12), 1 × 8 × 8¾", redwood
Seats (4), 1 × 8 × 62", redwood
No. 8 × 1¼" brass roundhead wood screws

Tools
Table saw, hand saw, or portable circular saw
Screwdriver
Hand sander

Level of Difficulty
Easy

Length of Time Required
Afternoon

Safety Precautions
Safety goggles, gloves
Filter mask

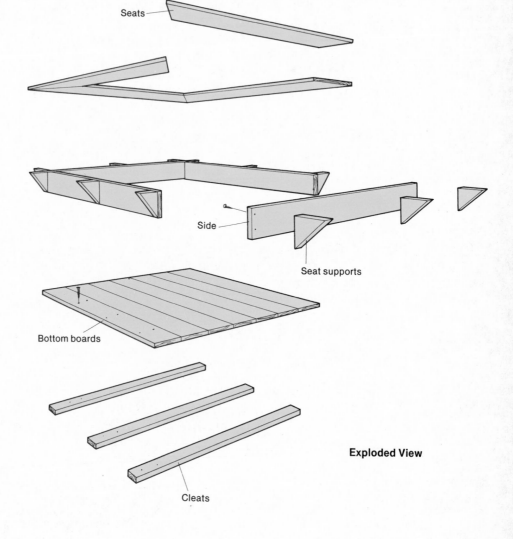

Seats

Side

Seat supports

Bottom boards

Cleats

Exploded View

A sandbox is one of the classic backyard projects, and one of the best ways to keep young children happy at play for hours. You can bring a piece of the beach into your backyard in just an afternoon. It is simply a large wooden box with a seat running around the outside; the bottom is reinforced with cleats that sit on the ground. The entire project is made with clear, heart-grade redwood 1 × 8's. The project is simple to make, but you will need help moving the finished project. When you are ready to fill the box with sand, call around to local lumberyards to find the cleanest grade of sand you can.

STEP 1
Building the Box
Cut the side pieces to the given dimensions. Fasten the sides together with No. 8 × 1¼-inch brass wood screws, butting sides to create a 4-foot-square box. Cut the bottom pieces to the given dimensions and fasten them across the bottom of the box with the same-sized screws, making sure the box remains square as you work. Finally, cut the cleats to the given dimensions and fasten them with the same-sized screws across the bottom boards to keep the boards from warping and cracking. The cleats also add strength to

the whole box and keep it from twisting out of shape.

STEP 2
Adding the Seats
Cut the seat supports to the dimensions given in Detail A and fasten them in place at each corner and the center of the sides with two No. 8 × 1¼-inch countersunk brass wood screws driven from the inside of the box. Be sure that the heads are well below the surface of the box and that no burrs are sticking up to snag a child's hand. For extra safety, you can fill the screw holes with plugs or wood putty. Cut the seatboards to

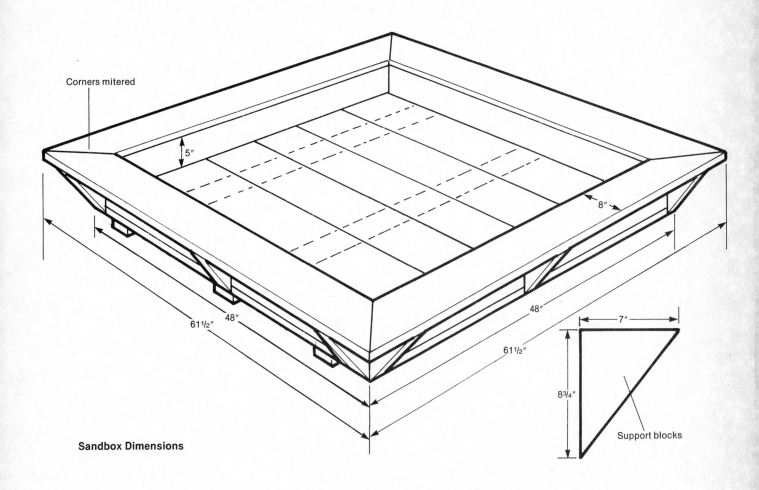

Corners mitered

5"

8"

61½"   48"

48"

61½"

7"

8¾"

Support blocks

Sandbox Dimensions

the given dimensions and miter the corners at a 45° angle. Fasten the seats to the edge of the box and to the supports with the same-sized countersunk wood screws driven down through the seat into the edge of the box and into the supports (two screws for each support).

STEP 3
Finishing the Box
Use a hand sander to round all the edges on the seats, smooth the seats themselves, and sand the inside of the box. Place the completed sandbox on level ground, fill with clean sand, and watch the kids climb in and have a ball.

Index